AF606867

STEINSTUECKEN

STEINSTUECKEN

A Little Pocket of Freedom

By Donald Smith

Acclaim Press
MORLEY, MISSOURI

P.O. Box 238
Morley, MO 63767
(573) 472-9800
www.acclaimpress.com

Book & Cover Design: Rodney Atchley

ISBN: 978-1-948901-80-2 | 1-948901-80-3
Library of Congress Control Number: 2020952282

First Printing: 2021
Printed in the United States of America
10 9 8 7 6 5 4 3 2 1

This publication was produced using available information.
The publisher regrets it cannot assume responsibility for errors or omissions.

CONTENTS

FOREWORD

Small places often have an outsized impact on the course of history. Steinstuecken is one such place, and this book documents its importance and my grandfather's role in it.

General Lucius Clay, who died in 1978, is sometimes described as cold or imperious. A recent book review in the *Wall Street Journal* described him as courtly. As children, of course, we idolized him. He was formal, and his eyes were intimidating. His voice was deep from years of cigarette smoking, but he had a gentle Southern accent that was warm and quite comforting.

As children we were lucky to spend many summers at his home on Cape Cod. Following his Army career, General Clay had second careers as Chairman of Continental Can Company and as a Senior Partner at Lehman Brothers. Friday evenings would bring him to the quiet Chatham airport in one of the converted B-26s or B-25s, which Continental Can used as business planes. My grandmother, Marjorie McKeown Clay, and all the grandchildren would pile into the car to greet him. It was always quite a show.

As we got older we came to appreciate his remarkable intellect. A drink in the sunroom was followed by dinner, which was always a formal affair. These dinners gave us an opportunity to listen and ask questions. Any attempt at debate was usually a losing proposition. The breadth of his knowledge was simply astounding. I was impressed to find that he had read most of the books on my college reading lists. His literary criticism could be harsh, especially if he thought the books were pretentious or too long. Any games, such as cards, checkers, or chess, in which odds or options could be calculated, were over almost before they began.

For those of us lucky enough to be present, my grandfather would occasionally give a 30-minute summary of American history, going through each U.S. President, summarizing their accomplishments, their failures, and the problems of the day.

Lucius Clay remained a prodigious reader all his life. As his health deteriorated, his activities grew limited. One day I surprised him by identifying some songbirds in his backyard. My grandfather was startled, not so much by the idea that I knew something that he did not, but by the idea there was a field of knowledge right in front of him, to which he had never paid attention. Of course, the next time I visited him, he knew the details of every species of bird that had ever visited Cape Cod.

In his professional life, Gen. Clay was known for rapid evaluations and quick decisions that could sometimes result in bruised feelings. On a family level, he always maintained a close interest in all his grandchildren. He tried to resolve the usual family problems. He always helped with education and school tuitions and tried to ensure that each of us had an equal opportunity. I think my grandfather also firmly believed that the people of Steinstuecken, Berlin, and Germany deserved to be free with their own opportunities under their chosen government.

In my grandfather's own words, from his essay "The Creed of a Soldier":

> "In the middle of the war against Hitler, if somebody had told me that I would one day be standing in the heart of Berlin before several hundred thousand of the citizens demonstrating their desire to be free, I would have said the person was crazy. Yet that very thing happened to me when I returned to the former German capital with the Freedom Bell, the symbol of the American campaign to pierce the Iron Curtain with the propaganda of truth. In open and dangerous defiance of the Russians and their East German puppets, thousands of West and East Berliners gathered in the middle of the city in a moving demonstration against tyranny. If they had believed in tyranny a few years before, they believed in it no longer. They had seen what democracy could mean and they wanted it."*

—Lucius D. Clay III, M.D., July 16, 2021

*Clay, Lucius: "The Creed of a Soldier" essay excerpt from *This I Believe: The Personal Philosophies of One Hundred Thoughtful Men and Women*. Morgan, Edward P., Editor; Simon and Schuster, NY, 1952, pg. 29.

INTRODUCTION

When the Cold War split Berlin in half, between East and West, one neighborhood was trapped in the middle. For more than twenty years, the West Berlin neighborhood of Steinstuecken was caught in a tug-of-war between the Americans and the Communists. This book tells this hamlet's story; it also shows how its experiences impacted the Cold War in Western Europe. This was a unique, interesting episode in Cold War history.

Steinstuecken officially belonged to the U.S. Occupation Sector of Berlin. However, it was located outside the city boundaries, completely surrounded by East German territory. No West Berlin-owned roads or trails connected it to the city. It was a de facto Western island in a Communist sea.

From 1951 to 1972, Steinstuecken's residents resisted Soviets and East Germans attempts to absorb their home into the Communist zone. East German troops blocked mail deliveries, denied access by West Berlin police and firemen to the village, and even threatened to kidnap villagers. Through it all, the people of Steinstuecken remained defiant, courageous, and loyal to the West.

America could have turned its back on Steinstuecken—but it didn't. U.S. officials in Berlin rose to the hamlet's defense. American diplomats interceded often with the Soviet occupation authorities on its behalf. During the Berlin Wall crisis, the Americans sent a Military Police (MP) patrol to the village to ensure its safety. The Army maintained that presence for *eleven years*, with Army helicopters ferrying the MPs in and out. Steinstuecken's plight even drew the personal attention of President Kennedy, who personally issued guidance on how the village should be defended.

General Lucius Clay, the hero of the Berlin Airlift, made a dramatic helicopter flight there, in the midst of the Berlin Wall crisis; this gave the West a huge morale boost at a time when Western fortunes seemed on the wane in Berlin. Protecting Steinstuecken allowed the U.S. to demonstrate to its West Berlin and West German allies that America's promises to safeguard West Berlin were sincere.

This book does more than tell what happened in one tiny Berlin neighborhood. It explores the wide variety of challenges America faced in protecting and sustaining West Berlin. It also describes some of the benefits Berlin gave to the West during the Cold War, and the courage many West Berliners showed when facing the Communists.

Steinstuecken's story is a success story that arose from a partnership between Americans and Germans during the Cold War. People who value the friendships Germans and Americans built after World War II will find this neighborhood's experiences interesting, and even uplifting.

Steinstuecken was a place where Berliners were brave, and Americans did the right (instead of the easy) thing. Its legacy deserves to be remembered, fondly and proudly. That is why I wrote this book.

—Don Smith, December 2020

CHAPTER ONE

"What was that little place?"

Jacques Reinstein was a career State Department official. He played key roles in US-German affairs during the Cold War. From 1955 to 1958 Reinstein was the Director of the Office of German Affairs. As his career ended, the Association for Diplomatic Studies and Training interviewed him to record his memories and experiences.

Reinstein recalled the challenges of one of his duties—responding to urgent requests for guidance from American officials in Berlin. Because Berlin was a Cold War hotspot, even small incidents could cause big problems. So, staff in Berlin often asked Washington for instructions. Reinstein fielded many of these calls.

> These things would drive you crazy because what would happen was there would be an incident. It would get reported to the military, the military would talk about it, they would then report to the political people, the political people would then consult about it and they would come up with a conclusion as to what should be done, and a telegram would come around about six o'clock in the evening, which had to be answered right away—which was a damn nuisance. There was a period of time when I swear I never got home for dinner because of these wretched telegrams coming in night after night.[1]

Then, Reinstein recalled one particular place in Berlin. A place that apparently caused him and others in the State Department frequent grief.

> "What was that little place that was disconnected" from, but part of "Berlin? I can't remember the name of it. We used to fuss about that."

That "little place" was undoubtedly[2] Steinstuecken, a small neighborhood that belonged to one of Berlin's suburbs. Steinstuecken caused quite a bit of fuss during the last half of the twentieth century, for Americans, Soviets, and Germans alike.

Prior to the Cold War, it was simply one of many communities in Greater Berlin. Once the Cold War heated up, though, it became a flashpoint. The little neighborhood's name often appeared in newspapers across the world, as the scene of another warm (or hot) incident in the ongoing struggle between the Communists and the West.

What made Steinstuecken contentious? It wasn't the seat of any government. It had no industry, and it controlled no major roads, railways, or rivers. Steinstuecken became critical (and therefore famous) not because of *what* it was but *where* it was.

Steinstuecken was officially part of a Berlin *Bezirk* (borough) that belonged to the US Occupation Sector. But it sat about one kilometer *outside* the city's outskirts in the state of Brandenburg. Brandenburg fell within the occupation zone for the Soviet Union. All the land in between Berlin and Steinstuecken belonged to Brandenburg. No Berlin-owned road or strip of Berlin-owned land connected the hamlet to the city.

In other words, a neighborhood under American protection was surrounded by Communist territory, cut off from the rest of Berlin. Once the Cold War heated up, this situation was sure to cause problems. And it did, over and over again.

Steinstuecken's unique situation stemmed from two factors—a quirk in nineteenth century German real estate practices and a poorly drawn World War II map. Its path to fame started years before the Cold War began.

In 1943, the Allies began planning how to handle Germany once they defeated it. The Allies had no interest in negotiating with Hitler or allowing any prominent Nazis to govern the country. Instead, the Allies would demand Germany's unconditional surrender. Whatever remained of the German national government would be swept away. The Allies would then run Germany themselves. Each of the Allied Powers agreed to provide troops to occupy the country.

The Allies portioned Germany into occupation zones. The Soviets got the eastern third of the country, the British took the northern regions near Scandinavia and the North Sea, the Americans received southern Germany, and the French were given some territory that bordered France. Each Allied power would be the governing authority within its own zone. Berlin, the Nazi capital, fell within the Soviet Zone.

However, Berlin *itself* was not part of the Soviet Occupation Zone. The Allied Powers thought of Berlin as a unique, especially important place. It was more than just the Nazi capital. Berlin had been the capital of the German state (and former kingdom) of Prussia. Prussia had been the driving force behind the modern German nation, which was created in 1871 from several Germanic territories and kingdoms. In the late 1800s and early 1900s, the German emperors (or "Kaisers") who launched wars across Europe ruled from Berlin. It was a center of industry and culture, one of the great cities of the European continent. The US and Great Britain were not content to let the Soviets absorb Berlin into their occupation zone. So, Berlin became a unique occupation zone of its own.

The "Protocol on Zones of Occupation in Germany and Administration of the 'Greater Berlin' Area," approved by the Allies on September 12, 1944, declared that Berlin "will be jointly occupied by armed forces of the U.S.A., U.K. and U.S.S.R."[3] The protocol divided the boroughs (*Bezirke*) of Berlin among the occupying powers. Eastern Berlin was the USSR's Occupation Sector, northwestern Berlin became the British Sector, and southwestern Berlin was the US Sector. (Later, the Allies gave France its own sector, in the northwest of the city.)

By May 1945, Nazi Germany was finished. British and American forces marching east met Soviet forces driving west, and German armed resistance collapsed. In two ceremonies, one in Reims, France, on the seventh and another the next day in Berlin, the German military surrendered. World War II in Europe was over. The next month, on June 5, the victorious Allied Powers issued a "Declaration Regarding the Defeat of Germany and the Assumption of Supreme Authority."

> The German Armed Forces on land, at sea and in the air have been completely defeated and have surrendered unconditionally and Germany, which bears responsibility for the war, is no longer capable of resisting the will of the victorious Powers. The unconditional surrender of Germany has thereby been effected and Germany has become subject to such requirements as may now or hereafter be imposed upon her.

The Allies assumed "supreme authority" over Germany. This "supreme authority" included, in the Allies' eyes, "all the powers possessed by the German Government, the High Command and any state, municipal or local government or authority."[4]

By early June, Berlin had been in Soviet hands for a month. The capital fell to Soviet troops on May 6, after a two-week-long battle. Approximately 90,000 German defenders—soldiers, Hitler Youth, and civilians—tried to hold back more than *two million* Soviet troops. It was a titanic fight. Researchers estimated Soviet deaths at over 80,000.[5] Hitler committed suicide in his bunker. The Soviets, who had lost upwards of 20 million people at the hands of the Nazis, occupied the capital city of their tormentors. They hoisted their hammer-and-sickle banner atop the *Reichstag*, a German government building that was a symbol of the Nazi regime. Two months later in July, American and British troops arrived in Berlin to assume control of their occupation sectors.

They found a devastated city. Soviet artillery and tanks weren't the first Allied forces to pound Berlin. Bombers had pounded it for years. The Americans and British air forces had made Berlin a priority target of their strategic bombing campaign. In 1945 they intensified their attacks. They wanted to disrupt German efforts to reinforce and resupply Nazi forces trying to stop the Soviets; they also hoped that an unrelenting rain of bombs might induce the Germans to surrender. A typical American or British air raid on the city in 1945 dropped over one thousand tons of bombs.[6]

As a result, Berlin was blown to bits. American General Lucius Clay, the first American Deputy Military Governor of Germany, first saw the city on June 5. "Wherever we looked there was desolation. The streets were piled high with debris which left in many places only a narrow one-way passage between high mounds of rubble, and frequent detours had to be made where bridges and viaducts were destroyed." The German civilians "seemed weak, cowed and furtive, and not yet recovered from the shock of the Battle of Berlin. It was like a city of the dead."[7] Locals hired to repair damaged buildings that the Americans planned to use for their headquarters "fainted from exhaustion on the job" and had to be fed by the Americans.[8] "Suffering and shock was visible in every face," wrote Clay. "The city was paralyzed."[9]

Clay's memoir describes the extent of Berlin's devastation. [All information in brackets was added by the author]

> There were only 20 fire department stations in operation, compared to a normal total of more than 80. Almost 3,000 breaks in water mains were still to be repaired and gas was available to only a small portion of the city. Hospital beds were limited in number and far below demand. Medical supplies were scarce and many of the hospitals were completely out of narcotics. Motor ambulances were not available and transportation of the dead and wounded was by hand stretcher or cart. Dead bodies still remained in canals and lakes and were being dug out from under bomb debris. It was a common sight to see a headstone of wood on top of a mound of debris with flowers placed at its foot. Large quantities of untreated sewage had to be discharged in the canals, creating an additional health hazard, and only 23 of 84 pumping stations were in operation. In Steglitz [one of the *Bezirke* in the US Occupation Sector] it was estimated that out of 14,000 homes, 3,260 had been destroyed, 3,200 uninhabitable, and in the remaining 7,500 which were considered habitable, 10,000 out of 43,000 rooms were seriously damaged. In the [borough] of Schoneberg, 45 percent of the housing was completely destroyed, 15 percent heavily damaged and only 5 percent undamaged.[10]

Much of Germany was damaged as badly as Berlin, especially the major cities. "All central and state government had stopped; county and city government no longer existed" wrote Clay.[11] Thousands of refugees clogged the roads. "The scenes on highway and railway were indescribable," he wrote, and "the roads were filled with destitute human beings desperately looking for a place to live."[12] People had to barter for food. Society seemed ready to collapse. Germans coined a special term for their situation: *Stunde Null* (zero hour), a time when the way of life everyone knew came to an end, and a new way of life began.

The Allies' joy in winning the war was dampened as they realized the extent of Germany's devastation. "Supreme authority" meant *they* had to run Germany. Immediately. Soldiers trained for war now had to keep the peace, hunt war criminals, and solve an endless list of problems arising from the war.

The four occupying powers shared responsibility for governing Berlin. Each of the powers was the primary governing authority within its own occupation sector. Berlin's citywide affairs, though, would be run by a "quadripartite" or Four Power government. The Western Allies chose to create a separate military government organization that the Four Powers would operate together, in cooperation with each other. The primary administrative body of that organization had a catchy name—the *Kommandantura*, which means "headquarters." The British, French, Russian, and American soldiers and civilians in Berlin now had to take a lofty concept— four different nations running a single city that was in ruins and in a foreign country—and implement it.

They quickly encountered a host of problems. Among them were shortcomings with the maps the Allies had of Berlin and vagueness in the prewar agreements on how to divide the city. The agreements specified which *Bezirke* in Berlin belonged to which occupying power. But the Allies' maps and prewar planning sessions hadn't accounted for all the territory the city owned. Specifically, the Allies hadn't thought through how to deal with Berlin's exclaves.

An *exclave* is a place that lies within one government's territory but officially belongs to another government. (Normally, a place is described as an "exclave" if it belongs to one country, but is surrounded by the territory of a different country.) Exclaves are *completely* surrounded by another country's territory. Essentially, they're little legal islands. *Enclave* is a more common term for isolated pockets of territory. But enclaves typically have some physical connection to their country—a corridor of land that links back home or a coastline on a body of water that leads to the homeland. Exclaves, on the other hand, are totally enclosed by the land of another country. If exclave residents want to travel to their home country, they must cross through the territory (or airspace) of a foreign nation.

The countries currently on the European and Asian continents differ greatly from the ones there only a few hundred years ago. Over the centuries, nations conquered other nations, small kingdoms merged into larger countries, and kings swapped territory. Countries changed their borders or even ceased to exist.

From time to time, a small area of land would lose its physical attachment to its homeland. Normally, that area would be absorbed into the country that now surrounded it. Occasionally, though, the now-isolated area maintained its allegiances *and* its legal status to its home country. This could happen for a variety of reasons. Perhaps the residents of the area passionately didn't want to be citizens of the new country, and that new country didn't object. The area might house a memorial, religious shrine, or some other site important to the original home country. Or an ethnic group with close ties to the home country might live in the area. As a result, exclaves weren't unheard of in Europe and Asia.

Steinstuecken's journey to becoming the most famous exclave of the Cold War started in the early 1800s. Residents of the village of Stolpe, which sat on the banks of the Wannsee, one of modern Berlin's largest lakes, began to acquire plots of farmland in an area approximately two miles to their south.[13] As the years passed, people built houses on the plots, and a small village grew. The soil was rocky, so the village acquired the name *Steinstuecken*, German for "pieces of rock" or "stone pieces."[14]

Although the two areas were miles apart, German law and custom treated Steinstuecken as part of Stolpe. "The fragmentation of land and administrative areas is an ancient feature of German rural settlement," wrote Central Intelligence Agency (CIA) analysts in 1967 in a report on the major exclaves around West Berlin.[15] "Because of tradition and the inheritance laws, farmland was cut up into very small parcels" said Frederick Sackstedter, a State Department liaison to the Germans. An average farm might total only twelve acres, but that acreage "might be in as many as 35 little parcels scattered over a wide area."[16] In 1898 Stolpe merged with another village, Alsen, into the parish of Wannsee.[17]

In 1920, the city of Berlin grew dramatically. On April 27, the Prussian government passed a law titled the "Formation of the New Municipal Community of Berlin." "94 formerly independent administrative areas," wrote the CIA in its report on West Berlin's exclaves, "ranging from large urban settlements to small villages and rural estates" were combined together[18] in the new city of "Greater Berlin." The law, commonly called the "Greater Berlin Act," caused Berlin to explode, growing from 65 to 876 square kilometers.[19] Wannsee was incorporated into the Zehlendorf *Bezirk*. Steinstuecken, as part of Wannsee, thus became part of the city—legally, but not physically.

Neither the Greater Berlin Act nor subsequent legislation in 1938[20] precisely defined the city's borders. The city boundary that Germans came to accept left Steinstuecken *outside* the Berlin city limits. Steinstuecken's northern border was separated from the city limits by about 1200 meters. The Zehlendorf *Bezirk* lies at the southwestern corner of Greater Berlin. Zehlendorf borders the state (*Land*) of Brandenburg.

Steinstuecken ended up completely surrounded by Brandenburg territory, with no officially-recognized strip of Berlin territory connecting it to Zehlendorf.

A small neighborhood, Steinstuecken had approximately forty houses and 300 residents in 1945. The village covered only thirty acres,[21] about the size of a college football stadium complex. A railway line feeding into Berlin bisected the neighborhood. Wooded areas lay outside the exclave to its east, the town of Babelsberg to its west.

Before World War II, Steinstuecken's status as an isolated pocket of Berlin didn't matter much to its residents or their neighbors. It was one of many neighborhoods around the city's outskirts. Its residents commuted to jobs in the city, and Steinstueckeners mingled daily with the residents of two neighboring towns in the state of Brandenburg, Babelsberg and Potsdam. Many thought Steinstuecken was a neighborhood of Babelsberg. Its legal status as part of Berlin mattered mostly at tax time.

The occupation changed that. The Allied Powers tightly controlled travel between the occupation zones. Normal commerce routes between towns and cities and across Germany were now blocked by Allied checkpoints. All Germans relied on ration cards for their food—cards that the victorious powers controlled. The quantity and quality of the food Germans got varied, based on how generous (or stingy) their occupier was. In the latter half of the 1940s, your quality of life as a German depended on the occupation zone or sector where you lived.

Steinstuecken was not Berlin's only exclave. Several plots of land outside of Greater Berlin had the same problem—legally part of the city but physically outside it. Historian Honore' Marc Catudal Jr.[22] wrote a book that, to this day, is the best record of Steinstuecken's experiences in the early Cold War years. Catudal counted ten major exclaves around Berlin. They were mostly farmers' fields, vacation cabins, gardens for Berlin residents or abandoned plots. Few were inhabited full-time. Steinstuecken was the only exclave with enough permanent residents to truly be thought of as a neighborhood.

The Allied maps of Berlin didn't show these exclaves very well, if at all. In all their prewar planning for how to govern Berlin, the Soviets, Americans, and British hadn't thought much about how to handle the exclaves. That might seem like a huge, hard-to-understand oversight. Remember, tho-ugh, that before World War II, the legal status of these neighborhoods/fields/cabin sites and garden plots was essentially a technicality. For most Berliners (including their mapmakers, apparently), these places were just part of Greater Berlin. Technically, an "exclave" is part of one *nation* that sits totally inside the territory of another *nation*. The Greater Berlin exclaves, Steinstuecken included, had never been foreign lands to Berliners. After the war, that changed. As the four Allied Powers tightened control over their occupation sectors and zones, the boundaries between those sectors and zones often seemed like international borders.

From 1945 until the end of the decade, Steinstuecken's status didn't concern American occupation officials very much. They had more pressing problems. Berlin was in shambles, with its people living in ruined homes and on meager rations. The Americans had to figure out how to rebuild and run Berlin in partnership with three other nations. And toward the end of the decade, another issue arose that would dominate Berlin for the last half of the century—the Cold War.

As the postwar years passed, relations between the Soviet Union and the Western powers (France, Great Britain, and the United States) soured. Eventually the West realized that the Soviets planned to turn Eastern Europe into a Soviet-controlled buffer zone. Less than one year after the Allies occupied Berlin, Winston Churchill gave his famous "Iron Curtain" speech in March 1946. At Fulton College in Missouri, Churchill warned that:

> an iron curtain has descended across the Continent. Behind that line lie all the capitals of the ancient states of Central and Eastern Europe. Warsaw, Berlin, Prague, Vienna, Budapest, Belgrade, Bucharest and Sofia; all these famous cities and the populations around them lie in what I must call the Soviet sphere, and all are subject, in one form or another, not only to Soviet influence but to a very high and in some cases increasing measure of control from Moscow.

Behind that Iron Curtain, more than one hundred miles from the British and American Occupation Zones in West Germany, lay Berlin. The French, British, and American Occupation Sectors of the city soon became "exclaves" themselves—Western-controlled pockets surrounded by Communist-controlled territory. Given everything else they had to worry about, it's not a surprise that the Americans paid little attention to the legal status of one tiny neighborhood.

Some Allied officials considered giving Steinstuecken to the Soviets. In his book, Honore' Catudal Jr. says that one American and one British official remembered the Americans trying to give away the hamlet.[23] The Allies discovered many problems with the occupation zone and sector boundaries. Sometimes the boundary lines crossed canals and lakes, leaving small pockets of land that technically belonged to one occupying power on the shoreline of another power's zone. Or a neighborhood would be connected to its owning *Bezirk* by just a street or a narrow sliver of land. These zigs and zags in the boundary lines caused headaches for the occupation forces, who had to patrol those lines and govern those sectors. So, from time to time, the Allied Powers traded bits of land. They did this to smooth out boundary lines, make gestures of goodwill, or compensate for other considerations. When you think of Steinstuecken's situation that way, trading it to the Soviets—who controlled the German state where the village actually *was*—sounded rational.

(The Western Allies even had Soviet-controlled pockets *within* their sectors. The Soviets didn't completely evacuate the Western occupation sectors when the Western Allies arrived. For example, the Russians kept the facilities for Radio Berlin, the main Nazi radio station, so they could operate it themselves. Those facilities were in the British Sector. They also established several memorials to their war dead in West Berlin. The Soviets kept some of these outposts throughout *the entire Cold War* As a result, Soviet personnel and symbols were regular fixtures in West Berlin. Whenever East-West tensions arose, the Western Allies and West Berlin authorities found themselves in a ticklish position—having to protect Soviets from angry Western citizens.)

In the summer of 1945, the occupying powers established a committee to look at the troublesome spots on the boundaries. That August, the committee recommended that three exclaves belonging to the Zehlendorf *Bezirk*—Steinstuecken, plus two uninhabited farmer's fields—be transferred to Soviet control. In return, the Americans would take two areas on a Wannsee Lake island in the US Sector, where Soviet sentries remained. However, for reasons long since lost to history, the committee's recommendations were never implemented.[24] The Russians stayed on the island, and the US kept Steinstuecken.

The Americans even disagreed among themselves whether Steinstuecken was part of the US Sector or not. The records of OMGUS (Office of Military Government, US), the military command that administered occupied Germany, are stored in the National Archives outside of Washington DC. They contain a letter from Colonel William Babcock, OMGUS Deputy Director, to a Steinstuecken resident, dated April 27, 1948. The resident wanted to get food and consumer goods from American occupation authorities instead of the Soviets.

In his reply, Babcock told the Steinstuecken resident that "We [in the US occupation authority] understand that you are actual Berliners." Babcock acknowledged that "when we first occupied the American Sector of Berlin, we considered Steinstuecken as part of our administration. However, about six months ago, we discovered that, at the time Berlin was divided between the Occupying Powers, Steinstuecken was not included in the U.S. Sector but was included in the Soviet Zone for purposes of administration."[25] Therefore, Babcock said, the Steinstuecken resident would have to take his requests to the Russians.

Karl Mautner, a State Department official stationed in Berlin, and some of his colleagues disagreed with Babcock. They firmly believed that Steinstuecken belonged to the US Sector. As with Jacques Reinstein, the State Department later interviewed Mautner to record his memories of his career. Mautner recalled a question that arose during the early years of the occupation: Should Steinstuecken residents draw food rations cards from the US or the Soviets? That exposed the larger disagreement within OMGUS about Steinstuecken's status:

> Colonel Babcock, who was [the] deputy [to General Frank Howley, head of U.S. Military Government in Berlin], proposed to give Steinstuecken away. [Ulrich] Biehl, [one of Mautner's colleagues] wrote a letter, a memorandum, which went all the way up, stating that neither Babcock nor Howley nor General Clay [by then the US Military Governor of Germany] could give Steinstuecken away because it was legally a part of West Berlin. That really prevailed. Then I followed up by pushing the city to giving them ration cards. We thus saved Steinstuecken [from Communist control].[26]

During the 1940s, neither the Americans nor the Soviets moved definitively to assert their authority over the neighborhood. In 1946 the Russians evicted the residents of sixteen houses in Steinstuecken, turning their houses into quarters for Soviet officers. However, neither occupying power stationed troops there. Initially, Steinstuecken residents received US Sector ration cards from Zehlendorf. But in 1947, the US stopped issuing them to Steinstuecken residents, forcing the Steinstueckeners to get ration cards from the Soviets. This continued until April 1950. Then, the Soviets stopped issuing cards, "pending a decision as to whether the area belonged to Berlin or Brandenburg."[27] Eventually the Americans resumed giving ration cards to the villagers.

For the first few years of the occupation, Steinstuecken was a hamlet stuck in limbo. No one determined conclusively who should govern it. The Allies didn't resolve the ambiguities about the village's status, and German officials lacked the authority to do it themselves. The hamlet's problems seem to have gotten lost in the whole mass of crises engulfing postwar Berlin—feeding the millions of city residents, fixing critical services, and dealing with swarms of refugees, the Berlin Blockade of 1948, and the start of the Cold War. Steinstuecken would stay in limbo until the 1950s. By then, changes in Germany and throughout the world would bring this little neighborhood to the forefront of the Cold War in Berlin.

CHAPTER TWO

OFFICE OF THE UNITED STATES
HIGH COMMISSIONER FOR GERMANY
BERLIN ELEMENT
PUBLIC SAFETY DIVISION
SPECIAL BLOTTER—18 October 1951

1615: Soviet Zonal leaflets announce incorporation of Steinstuecken Enclave in DDR.

According to reports received, leaflets were found at Steinstuecken, U.S. Sector Enclave in Soviet Zone (500 meters south of Griebnitz station, coordinates 1b R01) which announce that this area is incorporated in the German Democratic Republic as of today. West marks are out of circulation, all laws of the Soviet Zone are put into effect. The population is to report to Potsdam to receive ration and coal cards. The announcement is signed by the Minister of the Interior of Brandenburg.[1]

On the afternoon of October 18, 1951, a Thursday, Steinstuecken residents found their mailboxes broken open. Inside was a proclamation from the Brandenburg state government. "In order to eliminate the unnatural state of administration and maintenance of the Steinstuecken area," the hamlet was being "temporarily incorporated into the administration of the City of Potsdam." Steinstuecken now belonged to "Potsdam-Babelsberg" and was now part of the "German Democratic Republic (GDR)," the Communist national government in East Germany.[2] (DDR stands for *Deutsche Demokratische Republic.*)

The Communists had come for Steinstuecken. They were trying to sever the hamlet's links to West Berlin and absorb it into the Soviet Zone. The Americans now faced a direct challenge to Steinstuecken's status as a part of Berlin and the American Occupation Sector. They also faced a test of the US force's ability—and willingness—to defend the exclave. The events of the next few days would determine whether the hamlet remained free or fell into Communist hands.

For his book on Steinstuecken, Honore Catudal Jr. interviewed many of its residents and made several trips there. (The East Germans eventually banned him from the exclave.) Catudal writes that, by October 1951, Steinstuecken residents had grown accustomed to East German *Volkspolizei,* or "Vopos," patrolling outside their village. Steinstuecken's odd status naturally attracted GDR and Soviet attention. Vopos on guard duty were now part of the scenery around the exclave.

Two weeks earlier, though, something ominous had happened. At this point in the Cold War, the Communists hadn't yet sealed off Steinstuecken from the Soviet Zone. No walls or fences surrounded it. People could still walk between the hamlet and the surrounding areas. Vopos hardly ever entered Steinstuecken, and Soviet officers even less. But in early October, residents saw several Soviet officers, accompanied by Vopos, walk throughout the village. They seemed to be registering houses and compiling lists of inhabitants from the names on mailboxes. Now those same mailboxes had been pried open, and the mail inside them was gone. The villagers were sure the Vopos had it. Everyone hoped there was nothing in the mail that might anger the Communists.

Posters appeared, announcing the village's annexation. They invited residents to a meeting that evening. There, the mayor of Potsdam would greet his "constituents" and answer their questions about their new life as citizens of the GDR.[3] American observers reported that "the zonal border is [now] guarded by reinforced Volkspolice patrols. Apparently this is designed to prevent anyone of the population to escape or take property into the U.S. Sector."[4]

The seizure of Steinstuecken was an example of Communist "salami" tactics. The Western Allies coined that term to illustrate how the Russians carved away, in small slices, Western rights in Berlin. The Soviets and their GDR minions constantly imposed new restrictions on West Berlin. They blocked the *autobahn* to West Germany or levied new taxes on barge traffic or declared (with no warning) that certain goods couldn't be shipped by parcel post any more. These actions steadily reduced West Berlin's breathing space as a free community. Each new provocation was like another slice being carved off free West Berlin.

In 1951, the salami metaphor became real. The Soviets and the GDR seized areas on West Berlin's outskirts that, up until then, had been treated as West Berlin (and Western Allied-occupied) territory. On January 30, Soviet troops occupied the Neuer Gusthof farm in the Frohnau section of northern Berlin. The farm was officially part of the Soviet Zone, but since 1945, it had been administered as part of the West Berlin *Bezirk* of Reinicksdorf in the French Sector.[5] Three days later, on February 2, the GDR seized a much larger area—the British Sector village of West Staaken, with over 5,000 residents.

"Reds Occupy Area in Berlin" was the headline for *Stars and Stripes*' February 3 article on the West Staaken takeover. *Stripes* correspondent Norber Ehrenfreund wrote that the village's residents, "who have been living as West Berliners for five years, awakened yesterday to find they were residents of the Soviet Zone. A squad of 20 'people's policemen' moved in during the night, occupied the area and nailed up posters announcing the change. Teachers in the West Staaken school were dismissed and the Soviet Sector school council said new teachers from the Soviet Zone would take over."[6] Previously, wrote Ehrenfreund, "West Staaken has been administered to a great extent by the British Sector. All business was transacted in West marks, and residents voted in West Berlin municipal elections." The Communist takeover "virtually cut off West Staaken from the West sectors."[7] In the eyes of West Berliners, West Staaken was West Berlin territory. When the GDR seized the village, the West Berlin government howled in protest and urged the Western Allies to do something.

To their surprise (and dismay), West Berliners soon learned that the Soviets had the best legal claim to both Frohnau and West Staaken. In 1951, the "High Commission for Germany," or "HICOG," was the organization that ran American occupation activities. A February 14 dispatch from the Berlin HICOG office admitted that the disputed Frohnau area was "legally part of the Soviet Zone," and the main road from Berlin to Frohnau crossed 200 meters of Soviet Zone territory. Initially, the Russians hadn't objected when Westerners used the road to Frohnau.[8] As the years passed, many locals apparently assumed that the road and the entire area around the Neuer Gusthof farm was part of the French Sector. It wasn't.

For West Staaken, the news was worse. In the summer of 1945, all four occupying powers had reviewed the occupation sector borders.

The British agreed to transfer West Staaken to Soviet control. (In return, the British would receive a portion of a Berlin airfield, Gatow, which fell within the Soviet Zone.)[9] The transfer never occurred; it's unclear why. The Russians never asserted control over West Staaken. The neighborhood continued to function as a *de facto* part of the Spandau *Bezirk* in the British Sector. (Until February 1951, that is). When the Soviets finally did take West Staaken and Frohnau, the Western Allies couldn't do much about it. The Russians had asserted their authority over territory that was officially theirs.

The episode left West Berliners and their elected officials stunned and frustrated. It also spotlighted an ongoing source of irritation for the West Berliners—they didn't control their own city's boundaries. Berlin was still an occupied city. The occupying powers were the final authority on whether a certain neighborhood did (or didn't) belong to Berlin and which occupying power controlled that neighborhood.

In 1951, the West Berlin government didn't know exactly what (in the Allies' eyes) the boundaries of Berlin really were. The Allies hadn't allowed West Berlin officials to see all the official Allied maps of Greater Berlin or the records of the Allies' discussions on the exact boundaries of the occupation sectors. (The Allies had good reasons for not sharing. Many of those discussions had touched on sensitive issues, and the Allies didn't want to share those details with the West Berliners.) That put the West Berlin government in a tough spot. It didn't definitively know where the dividing lines were between Greater Berlin and the surrounding Soviet Zone or the boundaries of the four occupation sectors within the city.

This caused the West Berlin government to be publicly embarrassed over West Staaken. In Catudal's account of the West Staaken episode, West Berlin officials initially made some very strong statements against the GDR's move on the village. Then, when the details of the 1945 deal between the British and Soviets became known, those same West Berlin officials had to back down publicly. They "had been made to look foolish before the population of the city," wrote Catudal. "In turn, Western prestige had suffered."[10]

After the West Staaken affair, West Berliners "were officially assured that there are no more points of controversy" along the borders, wrote the West German paper *Der Tagesspiegel.*[11] Another West German paper, *Der Kurier,* reported that "the Western Allies had assured them at the time that these border lines were the same as those agreed upon in 1945 between the four occupation powers."[12] But many Allied occupation maps, as mentioned in Chapter 1, did not show Steinstuecken as part of the Zehlendorf *Bezirk*. (West Berliners didn't know this because they weren't permitted to see those maps.) And now, despite all the Allied assurances, the Communists had struck again. As the Vopos encircled Steinstuecken, it looked as if another part of West Berlin had been sliced away.

Mayor Ernst Reuter and the rest of West Berlin's leadership feared a replay of West Staaken. A quick look at the city's borders showed quite a few bulges or fingers of West Berlin land jutting into the Soviet Zone. If the Soviets could hold on to Steinstuecken, what might they try to carve off next? West Berlin's leaders made it clear that they weren't going to sit quietly, cross their fingers, and hope for the best.

On Friday, October 19, the morning after the Vopos surrounded Steinstuecken, emergency sessions of the Zehlendorf *Bezirk* and West Berlin city governments convened. They met again on Saturday the twentieth. Reuter and other city leaders denounced the GDR power grab and demanded that the Western Allies reverse it. "We must insist that the right be re-established that has been violated by the occupation of Steinstuecken," said Reuter on Friday the nineteenth, after meeting with Zehlendorf officials.[13] That same day, *Der Tagesspiegel* said West Berliners saw a familiar pattern in the Communist land grabs, a pattern they called "the system of rationing small provocations." *Der Tagesspiegel* wrote that West Berliners were sure that the Soviets would continue to test "how often and how heavily they can deal blows to the West" before the Western Allies struck back meaningfully.[14]

HICOG staff produced English-language summaries of major West Berlin and West German press stories. The summaries of this weekend's German press carried plenty of strong words from Reuter and his colleagues. "Steinstuecken Belongs To Berlin" thundered a headline from *Der Tagesspiegel* on Sunday the twenty-first. The article reported Reuter said, "There are things in Berlin which cannot be tolerated and would not be tolerated by anyone in the long run." "There is a limit to arbitrariness," was a Reuter quote in Sunday's *Der Tag*. In an unmistakable reference to West Staaken, the mayor announced that "This time, we will strike back." Again, in that Sunday's *Der Tagesspiegel*, a West Berlin official (presumably Reuter) said, "There cannot be any attack on West Berlin territory without our defending it with our life and our existence." Dr. Otto Suhr, president of West Berlin's House of Representatives, was just as dramatic. "If we do not fight for the enclave of Steinstuecken today, the enclave of West Berlin will be in danger tomorrow."[15]

City leaders and West German journalists left no doubt that West Berliners expected the Western Allies to free Steinstuecken. An article in *Der Telegraf* called the takeover a "serious violation of the Four-Power status of Berlin."[16] Politicians and reporters reminded everyone that, in the past year, the Western Allies had publicly guaranteed the security of West Berlin. "Steinstuecken is a case of test" for the Western Allies, wrote Sunday's *Telegraf*.[17]

"The annexation of Steinstuecken," wrote Catudal, "had clearly developed into an emotionally-charged issue. The future of the cutoff West Berlin hamlet, it was asserted, not only involved Western prestige, but a bond of trust between Berliners and the three protecting Powers now existed. The life of a small part of the Free World was as stake and it must be defended."[18]

Meanwhile, the East German press exulted over Steinstuecken's annexation and mocked the West. "Steinstuecken Can Breathe," crowed the *Berliner Zeitung* that Saturday:

> The racketeers, black marketeers and currency speculators of West Berlin, who are the stakeholders here, have intoned a big outcry in the press. What has happened?
>
> Steinstücken, previously a West Berlin enclave in the territory of the GDR—a small, disconnected segment of another West Berlin district going back to the days of stagecoaches—has now been included, in accordance with the international treaties, in the administrative area of the city of Potsdam. This long overdue step was taken in order to bring the small community, which lies within the territory of the GDR, in normal connection with their surroundings.
>
> How has Steinstuecken looked, up to now? Black marketeers and currency speculators had considered this place as their sanctuary. Several of the small households in this small village were completely at their service. The criminal elements took advantages of the farmers who lived in Steinstuecken. No wonder, then,

> that the people of Steinstuecken were unhappy over the heavy loads they had to bear.
>
> Now, finally, decent conditions have been established in Steinstuecken. Honest work is once again respected, the interests of the farmers are being protected by the authorities, and the members of the community are able to participate in the developmental successes of the GDR. Steinstuecken's experience is similar to that of Staaken, a community that was also subject to bankrupt Western administration, contrary to international agreements. But, now that they can flourish and thrive under the management of their rightful government, the Steinstueckeners can look forward to this change with confidence.[19]

Neues Deutschland, another GDR newspaper, echoed the *Berliner Zeitung's* "objectivity" with its headline: "Finally, normal conditions for honest citizens!"

The Communist press painted Steinstuecken as a haven for smugglers and currency speculators. *Neues Deutschland* called the village a "bootlegging headquarters." "Who was interested in the previously abnormal situation in Steinstuecken," asked the paper? "Only criminals and speculators. The West Berlin politicians and newspapers that howl over the elimination of this criminal center, only show once again that all West Berlin politics is driven by the morality of criminals and gangsters."

Pointing to high unemployment in the Western sectors, the East German press accused West Berlin and Western Allied leaders of using the Steinstuecken affair to distract West Berlin citizens' attention from the failures of their own government. "They, who don't have the ability to give hundreds of thousands of unemployed people in their own administrative districts labor and bread, nor prevent the constant increase in food prices," crowed *Neues Deutschland,* "do not have the slightest right to be indignant about measures that were taken in Steinstuecken."[20]

No matter how indignant the West Berliners were about the "measures" the Communists took in Steinstuecken, they were powerless to reverse them. If Steinstuecken was to be freed, the Western Allies would have to do it. Specifically, the Americans. America was, by far and away, the most powerful and influential of the Western Allies.

And Steinstuecken was an American responsibility. The Western Allies claimed that the hamlet belonged to Zehlendorf, a *Bezirk* in the American Sector. The Communists' salami knife had now targeted a section of US territory—and put the US Army and the HICOG on the spot.

The HICOG quickly realized they'd have to wage a legal and public relations fight with the Soviets, over who had the better claim to Steinstuecken. "If and when this Steinstuecken business comes to the point of conversations with the Russians," said a HICOG memorandum dated October 24, 1951, "the legalistic aspects are certain to come in for extensive and intensive discussion."[21] HICOG staff researched the village's history, before and after the war. Some documents created from that research still exist in the National Archives in Washington.

The October 24 memorandum explained how Steinstuecken ended up under American control in the first place. When the Allies divided Berlin into occupation sectors, they didn't draw boundary lines on a map. Instead, they assigned specific *Bezirke* to each occupying power. Berlin *Bezirke*, like the boroughs in New York City, had their own governments and civil servants. The Allies could use those governments to help them run the city. Zehlendorf was allocated to the Americans.[22] According to West Berlin records and city maps going back to the early 1920s, Berliners always treated Steinstuecken as part of Zehlendorf.[23] Therefore, according to the Allies' formula for establishing the occupation sectors, Steinstuecken belonged in the US Sector.

A memorandum addressed to Cecil Lyon, the HICOG director in Berlin, gives a quick review of Steinstuecken's history and its connection to the US occupying forces. It is dated October 19, the day after the village's seizure. This memo was probably written to advise HICOG leadership of key background information relevant to the crisis.

The memo cited evidence of the village's ties to the Western sectors—evidence that would bolster any American claim to the hamlet. Steinstuecken residents paid taxes and telephone and utility bills to West Berlin. They registered births and other official events with the police station in Wannsee, and residents voted in the West Berlin elections in 1946, 1948, and 1950. They read West Berlin newspapers, which were forbidden in the Soviet Zone.[24] The one store in the village took West marks, and Zehlendorf paid the villagers' unemployment and old-age pension benefits.[25]

The Allies' case had weaknesses. Steinstueckeners paid their taxes in East marks, not Western currency.[26] They often shopped in Babelsberg and Potsdam—taking advantage (as many West Berliners did) of the splendid exchange rate between East and West currency.[27] (One Western "DeutscheMark" was normally worth between four and six East German marks). There were also the issues covered in Chapter 1: the Soviet occupation of sixteen houses in the village, the August 1945 ruling by a Four-Power committee (never implemented) that Steinstuecken should go to the Russians, and Colonel Babcock's letter saying that, as some Americans saw it, Steinstuecken belonged to the Soviet Zone.

There was more. *Der Spiegel,* a West German magazine, reported that the Zehlendorf government had copies of letters that Colonel Babcock had sent to the Soviets during the Berlin Airlift. The letters asked the Russians to take over the exclave—and reimburse the Americans for past support costs! The article claimed Babcock had wanted to lessen Allied supply burdens during the blockade and hoped to offload Steinstuecken onto the Russians.[28]

Walter Steinweg was the unofficial mayor of Steinstuecken. In his memoirs, he said there had been "hard resistance" to Steinstuecken's inclusion in the US Sector from some American officials—and some West Berlin officials as well. Some Zehlendorf representatives claimed that Steinstuecken wasn't their *Bezirk's* responsibility. Some objected when village residents became eligible for new West German currency issued in 1948. One *Bezirk* administrator defended his opposition by referring to Soviet Zone newspapers. The administrator pointed to a Soviet Zone article on mass Communist demonstrations against the new West marks. The administrator told Herr Steinweg that he (the administrator) would be blamed "if something were to go awry on the basis of his decision."" If Steinstueckeners got West marks and trouble resulted, he would be "in danger of being banished into the [political] desert." Another Zehlendorf politician met with villagers to hear their concerns—and ask them to join his political party.[29]

In his memoirs, Steinweg remembers two Americans in particular, who were very helpful to Steinstuecken and showed obvious concern for its residents—Karl Mautner and Ulrich Biehl, the two State Department officials mentioned in Chapter 1. Mautner, recalled Steinweg, was "one of the few who had an ear for my pleas, and even made himself available to me for Steinstücken matters without an appointment."[30]

Steinweg remembered how, on one occasion, Biehl called Zehlendorf officials to HICOG headquarters, hoping to get West Berlin ration cards for exclave residents. The effort failed. Afterwards, Biehl told Steinweg that the Zehlendorf officials had not supported Biehl's endeavors. Steinweg says that Mautner was instrumental in Steinstuecken eventually getting West Berlin ration cards again.[31]

The Soviets, for their part, hadn't exactly been clamoring for Steinstuecken. HICOG records showed no evidence that the Russians had tried to implement the 1945 *Kommandantura* recommendation that the village be incorporated into the Soviet Zone. They rebuffed Babcock's request to take over the village and reimburse the Americans for past support costs. As mentioned in Chapter 1, in the spring of 1950 the Russians stopped issuing ration cards to village residents. They claimed it wasn't clear that Steinstuecken was really a Soviet responsibility. And, the Russians had never paid rent to the owners of the houses they confiscated. The occupying powers often paid rent for buildings requisitioned from German citizens and companies. However, the Russians refused to pay rent for the Steinstuecken houses. Why? The authorities in *Land* Brandenburg claimed Steinstuecken belong to West Berlin.[32]

As the HICOG staff looked at the hamlet's history, they found a mixed bag. The Americans and Russians could both point to evidence that justified their claims to the village. Both could cite times where the other power denied it had authority over Steinstuecken.

As for the realities on the ground, the Russians held many of the better cards. They could ignore West Berlin public opinion. They could wave off American claims to the village by saying that Four Power agreements on Berlin boundary lines were vague or incomplete. They could argue that Germany's total defeat made Steinstuecken's past ties to Berlin irrelevant.

Millions of ethnic Germans were evicted from their homelands after the war ended. (Eastern European nations essentially cleansed themselves of residents with German ancestry.) The victorious Allies changed German borders and took German territory. The Allied Control Council even abolished an entire German state—Prussia! In 1947, the Allied occupation authorities dissolved Prussia, the *Land* that symbolized the country's aggressive past. Calling the state "a bearer of militarism and reaction," the Allies distributed Prussia's lands among other

Laender.[33] Considering all that, why make a huge fuss over one small neighborhood in one city?

Another problem for the Americans: Steinstuecken was a *de facto* island. No strip of West Berlin territory connected the village to the rest of the American Sector. No Allied or West Berlin authorities disputed the fact that the territory in between Steinstuecken and Zehlendorf belonged to Brandenburg. If the Americans wanted to send troops to rescue Steinstuecken, they'd have to cross Soviet Zone territory. That might lead to Americans and Russians pointing guns at each other.

Ernst Reuter was willing to risk a confrontation. On the afternoon of October 19, the mayor paid a visit to Major General Lemuel Mathewson, the US Commandant of Berlin (USCOB). The USCOB was the senior American military commander in Berlin. Copies of two messages from Mathewson to HICOG headquarters in West Germany, which describe the meeting, are in the National Archives. One appears to be a quick summary of Mathewson's conversations with Reuter. The other is more detailed and is addressed personally to "Hays and Handy." Presumably this is General Thomas Handy, the commander of US European Command, and Major General George Hays, the Deputy HICOG.

"The mayor," Mathewson wrote in his note to Hays and Handy, "urges prompt and strong counteraction on the part of U.S. authorities. He has even suggested that I should cross the narrow strip of the Soviet Zone with a military convoy and occupy the Steinstuecken community in force."[34] In the summary message, Mathewson said that Reuter called for the "marching of a military column into Steinstuecken." Reuter also proposed that the Western Allies seize two Soviet-occupied buildings in West Berlin—the *Reichsbahn* (railway) offices in the US Sector or the *Rundfunkhaus* (Radio Berlin offices) in the British Sector. Reuter called these "Soviet enclaves in West Berlin."[35]

In his personal message to Hays and Handy, Mathewson commented on the village's predicament within the context of the overall geopolitical situation in and around Berlin:

> Steinstuecken is a small enclave in the Soviet Zone, lying about 500 meters south of the U.S. Sector-Soviet Zone boundary. It has always been administered by, and considered to be a part of, the district of Zehlendorf, a major subdivision of the U.S. Sector.

> While its legal status was fairly clear in 1945, it has been since then subject to such contradictory actions and conflicting opinion on our side, that our position today is somewhat indeterminate. Community today only contains about 200 residents and, from a practical point of view, might well be absorbed by the Soviet Zone. However, it represents another encroachment by the Soviets on the territory of Greater Berlin, and weighs heavily on public opinion.[36]

"Reuter states that the West Berlin population is extremely concerned by the Steinstuecken incident," wrote Mathewson, "and is wondering how long the Soviets will be permitted to take unilateral action without retaliation."[37]

Mathewson told Reuter that he "agreed that retaliatory action was desirable." However, the Western Allies "must refrain from any move which they could not be sure of following through to a successful conclusion." Any action against Soviet-held buildings in West Berlin required British and French approval.[38] The American general didn't send a column of troops to Steinstuecken. Instead, he told Reuter that he would send a note to the Russians "protesting the Soviet action, and was considering other means of making clear to the Soviets that we would not tolerate continued Soviet encroachment on the territory of Berlin."[39] Mathewson told Reuter that he would meet with the British and French commandants the next day, October 20, to discuss the situation.

Ernst Reuter was mayor of an occupied city, but he wasn't someone the Western Allies could simply dismiss. Ernst Reuter was a Cold War hero. Great leaders can help people make it through the most difficult of times. In the years immediately after World War II, the people of West Berlin desperately needed a great leader. Fortunately, they had one in Reuter.

A former communist, Reuter had been mayor of the East German city of Magdeburg. When the Nazis came to power, Reuter had to flee Germany, settling in Turkey during the war. At war's end he returned to Germany, eventually emerging as a leader of the Social Democrats (SPD), the primary West-leaning political party in Berlin. The French were unfriendly to Reuter—they distrusted any strong German leaders. The Soviets, unhappy that Reuter had abandoned communism, criticized him constantly, calling him an American lackey.

The Americans, though, found him impressive. "Dr. Reuter is a courageous political leader, a man of powerful intelligence and an experienced and capable municipal administrator," wrote General Frank Howley, the USCOB during the Berlin Blockade.[40] Karl Mautner recalled Reuter as "an extremely astute man, very intelligent, and obviously a leadership figure."[41] He "had a political sense that held everything together," said State Department official Martha Mautner (yes, the wife of Karl).[42]

After the 1946 city elections, SPD members of the City Assembly reacted harshly when the new mayor, an SPD member, acted overly friendly toward the Communists. In early 1947 they held a "no confidence" vote. When the mayor lost the vote, he resigned, and the SPD tried replacing him with Reuter. The Soviets blocked the change. Major German political moves in Berlin required unanimous four-power approval, which the Soviets refused to give. Reuter thus acted as an unofficial, *de facto* mayor for West Berlin until the 1948 elections. By then, the Berlin Blockade was in full swing, and East and West Berlin had separate city governments. Reuter became the official mayor of West Berlin.

Reuter's leadership was at its most powerful when the Allies most needed it—during the Berlin Blockade. In *Berlin Command*, Howley's book about his time in Berlin, he recalled when Reuter met with John Foster Dulles early in the blockade. Dulles, who would be Secretary of State in the Eisenhower administration, was visiting Berlin to gauge whether the West Berliners could hold up under the strain of the blockade:

> 'Will the Germans stand fast during the winter?' Dulles demanded, wasting no time on preliminaries. 'Or will they give up, accept Russian aid and get us out of Berlin rather than take more suffering?'
>
> Reuter's reply was emphatic and had the unmistakable ring of sincerity. 'The people of Berlin are accustomed to suffering,' he reminded Dulles. 'We are willing to suffer a great deal more to escape Russian domination.' Dulles seemed impressed.[43]

On September 9, 1948, hundreds of thousands of Berliners rallied to show their determination to resist the Soviets and endure all the hardships of the blockade. Reuter was one of many Berlin leaders to address the crowd. His speech, though, is the one most people remember. It was, arguably, his most dramatic public accomplishment as the leader of free West Berliners.

"*Ihr Völker der Welt, ihr Völker in Amerika, in England, in Frankreich, in Italien*!" thundered Reuter to the thousands gathered around the *Reichstag*. ("People of the world, people in America, in England, in France, in Italy.") Then, Reuter raised his palms to the sky.

> *Schaut auf diese Stadt! Und erkennt, daß ihr diese Stadt und dieses Volk nicht preisgeben dürft und nicht preisgeben könnt!*
>
> (Look upon this city! And recognize, that you cannot, you must not forsake this city and its people.)[44]

"Reuter was more than just a mayor," said Martha Mautner. "He was a symbol."[45]

Reuter was strongly pro-American. During the Berlin Blockade he toured the US. "The American public and American government will not abandon us in this struggle," he reported to the Berlin city government upon his return. "This is the firm conviction I gained after numerous contacts in the United States.... We shall not be abandoned, and we shall not be surrendered. We shall be and remain a free city."[46]

Two years later in May 1951, Reuter visited America again. Afterwards, he wrote an article for a HICOG monthly information bulletin. Titled "As I See America," Reuter shared his impressions:

> Some of what I saw and experienced in the United States is as certain and solid as a rock. This country, the size of a continent, is not only great from the geographical point of view or because of its economic potential, not only because it is about to develop great military strength in all fields: no, this country is great because it has realized its task and it is determined to tackle it.
>
> This perception and this determination are what I encountered wherever and with whomever I spoke. The people of this country are open-minded; whenever opportunity offers, they endeavor to learn from experience, both past and present. America has gained immense political maturity, through her historical development and through her bitter experiences in two world wars.

> This impression, of all that I gained during my stay on the other side of the ocean, stands out. It is a fact that is all the more important since America is a real democracy and boasts a public opinion that is shaped neither by propaganda nor by pressing a button to make people follow a given line. In the United States, people strive to comprehend significant problems. Hundreds of thousands, even millions, concern themselves with economic and political questions; they discuss them, they try to hear the views and opinions of other parties, and then they judge and form their own opinion.[47]

For the Western Allies, who were trying to convince West Germany to align itself with the West in the Cold War, Reuter's words must have sounded like pure gold. Now, five months after that article appeared, the man who had said those wonderful words demanded that the Americans save Steinstuecken. Ernst Reuter was not a man that the HICOG wanted to disappoint or disillusion. Millions of West Berliners and West Germans heeded his words.

"We are at present considering what retaliatory steps are available to us," Mathewson said in a message to HICOG headquarters. Based on what the message said, Mathewson felt his options were limited. "My immediate decision is to address a strong letter of protest to the representative of the Soviet Control Commission in Germany in Berlin, which I am doing this afternoon. While I see no other course of action available to me with respect to Steinstuecken, I do feel that we should resort to some form of retaliation in the immediate future." He then proposed something minor—demand the Soviets remove a small group of sentries who had been allowed to man a guard post just inside the US Sector. "I can't admit too much enthusiasm for this plan," Mathewson wrote, "but I feel that it is preferable under the circumstances to the negative action which I will otherwise be forced to take. Your immediate instruction would be appreciated."[48] (It is unclear what Mathewson meant by "negative action.")

The British and French commandants weren't ready to march on Steinstuecken either. A copy of a telegram from the British Control Commission for Germany (the UK's equivalent of the HICOG) is in the National Archives. The telegram summarizes, from the British point of view, Mathewson's meeting with the Commandants on October 20: "The Commandants considered the situation created by the occupation of Steinstuecken by the East Zone police, and irrespective of the legalities or illegalities of the issue and the possibilities of similar moves at other exclaves, have agreed that counter-measures should be taken at once in order to maintain Berlin morale and to reaffirm the Western Allies position in the City vis-à-vis the Russians." The message then mentions "the two most appropriate counter-measures available—the *Reichsbahn* building and the *Rundfunkhaus*."[49] The CIA's Office of Current Intelligence said, in its Daily Digest of October 25th, that the Western Allies had considered "retaliatory action, in the form of denying the Russians access to the important radio building which they now occupy in the British Sector."[50] If the commandants had considered a military response, they apparently decided not to pursue it.

Unfortunately, Lemuel Mathewson didn't keep a diary during his command in Berlin. And the HICOG records in the National Archives are limited. So, that forces us to do some guesswork to try to deduce what Mathewson was thinking during that weekend in October.

It seems obvious that the USCOB wasn't ready to risk armed conflict over Steinstuecken. Neither his messages nor the British's indicate any intent to respond with force. Nor do they show a strong Allied resolve to rescue the village. The Western commandants clearly felt it necessary to retaliate over Steinstuecken. They needed to send a strong message that future Russian "salami tactics" would have consequences. They also needed to reassure West Berliners that they could trust the Western Allies to protect the Western sectors of the city.

But it appears the Western commandants might have been willing, albeit reluctantly, to let the East Germans keep Steinstuecken if they couldn't convince the Soviets to back down. "We could have sent our own troops and driven them out," recalled Cecil Lyon. But "like so many things in those days, we were terrified that if we did the balloon would go up, and we'd get into a real row."[51]

Here is the protest letter that General Mathewson sent to the Soviet Control Commission (the Soviet's version of the HICOG) on the afternoon of October 19:

> I am informed that, by order of the German authorities under Soviet control, the village of Steinstuecken was declared on 18 October 1951, to be "administratively incorporated into the City

> of Potsdam." This unilateral and arbitrary act is a violation of the European Advisory Commission Agreement of 1944, whereby the district of Zehlendorf, of which Steinstuecken is a part, was included in the U.S. Sector of Berlin. The illegal action against Steinstuecken was taken without consulting the U.S. authorities under whose jurisdiction it belongs, and in utter disregard for its inhabitants.
>
> I therefore demand that the Soviet occupation authorities instruct the German authorities under their control to revoke their actions against Steinstuecken and permit its inhabitants to resume their former pattern of their lives as members of the West Berlin community.[52]

Once Mathewson sent his note, he and the other Western Commandants waited to see how the Soviets and East Germans would respond. They also watched developments in Steinstuecken over the weekend.

The village remained surprisingly calm. No reign of terror fell on the hamlet. No NKVD or Vopo teams stormed into houses or rounded up "revanchists" or "bootleggers." In fact, no one was arrested. Nor did the GDR occupy the town. Catudal questioned Steinstuecken residents on exactly what did or didn't happen in the village after the Communists surrounded it. In his book, he emphasized that the Vopos never blanketed the neighborhood with troops. One West German newspaper reported that some Vopos and Soviet soldiers had shopped in the village's store, looking for chocolate and cigarettes.[53] But the East German police stayed mostly on the outskirts of town.

In fact, Steinstuecken was never completely sealed off from West Berlin. The primary way that residents traveled to and from Berlin was over a country road known as the *Waldweg* ("woodland path"). The Vopos never completely blocked the *Waldweg*. The morning after the Communist proclamations appeared, several Steinstuecken residents were able to walk past the beefed-up Vopo patrols and go to Zehlendorf, where they met with city officials to report conditions in the village. On Saturday the twentieth, several village residents were able to travel to Zehlendorf again. They met with Mayor Reuter and other West Berlin officials to personally (and publicly) plead for help.[54] The GDR's handling of Steinstuecken was not as ruthless as it could have been. It was as if the Communists were waiting to see if the West really would push back this time, in this latest episode of salami tactics.

Things were tense, to be sure. Vopos walled off the town and the path to Zehlendorf with barbed wire. They cut the phone lines to West Berlin. The villagers, scared and uncertain of what might happen next, mostly stayed in their homes.[55] Outside the village limits, in full view of the residents, Soviets set up anti-aircraft guns and conducted battle drills.[56]

The residents were scared, but they were also defiant. They didn't cower before the Communists. Before the East Germans cut the phone lines, the Zehlendorf police managed to call Steinstuecken residents and get updates on their situation. The police were told that the village's residents "unanimously decided not to comply with the announcement of the Council of the City of Potsdam," annexing the village to Brandenburg.[57] Most village residents refused to go pick up GDR food ration cards in Potsdam, even though GDR representatives told them to do so. Nor did they surrender their West Berlin identity cards. They didn't buy goods from the East German grocery trucks that came to the village.[58] And they boycotted the meeting with the mayor of Potsdam—"their" new mayor—on the night of Thursday the eighteenth. The Zehlendorf police learned, in one of the last phone calls from the village, that the residents had chosen not to attend en masse. They sent just a few observers instead.[59]

The meeting was held at Walter Steinweg's tavern; he was one of the observers. As promised, the mayor of Potsdam addressed [in his words] the "dear citizens of Steinstuecken." A "large contingent of Socialist Unity Party (SED) functionaries" accompanied him. (The SED was the primary Communist-backed political party in Germany). Steinweg wrote that, although the villagers had been "ordered to come" to the meeting, they "wisely stayed away, and the restaurant was mainly filled with SED envoys."

"I still remember clearly," wrote Steinweg, "that one of the ranking functionaries invited me to have a glass of beer." The official "described to me in the most colorful terms how the business in our grocery stores and pubs" would improve, now that Steinstuecken was in the GDR. "All I had to do was welcome the new arrangement with the GDR warmly." Steinweg replied that he was waiting to see how the West Berlin government would react. The man wasn't pleased. His "mood turned sour, and he snapped 'You can be sure that Steinstuecken will remain in the GDR.'"

The Communist then admitted that "anything might still happen." The West might break the GDR's hold on Steinstuecken. If that happened, the official remarked, then "perhaps some printer's ink might be spilled about a kidnapping, and that will be that."[60] When West Berlin citizens vanished—most likely because the Communists had kidnapped them—the authorities or their loved ones often printed "Have You Seen Me" posters. Steinweg took the "printers' ink" comment to mean that, if the GDR failed in Steinstuecken, some villagers—himself included, perhaps—might vanish.

Possession is nine-tenths of the law. The Communists didn't actually possess Steinstuecken, but they had surrounded it. The village with its brave and inspiring residents was still an island. The Western Allies could build an airtight legal case for their rights to the village, and it might not matter. If the GDR (supported by its Soviet overseers) was determined to seal off Steinstuecken, the West's options were limited.

"You don't realize how intolerable it is to us having you in Berlin where you can prevent us from consolidating that area."[61] General Vasily Chuikov said that in 1949 to a State Department official. Chuikov had commanded the Soviet 8th Guards Army, which had participated in the capture of Berlin. The Russians shared Chuikov's frustration. It must have been very hard to convince the Soviet Zone's Germans to support the Soviet side and embrace communism when those same Germans could travel to West Berlin or talk with their friends who lived in the Western sectors of the city and see a much better (and much freer) way of life. The Russians harassed the West in Berlin whenever and wherever they could. Imagine all the grief they could cause to one little Western neighborhood marooned in Communist territory. Those thoughts must have crossed American minds, as the HICOG pondered what to do with Steinstuecken over the weekend of October 20.

CHAPTER THREE

"Germany must be brought into the Western community"...
"as rapidly as possible. And it is folly to think of bringing
her in as a permanent second-class member."[1]
—US High Commissioner for Germany (HICOG) John J. McCloy

American officials in Germany and Washington worried that the Steinstuecken crisis might cause problems for the United States in Berlin, and beyond. West Berliners were watching the United States . . . but so were the West Germans and the Western Europeans. They all wondered whether the US had the will and staying power necessary to remain in Europe for years, even decades, and keep the Soviets at bay.

In the fall of 1951, Western Europe was struggling through major political, economic, and defense policy transformations. The Americans hoped these changes would improve Western Europe's economy and security and lessen America's overseas aid burden. But if the people of West Berlin, West Germany, or Western Europe doubted America's resolve, those transformations could stall or fail. Europeans watched the Americans intensely, looking for even small signs that the US wouldn't keep its promises to protect Europe. The HICOG and State Department feared that Europeans might interpret abandoning Steinstuecken as just such a sign.

One month earlier, American, Canadian, and Western European leaders had met in Ottawa to review the status of West European defenses. North Korea's invasion of South Korea had shocked and scared the West. Many feared the Soviets might attack Western Europe. In September 1950, US Secretary of State Dean Acheson announced that the United States was prepared to "participate in the immediate establishment of an integrated force in Europe, within the framework of the North Atlantic Treaty, adequate to ensure the successful defense of

Western Europe, including Western Germany, against possible aggression."[2] That "integrated force" would become NATO.

At Ottawa, NATO's growing pains were obvious. State Department records indicate the delegates felt Western defenses were inadequate. The British Foreign Secretary said the alliance would have to "weather a difficult period ahead until reasonable military equality between the East and West would be achieved."[3] General Eisenhower, who would become the Supreme Allied Commander in Europe in December, sent a report warning that "existing defense commitments were not being effectively met." It stressed the "vital necessity of having existing forces and those being raised be battle worthy." The alliance's level of battle readiness "required frank discussion."[4]

Frank discussions followed. Some NATO nations were struggling to achieve their force readiness obligations. A common complaint: Increased military spending would harm countries' finances and standards of living. The Dutch foreign minister said that "any further lowering of living standards would endanger social peace on the home front."[5] Denmark and Norway claimed their economies already faced inflation.[6] Secretary of State Acheson summarized the other nations' complaints in a message to the president on September 19.

> Most report a grave worry in European countries over deterioration of their internal economies under the impact of post-Korea defense programs. All have stressed that a military buildup at the accelerated rate that the US has been advocating would result in runaway inflation and economic chaos, would foster communism and thus be self-defeating.[7]

As for West Germany, its economy wasn't struggling; it was booming. By the 1950s, the German economy was on the path to becoming Europe's strongest. This economic revival had a colorful nickname—the *Wirtschaftswunder* ("economic miracle"). By the summer of 1951, German exports and employment had reached record levels,[8] and the dollar value of German exports exceeded the value of imports.[9] George Kennan, a legendary State Department Cold War figure, mentioned the German economic revival in a memorandum for the Secretary of State in September 1951. Kennan noted "the amazing rise in German strength and energy, which we have no choice but to recognize as a major European reality."[10] In a quarterly report to Washington, US High Commissioner for Germany John J. McCloy said, "Germany is the principal source of coal, steel and machinery for continental Europe."[11] The Americans wanted to tap that strength and energy. They wanted West Germany to build products for Western militaries.

That was easier said than done. John J. McCloy, as the "High Commissioner for Germany," was the senior American official in Germany. But he wasn't the boss of the Germans. And the Germans knew it.

In the years immediately following World War II, America's authority over the Germans was absolute. Germany hadn't been simply defeated—it had been crushed. At war's end, OMGUS, a U.S. Army-led organization, literally ruled the American Zone in Germany and American Sector in Berlin. German *Laender* and local governments had little authority. German civilians accused of common crimes weren't tried in their traditional hometown courts. The Allies suspended the entire German judicial system. Germans in the US Zone were tried by American military tribunals. All German political parties, newspaper articles, and radio broadcasts in the American Zone had to be approved by OMGUS. OMGUS even controlled when Germans could brew beer and go hunting.

By the time of the Steinstuecken crisis, though, OMGUS was gone. In the spring of 1949, the Berlin Blockade and the Cold War were in full swing. France, Great Britain, and the US decided to acknowledge the obvious: Germany would not reunify anytime soon, if ever. If West Germany was going to recover and eventually thrive, it needed its own national government. "The United States can tolerate no further delay in the restoration of political and economic health to Germany as an essential of European stability,"[12] wrote McCloy in one of his quarterly reports to Washington.

In September 1949, the Germans in the American, British, and French Zones elected a national parliament with two houses, the *Bundestag* (lower house) and *Bundesrat* (upper house). The Federal Republic of Germany, aka the FRG, came into being. The new country was soon known informally as West Germany. The parliament elected Konrad Adenauer, former mayor of Cologne, as the new country's first Chancellor.

Once the FRG was established, the Western Allies relinquished much of their day-to-day authority over West German life. In 1949 they enacted the "Occupation Statute." Here is its first sentence: "During the period in which it is necessary that the occupation continue, the Governments of France, the United States and the United Kingdom desire and intend that the German people shall enjoy self-government to the maximum extent possible consistent with such occupation."[13]

The Occupation Statute kept control of German foreign affairs, to include foreign trade, in Western Allied hands. The Western Allies maintained their own occupation courts and laws, and Germans had virtually no jurisdiction over refugees or Allied personnel. The statute also allowed the Western Allies to "resume, in whole or in part, the exercise of full authority if they consider that to do so is essential to security or to preserve democratic government in Germany or in pursuance of the international obligations of their Governments."

What the statute did return to the Germans, though, was much of the control over their society, local government, and lives. The statute returned most executive, legislative, and judicial power to German local and *Laender* governments. The Allies also removed almost all controls on German press and politics.

The Germans quickly exploited their new prerogatives and freedom of action. McCloy's quarterly reports show the Germans chafing against—and even outright resisting—Allied controls: "Passive resistance has developed to certain occupation-sponsored reforms (school, civil-service) induced by German awareness of the restricted nature of Allied authority under the Occupation Statute with regard to internal political matters," said McCloy in his report for the last three months of 1949. "There is a strong feeling in various quarters that the Western Powers are governing Germany in their own interest."[14] In his next report, McCloy told of a "noticeable stiffening of the German attitude toward the Western Occupation Powers."[15] More than a year later, in his report for the summer of 1951—immediately before the Steinstuecken crisis—McCloy wrote, "Growing German national consciousness found its expression in government and press statements criticizing various Allied actions."[16] The Germans had many complaints: forced dismantling of industrial plants, Allied controls on shipbuilding and foreign commerce, Western demands that the FRG pay pre-war German debts, etc.

The Occupation Statute ended military government. OMGUS was replaced by the United States High Commission for Germany, a State

Department organization. McCloy, HICOG's head, had been a corporate lawyer, president of the World Bank and Assistant Secretary of War during World War II. Diplomats and civilian administrators would now run the occupied areas. Personnel from the State Department and other civilian agencies replaced the Army, and the occupation switched from military to civilian control.

The HICOG had much less authority over the Germans than OMGUS did. HICOG staffers were authorized to "observe, advise and assist" the Germans in political, social, and education affairs. They could not restrict "the legislative, executive or judicial competence accorded to [German] governments in these matters." The occupation authorities were to exercise "minimum control over German trade and internal policies."[17]

As a result, the Americans' ability to out-and-out tell the Germans to do (or not do) something diminished drastically. "By the time we got there," recalled Harry Odell, a State Department official who came to Germany in 1951 to work at the town and county levels, "the real authority legally was still there, but in practice, there was very little power left. The Germans had by that time pretty much started running their own affairs up to a pretty high point."[18] Taylor Seelye, another State Department employee, echoed Odell's view. "By this time, the Germans had resumed control of the government and administrative machinery. The U.S. no longer operated by fiat."[19] McCloy and his State Department personnel would have to rely more heavily on persuasion, negotiation, and relationship-building with the Germans. Americans could no longer treat Germans as, in the blunt words of a State Department official, "somebody to be stepped on."[20]

The Americans needed Germany's support and cooperation in many areas. The US not only wanted Germany to build defense products. It also needed Germany to willingly align itself with the developing community of Western European nations. Having barely survived the last European war, the nations of Western Europe—and countries that kept getting dragged into European conflicts (i.e., the US and Canada)—hoped to prevent future wars in the region.

Western diplomats wanted to build a series of organizations and treaties that would bind the European countries together in multiple areas—economic, political, social, and defense. The North Atlantic Treaty (which led to NATO) was an example of that. In 1946 Winston

Churchill called for a "United States of Europe." Three years later, ten European countries created the "Council of Europe" in May 1949. The Council was an advisory organization; it couldn't pass laws binding on member governments. Instead, it promoted cooperation amongst European countries in democracy, legal affairs, and culture.[21]

The US wanted the FRG to join the Council of Europe and other Western European organizations. The thinking was, if West Germany was tied to its neighbors, it would be less likely to invade them again. At a US ambassador's meeting, McCloy "said he favored a policy of getting Germany 'enmeshed' in every possible international organization."[22] A State Department memorandum of February 1950 said the best way to prevent future German militarism was to "so weave Germany into a larger whole as to contain satisfactorily the energies, economy and political ambitions of the Germans." Accordingly, the State Department was "following a policy of bringing Germany into as many Western European and world organizations as possible."[23]

Many West Germans supported that approach. Others, though, worried that, if West Germany bound itself too tightly to the West, it would be hard (if not impossible) to reunite with East Germany anytime soon. The Soviets encouraged this kind of thinking. "The Communists clearly hoped to build up German opposition to any contribution to Western defense, and to strengthen sentiments favorable to the neutralization of Germany," said McCloy in his quarterly report for September–December of 1950. "Their propaganda held out as its ultimate goal the unification of Germany."[24] The Soviets and East Germans warned that, if the FRG aligned itself with the West, the two halves of Germany might never reunite. No Western leaders really feared that West Germany might choose the Soviet side in the Cold War. But it was possible that West Germans could hesitate to bind themselves to the West, opting instead for some sort of uneasy neutrality. McCloy told Washington that "many Germans were troubled by the seeming incompatibility between Western integration and German reunification."[25]

One organization the Americans wanted West Germany to join would require the West Germans to make a huge sacrifice—control of their coal and steel resources! In March 1951 the West German foreign minister joined diplomats from France, Italy, Belgium, the Netherlands, and Luxembourg and initialed the "Schuman Plan."[26] Named for its creator, French Foreign Minister Robert Schuman, the plan called for the six nations to cede control of their nation's coal and steel production to a new international organization, the European Coal and Steel Community (ECSC). The ECSC was "a great step in the modern history of traditionally war-torn Europe," said an article in McCloy's quarterly report for January–March 1951. "A union of West European coal and steel resources would, in the words of Schuman, 'make any war between France and Germany not only unthinkable, but in actual fact impossible.'" … "That six European countries agreed to relinquish some of their sovereign rights to a new European high authority proves that the idea of European unity is more than a dream."[27]

Six countries may have offered to sacrifice control of their coal and steel resources for the sake of peace. But no one thought, or even pretended, the sacrifice was equal. The Western Allies wanted the ECSC to supervise coal and steel production in the Ruhr, Germany's primary coal and steel region. Without control of the Ruhr, Germany would be hard-pressed to launch another war. The ECSC's goal was to deprive Germany of its future war-making potential. From the viewpoint of America and West Europe, that was a good thing.

Many West Germans didn't agree. Konrad Adenauer and his Christian Democrat (CDU) party supported the Schuman Plan. Many in the main German opposition party, the Social Democrats (SPD), did not. They felt Germany was sacrificing too much. Who could blame them? What country wouldn't care if other countries took over its natural and industrial resources? (How would twenty-first -century America react if the UN took control of Texas' oil resources?) "There is an increasing desire in German political circles," wrote McCloy, "to be able to pursue German policies in defense of what are deemed legitimate German interests and not to be merely a German instrument of Allied policy."[28]

In late October 1951, at the time of the Steinstuecken crisis, the *Bundestag* was still debating the Schuman Plan. The Western Allies expected the West German government to approve it, but it hadn't yet. At the same time, the FRG and the Western Powers were hashing out the details of new agreements that would formally end the Allied occupation of West Germany. These would be agreements between sovereign and co-equal governments, not orders from occupying powers to a defeated people. "Germans have 'developed a sort of "occupation fatigue" accompanied by grave doubts of the good will and intent of the Occupying Powers,'" the HICOG reported in its quarterly report for summer 1951. "To match new German responsibilities in connection with collective security, a new political status was essential. Neither as an occupied nor a satellite state could Western Germany be expected to make a whole-hearted contribution, but only as a partner in the community of free nations." The HICOG report said that "it was natural that the Germans should expect that equal duties should be balanced with equal rights."[29]

As for equality among the three Western Allies, there wasn't much. By this point in the Cold War, the US was clearly the strongest of the three Western Powers. France and Britain struggled to recover from the war. Both received Marshall Plan aid. The US assumed the lion's share of the costs for occupying Germany. In the early 1950s, the French Communist Party was strong enough to make American diplomats question how reliable a Cold War partner France could be. George Kennan, in September 1951, worried about "the continued inability of the French"..."to eliminate the communists from the dangerous [position] they have established" in French society.[30]

As for the British, their resources were exhausted and strained. Their economy had problems. The British Foreign Minister, Ernest Bevin, admitted in September 1950 that there "was a very critical economic situation in the UK."[31] Many consumer goods (meat, sugar, gasoline) were still being rationed.[32] British citizens still had to use ration coupons. Before the war, Great Britain had been a coal exporting nation; now it was having trouble meeting its own needs.[33] The British had colonies and interests around the world they had to manage and support. They couldn't focus all their resources on Europe.

"One of the striking things of the course of developments since the war has been the decline of the British and French as great powers" wrote the State Department's Bureau of German Affairs in February 1950. "It is all too clear that the French do not occupy this position and the British are increasingly unwilling to bear these responsibilities. Their unwillingness rests fundamentally upon the tremendous cost of doing so. This has affected not only their military position but their attitude toward many problems that arise from day to day." As a result, "the task of leading and organizing the whole of the non-Soviet world has fallen increasingly and ever more heavily upon the United States."[34]

The Germans saw this. They knew American money—and the willingness to spend it on a defeated people—made the Marshall Plan possible. Many of the world's prime grain and rice growing areas had been battlefields; this caused food shortages across the globe. Most of prewar Germany's prime agricultural areas were now in the Soviet Zone. American farmers and ranchers stepped up to fill the void. Food shipments from the US helped the Germans survive the lean years immediately following the war. Even as conditions in Germany improved, it still relied on imports for much of its food supply. (General Clay, in retirement, remarked on people who regretted the mass extermination of the buffalo herds as the American West was settled. "My God," said Clay, "those plains where the buffalo roamed fed the entire world after World War II.")[35]

West Berliners and West Germans recognized that if the United States couldn't (or wouldn't) hold back the Soviets, then no one could. That led West Berliners—and West Germans and Western Europeans—to watch the US closely, even obsessively. Many wondered if North Korea's invasion of South Korea was a sign that the Soviet Union was ready to turn aggressive in Europe. Western Europeans knew they needed American protection, but they wondered if America had the will and means to keep a strong military presence in Western Europe. America now had a war on the other side of the globe. Communist China was now an American problem. The United States wasn't a traditional colonial power on the scale of Great Britain and France. Isolationism, not colonialism, had characterized many Americans' foreign policy preferences in the years before World War II. Many Americans feared becoming entangled in overseas alliances and commitments.

Western Europeans knew all of that. They knew Americans were worried that a long-term European alliance might drain their country's finances and pull it into World War III. They knew America had its hands full elsewhere on the globe. Many different forces tugged on the United States in late October 1951, pulling it to divert its money and military away from Europe. That made West Berliners, West Germans, and Western Europeans sensitive, even hyper-sensitive, to any American action (or inaction) that might hint that the US's resolve to hold back the Soviets was weakening.

That's what made Steinstuecken important. Remember how General Mathewson, the USCOB, described the village's situation in his message to Generals Hays and Handy immediately after the crisis broke out. Mathewson made it clear the hamlet was strategically insignificant.

"From a practical point of view," he wrote, it "might well be absorbed by the Soviet Zone." Losing Steinstuecken wouldn't jeopardize the US's actual on-the-ground ability to defend West Berlin. It might, however, make people wonder how much steel really was in the American's spines. As mentioned in the last chapter, Mathewson said that the GDR push on Steinstuecken "represents another encroachment by the Soviets on the territory of Greater Berlin, and weighs heavily on public opinion.[36]

Steinstuecken, the Americans feared, might be a proverbial "canary in the coal mine." Berliners, Germans, and Europeans might interpret any American unwillingness to defend the exclave as a sign of a greater unwillingness to stand behind US promises to safeguard Western Europe. That might make West Germany and Western Europe hesitate to commit themselves to Western European defense and a Western European community. Steinstuecken was a test of American will. HICOG leadership knew that as they pondered what to do about the hamlet's plight.

The senior American official in Berlin was the USCOB, General Mathewson. (John J. McCloy was the senior American official in Germany, and Mathewson worked for McCloy. But in Berlin itself, Mathewson was senior). To get a sense of Mathewson's tenor and spirit, read some of his official correspondence to the Russians. The National Archives contains some of those letters and memoranda. They reveal a man who didn't shy away from using tough, and sometimes mocking, language with the Communists.

On April 23, 1951, Mathewson wrote Sergei Dengin, chief of the Soviet Control Commission in Berlin. Dengin had complained about West Berlin police arresting two railroad stationmasters. (When World War II ended, the Western Allies let the Russians keep authority over *all* railroad facilities in East and West Berlin.) The stationmasters allowed pro-Communist propaganda to be posted in West Berlin railway stations; the West Berlin police arrested them for unapproved political activities. Dengin wrote Mathewson, accusing the West Berlin police of "gross lawlessness."[37] Mathewson fired back. "I regret that you have permitted yourself to indulge in propagandistic misrepresentations," he wrote in his reply to Dengin. "Surely such distortions of fact can have no proper place in constructive correspondence between us."[38]

The Soviet Tanker's Memorial incident spawned an especially entertaining series of letters between Mathewson and Dengin. As a memorial to the tank crewmen who fought and died in the Battle of Berlin, the Soviets placed a Russian tank on a pedestal. The pedestal was in the US Sector. By the summer of 1951, the memorial had become a handy outlet for Berliners to vent their anger with the Soviets. On June 12, Dengin wrote to Mathewson:

> It has come to my knowledge that a band consisting of criminal elements desecrated the memorial to Soviet tankmen who gave their life in the struggle against fascism and in the great cause of international peace. These provocateurs destroyed the facing of the memorial, smeared the pedestal with black paint and, after pouring gasoline, set it on fire. Neither the American authorities who are responsible for the preservation of order in this part of the city, nor the West Berlin police had taken any steps in order to put a stop to this shocking act of provocation.
>
> I register an emphatic protest against the defilement of the memorial to Soviet warriors, and demand that the culprits be traced and subject to severe punishment at once. Please advise me of the measures taken by you.[39]

Mathewson replied to Dengin a few days later:

> In reply to your letter of 12 June 1951, I should like to say that I deplore, as do you, the defacement of the Soviet Tank Memorial in Potsdamer Chausee, U.S. Sector. I had already issued instructions, in fact, even before the receipt of your letter, that every effort should be made to apprehend the guilty persons.
>
> I feel that we must accept the likelihood, however, that, the continued presence of this monument in the U.S. Sector will only serve, under the circumstances, as a provocative issue to the German people and that it may conceivably be subject to even further indignities in the future.

Mathewson suggested that the Soviets move their memorial "to some location outside the U.S. Sector where its significance can be more appropriately observed."[40]

To put it mildly, Dengin wasn't happy with Mathewson's reply. On June 26 he wrote the USCOB and made it clear that the Soviets didn't see a memorial to their war dead as a "provocative issue":

> Your letter of 18 June, 1951, convinces me that the act of provocation on the Potsdam Chausee in the U.S Sector of Berlin, with regard to the Memorial to Soviet tankmen, was organized not without the knowledge of the U.S. occupation authorities.
>
> The assertion contained in your letter, that "the continued presence of this Memorial in the U.S. Sector ... will serve as a source of irritation to the Germans and may, therefore be subjected to renewed outrages in the future" is false through and through, and is calculated only to lend support to fascist elements in Western Berlin, who are engaging in all sorts of provocative activities and striving, thereby, to complicate relations between the occupation authorities. Such an attitude on the part of the U.S occupation authorities is meeting only with misgivings and an expression of condemnation on the part of the Soviet control organs, as well as provoking the resentment of Berlin's population, including that of the U.S. Sector, whose feelings are inspired by a sense of profound respect for the memory of the Soviet heroes who gave their life in the task of liberating the Germans and other European peoples from the fascist yoke.[41]

Betsy Bailey, Lemuel Mathewson's daughter, recalls her father's feisty attitude toward the Russians. "I remember him coming home from work, frequently complaining about 'those blankety-blank Russians.'" Ms. Bailey remembers the Tank Memorial incident in specific. "Dad said, with a twinkle in his eye, that he was tempted to just put chicken wire around the thing."[42]

That is exactly what the Americans did. From Dengin to Mathewson on August 17:

> I have been informed that on instruction of the U.S. occupation authorities the monument honoring Soviet tankmen on the Potsdam Chausee has been surrounded by metal netting. This new, inadmissible assault against the monument honoring warriors, who gave their lives fighting Hitlerite tyranny, evidences that the U.S. authorities not only did not take any steps with regard to my letter of 26 June 1951, but embarked upon a course of further provocations with respect to the monument.[43]

Mathewson displayed that same feisty spirit and willingness to poke at the Soviets when he responded to the Steinstuecken crisis. The Americans gave the press his October 19 protest letter to the Soviet Control Commission. *Stars and Stripes,* the *New York Times*, and other major American and European papers carried the USCOB's demand that the Russians leave Steinstuecken.

Making the letter public signaled that the US might hold the line on Steinstuecken. Once the Americans publicized the USCOB's hardline language to the Soviets—language that demanded the Communists "revoke their actions against Steinstuecken" and allow the villagers to rejoin West Berlin—if the Russians still refused to budge, the Americans would be humiliated. Keeping the protest letter's text within diplomatic channels, out of the public eye, would have given the Allies a little more wiggle room. But Mathewson took the bold, public route instead.

On Monday, October 22, *Stars and Stripes* ran an article about Steinstuecken on Page 1. Its title: "West to Act on Berlin Grab." (Emphasis added)

> Berlin, October 21: Maj Gem Lemuel Mathewson, U.S. commander in Berlin, said today the Western Allies 'do not intend to tolerate the Communist seizure of a part of West Berlin.'
>
> Mathewson told *14 visiting US editors and publishers* [emphasis added] that 'action on our part is necessary to indicate to the Soviets that we do not intend to tolerate such measures.'
>
> The commander also disclosed that he expected a decision would be reached within the next several days concerning 'effective countermeasures.' He did not state what this counteraction would be.
>
> . . .
>
> Mathewson said the reason for the seizure was that the Soviets are always looking for ways and means to embarrass the Western Allies and the West Berlin authorities.
>
> . . .
>
> Referring to a meeting of the Western Allied commandants yesterday, Mathewson said: 'The commandants are in full agreement that the Soviet Zone authorities have no right to assume control over the area.'[44]

The American journalists were visiting Berlin as part of a previously scheduled tour of US military installations worldwide. They didn't come to the Divided City just because of Steinstuecken. But by putting the Steinstuecken crisis front and center before leading American journalists, Mathewson put US prestige at risk. He also guaranteed that the village's plight would stay in the public eye.

The American press was already following the Steinstuecken story. "East German police made a lightning invasion of the American sector district of Steinstuecken here and declared it part of the Russian zone," said a Reuters wire report in the *Minneapolis Star Tribune* on October 19. This was the opening sentence in an Associated Press (AP) wire report in the *Baltimore Sun,* also on October 19th: "Soviet Zone police took possession tonight of a half-square mile strip of land long regarded as part of West Berlin and immediately placed 50 families under East German control."

The major news wire services, especially AP and the United Press (UP), reported daily on the events in and around Steinstuecken. Newspapers throughout the US picked up these stories. Here are some of the headlines that American newspaper readers saw in the days immediately following the GDR's envelopment of the hamlet: "East Reich Police 'Annex' U.S. Area" (*Minneapolis Star Tribune*); "East Berlin Police 'Correct' Border" (*Baltimore Sun*); "U.S. Protests Red Grab in Berlin" (*Pittsburgh Press*); "US Protests Soviet Real Estate Theft Try" (*Arizona Republic,* Phoenix); "Communist Police Troops 'Annex' US Sector Town" (*The Daily Clintonian,* Clinton, Indiana); "Reds Seize Town in US Area of Occupied Berlin" (*Daily Times*, New Philadelphia, Ohio); "Reds in Berlin Seize Sector of US Zone—No Countermeasures taken by Americans" (Louisville *Courier-Journal*); "Berlin Section Seizure Rapped" (*Palm Beach Post,* West Palm Beach, Florida).

Some of the stories weren't helpful to the HICOG's efforts to assert American rights over the exclave. This is an excerpt of an AP wire story from October 19th:

> Old maps confirmed today the Russian right to seize a small strip of land on the American sector border of divided Berlin.... West Berlin police, rechecking the official land register, said this morning the village—Steinstuecken—was traditionally a part of the East German state of Brandenburg until 1945. In the postwar

confusion, the village adopted American sector ways, used western currency and even voted in the West Berlin elections.[45]

Another AP wire story that day said that the "Soviets had made several such 'corrections'" to the Berlin borders "in the past two years, and have always been sustained by the zonal record agreed upon by the Allies."[46]

Other stories from Western wire services highlighted the challenges Mathewson and the Americans faced in reversing the Communists' grab of the hamlet. "A Western spokesman said there was virtually no chance that American troops will be sent into the seized Steinstuecken district because they would have to cross Soviet-controlled territory to get there," said UPI in an October 19 wire report.[47] A *New York Times* cable said that, "Privately, both Americans and German officials agreed that nothing more could be done unless the United States decides to force a major showdown by sending armed forces to establish a corridor across the mile-wide strip of Soviet territory separating the 50-house hamlet from the rest of West Berlin. There were no indications that such a move is under consideration." That same *New York Times* cable made it sound as if many in the West had already written the hamlet off as lost to the Communists. "It appears that Steinstueckeners have joined 18 million other East Germans under Soviet control."[48]

The East German press mocked Mathewson's protest to the Soviets. From *Neues Deutschland*, on October 21:

> The American commandant, General Mathewson has written a letter of protest to the Soviet Control Commission, in which he complains that the inhabitants of Steinstuecken can no longer continue (as he characterizes it) 'their previous lifestyles as West Berliners.' What might Mr. Mathewson have in mind when he coined this new term of 'West Berlin lifestyle?' What is so special about West Berlin that it forces people to develop a special way of life?
>
> Perhaps Mr. Mathewson is thinking of the ever-increasing unemployment numbers in that part of Berlin, which is separated by the machinations of Washington's force from its natural economic hinterland? Perhaps Mathewson is thinking of the predic-

tion by [an East German labor leader] that the number of unemployed West Berliners will, with the onset of winter, increase to over 400,000? Certainly, in the midst of such economic misery, one must develop a special 'lifestyle.'

...The population, not only of Steinstuecken but of West Berlin, would gladly wave goodbye to the 'West Berlin lifestyle' which the American Mathewson deems so desirable. The population of Steinstücken, and West Berlin, has had enough of the atmosphere of uncertainty, speculation, economic hardship and emotional depression. The 'little people' of Steinstuecken will finally build a life worth living, without Mathewson and his lifestyle.[49]

The Soviets didn't see things the same way that the writers of *Neues Deutschland* did, though. "In a surprise move," wrote Catudal, the deputy chief of the Soviet Control Commission, accompanied by a group of advisors, called on American headquarters on Monday evening to "extend an olive branch." "Obviously trying to head off a Western reprisal," the Russians "requested an immediate audience with General Mathewson to discuss Steinstuecken."[50]

Catudal's assessment that the Russians wanted to avoid Allied retaliation makes sense, given the Communists' light grip on Steinstuecken. They did not forcibly occupy the village or arrest any of its residents. Nor did they prevent villagers from going to and from West Berlin. It was as if the Soviets and East Germans wanted to see if they could slice off Steinstuecken without the Americans making much of a fuss. By the evening of Monday, October 22, it was clear that Mathewson and the Americans didn't intend to let the little village go quietly.

Foreign Relations of the United States, the State Department's compilation of key diplomatic records and documents, includes a Memorandum of Conversation that details the discussions between the Americans and Soviets in that "immediate audience" on the evening of Monday, October 22. The Russian delegation was led by General Anatoly Sussin, deputy of the Soviet Control Commission for Berlin, and a Mr. Bashkin, his political advisor. General Mathewson and Cecil Lyon, the senior HICOG civilian official in Berlin, led the American delegation.

Mr. Susin requested an interview this afternoon at 4:30 pm. He arrived at 5:00 pm, and apologized for his lateness on the ground

> that the fog had delayed his coming. He opened the conversation by stating that he had come instead of Mr. Dengin, who is away. General Mathewson asked whether Mr. Dengin was in Moscow, but Mr. Susin's reply was not clear. Mr. Susin then said that he wished to discuss General Mathewson's letter to Mr. Dengin of October 19th concerning Steinstuecken. He then proceeded to explain that about an hour ago the Soviet authorities had told the DDR to instruct the administrators of Land Brandenburg to withdraw the Volkspolizei from Steinstuecken and to have that community refer to its former status.
>
> Mr. Susin, then, referring specifically to General Mathewson's letter, said that according to this letter, Steinstuecken had been included in the American sector by the European Advisory Commission Agreement of 1944. Mr. Susin said that the Soviet records did not indicate this and inquired whether we had any documents to support our claim. General Mathewson said that it was the district of Zehlendorf which was referred to as being included in the U.S. Sector in the EAC Agreement. General Mathewson added that Steinstuecken was part of the district of Zehlendorf.
>
> At this point Mr. Bashkin took up the conversation and asked whether we had any documents to prove that Steinstuecken was in our sector. General Mathewson asked Mr. Bashkin whether he could produce any documents proving that Steinstuecken was not part of the U.S. Sector.

Mathewson reminded the Russians that, in 1945, the *Kommandantura* had recommended exchanging Steinstuecken for some Soviet-controlled territory. However, no one acted on those recommendations, so both sides kept their disputed areas. When the Soviets "persisted in wanting to discuss the legal status" of Steinstuecken, Mathewson "informed Mr. Sussin that he had no intention of discussing those legal matters at this meeting. After some more discussion:

> General Mathewson next asked what the status of Steinstuecken was at this time, 'ten minutes past 5:00.' Mr. Susin said that, had their orders been carried out, the Volkspolizei should have been withdrawn and Steinstuecken should have been returned to its former status.

> General Mathewson next said, 'If the Volkspolizei have been withdrawn, I assume that West Berlin police will have free access to Steinstuecken.' At this point, Mr. Susin hesitated and then nodded his head and said 'Yes' ('Tak.') Mr. Bashkin, on the other hand, shook his head and said 'No' ('Nyet').[51]

"So Mathewson looked at me: 'What do we do now'" Lyon recalled. "I made a gesture of tossing a coin." It must have been an amusing scene—for the Americans, that is. "I think it's a perfect example of how the Russians do things," said Lyon. "One says 'Da' and the other says 'Nyet'—take your choice."[52]

After General Susin confirmed once more that the Communists would let Steinstuecken go, the meeting ended. General Mathewson didn't let the Soviet delegation leave without one last parting jab:

> General Mathewson said [to Mr. Susin] that he appreciated very much Mr. Susin's coming, and his attempts to be cooperative in this matter of Steinstuecken, but that he felt he must say to him that he did not admire the advice which he, Mr. Susin, was getting from certain quarters.[53]

In its Daily Digest of October 25th, the CIA's Office of Current Intelligence commented that, "During the conversations, the Soviet representative gave the impression that they wished to extricate themselves from the whole affair by shifting blame to the East Germans."[54]

The Russians did what they said they would do. The front page of *Stars and Stripes* for Wednesday, October 24, carried this headline: "Red Cops Yield Control of Seized Berlin Area." The *S&S* article, dated October 23, said that "Communist-controlled East German police withdrew today from an area of the U.S. Sector which they had occupied for five days, the West Berlin city government announced." Steinstuecken residents, who'd been told days earlier by the Vopos they were no longer West Berliners, were now "told they belonged to the West again."[55]

The Western wire services covered the Communist retreat, too. "The Soviets, in the face of allied threats of counter-action, withdrew Communist police today from a disputed American sector and returned it to U.S. control," wrote the UPI on October 23.[56] The next day, an

AP wire report led off with this sentence: "East German Communist People's Police retreated from the village of Steinstuecken after a five-day occupation that had threatened a head-on political clash between Russia and the Western powers."[57]

By Tuesday morning, "Steinstuecken had returned to its former, pre-annexation status," wrote Catudal.[58] "East German People's Police had withdrawn from around the exclave, annexation posters had been torn down and the barbed wire" was gone.[59] The Vopos hadn't gone too far, though. Detachments "of East Zone police remained posted at various points along the accessway to Steinstuecken," checking identity papers.[60] "The police slipped out early this morning," wrote the AP, "as quietly as they slipped into Steinstuecken last Thursday night."[61]

Two villagers came to the Zehlendorf police office to answer questions on the situation in the hamlet. No Soviet or GDR personnel harassed the men as they traveled to West Berlin. "About the present situation in Steinstuecken," said the Zehlendorf police in their report to the HICOG, "both men stated that the present conditions are in every respect the same way they were until Thursday of last week." A temporary office of the Potsdam city administration, established in Babelsberg, had been closed. "Flags and bulletin boards erected there have disappeared."[62] An AP reporter contacted Berliners who had access to Steinstuecken; they said the only remaining "sign of the 'occupation' was a rude shelter erected as a state-owned, ration-free hot dog stand."[63]

The mailman from Wannsee was able to get through to the village. He "stated that the situation in Steinstuecken seemed to him normal as before." The Vopos allowed food trucks from Berlin to travel to Steinstuecken, and "the food store in Steinstuecken" was accepting West marks again.[64] Residents gathered at Walter Steinweg's tavern to celebrate their *Befreiungstag* (Day of Liberation.)[65]

West Berlin's leaders joined in the celebration. *Stars and Stripes* described them as "hailing the determined U.S. stand after the Red seizure of Steinstuecken." "'Our determination brought us victory,' said Mayor Ernst Reuter."[66] The mayor was just as jubilant in the German press. "The Western victory was possible because the Communists had been confronted by a closed front of courage and resolution," Reuter told *Der Tagesspiegel*. The *Berliner Anzeiger* carried a quote from a village resident: "We have the strength of the West to thank."[67] As for the Western commandants, they "made no official announcement of the return of Steinstuecken to the U.S. Sector," wrote *Stars and Stripes*. They "maintained a wait-and-see attitude"[68] and kept mostly quiet on the matter.

By Wednesday, the village's telephone lines to West Berlin operated again. Mayor Reuter called the village that afternoon. He "inquired whether we in Steinstuecken were satisfied with our liberation," wrote Walter Steinweg, and promised to visit the village himself the following day.[69] Reuter then asked if the police detachment he'd sent to the village had arrived. It had. Earlier that afternoon, Steinweg had looked outside his window and seen three West Berlin policemen on the hamlet's streets.[70]

CHAPTER FOUR

"I'm glad we're part of the U.S. Sector again."
– An eleven-year old resident of Steinstuecken,
interviewed by *Stars and Stripes,* October 27, 1951.

The three policemen weren't there on normal police business. Mayor Reuter had sent them to test the Communists. For years, the hamlet had no West Berlin police presence. According to a HICOG memorandum dated October 19,1951, a Zehlendorf policeman patrolled the village during the first years of the occupation. However, in December 1948, "the policeman was threatened with arrest by Vopos and Soviets if he showed up again in the area." The American military government then ordered the Zehlendorf police chief "to cease giving police protection to Steinstuecken."[1] The primary duty of any government is protecting its citizens. Yet for over three years, the Soviets had denied Steinstuecken's residents the services of West Berlin's police force.

West Berlin leaders claimed that had made it easier for the GDR to envelop the exclave. "If Steinstuecken was not an enclave in the Soviet Zone," said Reuter, "I would have ordered the West Berlin police to move in immediately."[2] "If Steinstuecken had been held by a corporal's guard of the West Berlin police," said the *New York Times* in a cable report, "it might have been at least theoretically possible" to send reinforcements once the Vopos appeared.[3]

When the GDR dropped its grip on Steinstuecken, Reuter decided to reassert his city's law enforcement authority there. He came up with a plan to reestablish a West Berlin police presence in the hamlet. A memorandum for record from the HICOG's Public Safety Division, which supervised the West Berlin police, describes what happened.

On the evening of Tuesday, October 23rd—the day the GDR withdrew from around Steinstuecken—HICOG Public Safety received a phone call from the Zehlendorf police chief. "Mayor Reuter had ordered the Police Chief to have three police officers in [civilian clothes] sneak and smuggle themselves across the border to Steinstuecken. They were to carry, concealed, a complete uniform but to be unarmed. Immediately upon arrival in Steinstuecken they were to dress in their police uniforms and proceed to patrol the area as Berlin Police Officials."[4]

HICOG Public Safety officials conferred with Cecil Lyon, then told the Zehlendorf police they could proceed. Reuter's plan would confirm if West Berlin police could now go to Steinstuecken. (When General Mathewson asked the Soviets that question in his conference with them, they had simultaneously—and comically—said "Yes" *and* "No.") The HICOG did order that "no police patrols be sent into Steinstuecken in civilian clothing, even if they wear uniforms in Steinstuecken in the performance of their duties, and strongly advises that any authorized patrols should be introduced in the hours of daylight."[5]

Reuter complied. The West Berlin police didn't "sneak and smuggle themselves" into Steinstuecken. They went in broad daylight in full uniform. That Wednesday, at 1300 (1 PM), three Zehlendorf policemen approached the GDR checkpoint at Kohlhasenbrueck, which controlled traffic on the *Waldweg* between Wannsee and Steinstuecken. A HICOG Special Blotter found in the National Archives chronicled the day's events.

The three Zehlendorf police told the two Vopos on duty they were en route to Steinstuecken. "The two Volkspolice said that they had no orders to interfere and told them to proceed. At 1320 hours these three police officials reported by phone their arrival in Steinstuecken, stating that they were in no way interfered with or molested. When arriving at Steinstuecken the inhabitants gathered and expressed their appreciation of seeing West Berlin Police." The policemen were "under orders to make arrangements for facilities to operate a police office," which would "maintain constant police service at Steinstuecken consisting of one man who will be relieved every 24 hours." The blotter notes that Mayor Reuter planned to visit the exclave later in the day.[6]

The mayor never arrived. The appearance of West Berlin police in Steinstuecken "triggered a major alarm," wrote Walter Steinweg. Communist security forces rushed back to the village. The HICOG Special Blotter noted that, at 1530 hours (or 3:30 PM), the West Berlin police in Steinstuecken reported that "the entire area of Steinstuecken is surrounded by VoPo and Soviet soldiers."[7]

When Steinstuecken was first seized, it was primarily a GDR affair; Soviet forces stayed on the sidelines. Communist troops didn't enter the village in large numbers. This time was different. Russian military police (MPs) accompanied the Vopos, and they entered Steinstuecken in force. The West Berlin police took refuge in a house; the Vopos and Soviets followed them.

According to the HICOG blotter, the house where the West Berlin police were hiding was "surrounded by Soviet Military Police armed with machine pistols." Several Soviet MPs entered the house. Once inside, they walked up to the entrance to the room where the West Berlin police were, looked into the room, and verified that the West Berlin police were indeed there—and then left the house. A blotter entry at 1540 hours (or 3:40 PM) said West Berlin officials had "confirmed that Steinstuecken is surrounded primarily by Soviet soldiers, but including VoPos." Inside the town itself he reported no Vopos—"only Soviet Military Police." The Soviets "were inquiring from the population where the West policemen are. Allegedly the population denied any knowledge of their whereabouts."[8]

While the Soviet reaction was forceful and intimidating, it could have been much worse. The Soviet MPs could have arrested the West Berlin police, but they didn't. They could have ransacked Steinstuecken or carried off some of its residents. They could have cut the phone lines to West Berlin. They did none of those things.

A blotter entry of 1745 hours (or 5:45 PM) said that the situation in the village had quieted down considerably. The West Berlin police detachment reported that no Vopos or Soviets remained in the village. Vopos established posts around the edges of town, and a small group of Soviet MPs and Vopos was seen outside the town's limits.[9]

The West Berlin policemen spent an undoubtedly uncomfortable night in that house in Steinstuecken. The next morning, Zehlendorf sent fresh police to replace them. "The relief party," notes the HICOG Special Blotter, "were told by the VoPo stationed at the Kohlhasenbrueck border that they had orders to let no West Police pass to Steinstuecken." The news wasn't all bad. The Vopos said "that the 3 men at Steinstuecken could return unmolested to the U.S. Sector with their weapons."[10]

After the Soviets relented to Mathewson's demands and agreed to leave Steinstuecken, many people probably expected the hamlet to fade out of the public (and press) spotlight. This new Communist incursion kept the Western press' attention on Steinstuecken. "Berlin Police Barred By Reds" was the headline for a UPI wire story in the *Bend Bulletin*, of Bend, Oregon, on October 25. "The communists today barred west Berlin police from traveling across 300 yards of the Soviet Zone to reach the American sector outpost of Steinstuecken. The red action cast doubt upon the validity of the Soviet promise to return the disputed 'island' sector to U.S. jurisdiction. The communist police said they were under orders to prevent 'illegal' trips through the Soviet Zone." "East Germans Again at Steinstuecken," wrote Reuters in the British newspaper the *Guardian*. "Russian military police, armed with tommy-guns and Communist German police yesterday reentered the disputed American sector hamlet of Steinstuecken on the outskirts of Berlin," wrote UPI.[11] "Red Patrols Seal Off Village from the West: 4 Marooned in Town" said the Louisville *Courier-Journal* in an AP wire report.

"Four" marooned in Steinstuecken? The HICOG documents only mentioned three people going to the hamlet—the three West Berlin policemen. However, at least one West Berlin journalist had also gotten mixed up in this incident. The AP wire report in the Louisville *Courier-Journal* said, "Three West Berlin policemen *and a newspaper reporter*" (emphasis added) had entered the village. The AP identified that reporter as Manfred Trebess, of *Der Tag*. He was trapped in Steinstuecken with the West Berlin policemen. In addition, "one other Western German newspaperman was reported arrested by the Soviet patrols in their foray into Steinstuecken."

That same AP wire report said US occupation officials "were angry and confused by the incident." The Honolulu *Star-Bulletin* wrote this headline for a UPI wire report: "Unexplained Move Leaves American Officials Baffled." The wire report said the fresh Communist incursion occurred "while United States and West Berlin German officials were congratulating themselves on having forced the Communists to withdraw from the three-square-mile area which they 'annexed' to the Soviet zone for five days." The Vopos' "retreat had been hailed as a western victory over the Communists."[12] UPI said that "Western sources were confused as to whether the reentry of the Red soldiers and police was a violation of yesterday's promise to return the district to the US sector administration or if it had some other purpose."[13]

General Mathewson convened the Western commandants to assess the new crisis. The commandants decided to refer the matter to their superiors, the High Commissioners for the U.S., U.K., and France.[14] Because the territory separating Steinstuecken from the rest of West Berlin belonged to *Land* Brandenburg, not East Berlin, the Western commandants wanted to see if the High Commissioners could solve the Steinstuecken question.[15] Mathewson also protested personally to the Russians.[16]

This time, the Soviets didn't back down. Having West Berlin policemen on daily patrol in full view of East German citizens who lived in the Soviet Zone neighborhoods surrounding Steinstuecken was apparently too much for the Communists to stomach. The stalemate continued, and the three West Berlin policemen remained marooned. After a few days, they were able to return to Zehlendorf. Neither the Soviets nor the GDR interfered, as they'd promised.[17] However, no other West Berlin policemen were allowed to enter the exclave. Steinstuecken would remain part of the US Sector but without the "corporal's guard" of police that Reuter and the village residents so earnestly wanted.

When the West Berlin policemen left, the GDR released the West German journalist they'd arrested—Hartmut Reiche, an AP reporter. "Reiche told newsmen he was interrogated but not mistreated by Communist police officials," said a UPI wire report in the *Brooklyn Daily Eagle* on October 28. "He said he was detained in police barracks and not in a prison cell, and that he received food." The Vopos seized the film he'd used to take pictures as the West Berlin police entered Steinstuecken, but they did let him keep his camera.[18]

Reiche's mild treatment was another indication that the Soviets didn't want the Steinstuecken situation to get out of hand. Many West German journalists had had a much rougher time with the Communists. "Western officials disclosed that 28 West Berlin German newspapermen had been arrested or kidnapped by the Soviets in the last six years," said the UPI in that same wire report that ran in the Brooklyn *Daily Eagle.* The UPI wire report also raised the possibility that the Communists feared bad press in the West. "It was believed [Reiche's] release was prompted by a strong protest of West German newspapermen to Gerhardt Eisler, Communist East German press chief. Reiche was set free two hours after a delegation of 12 German newsmen went to the seat of the Soviet zone government and told Eisler they would ignore invitations to Communist press conferences if Reiche was not released."[19]

With that, the Steinstuecken crisis of October 1951 finally ended. Life in the village largely returned to what it had been before Thursday, October 18. Workers went to their jobs and children to school in Wannsee. Mail and supplies came from Zehlendorf, and Herr Steinweg sold Western newspapers for Western marks. The Vopo detachments stayed on the outskirts of town.

While things settled down in Steinstuecken itself, the Eastern and Western press continued to discuss the village and its troubles. The tone of Communist news coverage, so triumphant before Susin's meeting with Mathewson, grew much more muted. A Communist news wire service report on October 23—the day *after* Susin promised to retreat from Steinstuecken—was (to put it mildly) brief and *very* short on specifics:

> According to what ADN has learned from usually well-informed circles, on Monday the Acting Representative of the Soviet Control Commission in Berlin, Mr. Sussin, has contacted the Commandant of the American Sector of Berlin, General Mathewson, and has conducted with him a conversation regarding the Steinstuecken community.
>
> *During the conversation General Mathewson proposed that the documentary evidence at hand dealing with the question of Steinstuecken's status should be studied by specialists to be named by both sides.* (Emphasis added).

As General Mathewson might have said, "those blankety-blank Russians!" Not only did the news wire report *not* admit that the Soviets had agreed to leave Steinstuecken, but it also made it sound as if General Mathewson had agreed to debate, and even reconsider, the legal status of Steinstuecken.

Two weeks later, on November 6, the East German newspaper *Neue Zeit* ran an article on the exclave. By then it was common knowledge that Steinstuecken had not become part of *Land* Brandenburg. Titled "The Facts Will Prevail!" the article repeated the charge that Steinstuecken had been a "smuggler's island," occupied by "racketeers." West Berlin's claim to the village "was expressly precluded by Allied agreements," and the GDR "only took over administration of the village purely for policing reasons." The article admits that the Soviets ordered the Vopos to withdraw from the village and were negotiating "now with the Americans about the formalities of this enclave." *Neue Zeit* called the Steinstuecken episode a "provocation" by the West Berlin and Western Allied leadership, part of an ongoing series of assaults against European peace and the desire of all Germans to see their divided country reunited again. It claimed West Berlin was "an advanced hedgehog position" and "an explosion center" that the West will use to trigger another war.[21]

Stars and Stripes ran a feel-good story on Sunday, October 28. Mockingly titled "Reds Ignored During Grab of Berlin Suburb, Girl Says," it described an interview of a Steinstuecken resident during recess at her school in Zehlendorf:

> Berlin, Oct 27: An 11-year old girl told how her family refused to obey Communist police after they occupied her village in West Berlin last week.
>
> The girl is one of the 220 residents of Steinstuecken, the little suburb on the East-West frontier which spent five days under Soviet Zone control.
>
> 'We just ignored the Communist orders,' the girl said. 'We knew we belonged to the U.S. Sector, and that is where we wanted to stay.'
>
> Her name is being withheld because she still has to cross about 500 yards of Soviet Zone territory every day to go to school in the U.S. Sector of Berlin.
>
> 'They told us to pick up new food ration cards and coal ration cards in the East zone but nobody did,' the girl said. 'They told my daddy to go to a party meeting, but he would not go. We all knew it wouldn't last long. We knew the West Berliners and the Americans wouldn't leave us like that.'
>
> 'When the police first came they put up posters everywhere,' she said. 'They did not bother us much, except with all those orders about papers and meeting and new money. We all went to school just the same in the U.S. Sector.'
>
> The girl said that after the police withdrew, some 'government men' came into town and took down all the Communist posters which has been nailed up five days before.

> 'They looked angry about that,' she said. The schoolbell rang.
> 'I'm glad we're part of the U.S. Sector again,' she said.[22]

The Steinstuecken affair of October 1951 turned out well for the Western Allies. It let them show the West Berliners—and West Germany and the entire world—that they wouldn't stand by and watch the Russians slice off chunks of West Berlin. After West Staaken and the Neuer Gusthof farm, Germans needed reassurance that the West would "hit back," as Mayor Reuter put it. Mathewson's firmness gave that reassurance. Everyone knew the Americans could have let Steinstuecken go. "The tiny district," wrote the AP in a wire report of October 24, "is of no strategic or economic value to the West."[23] The Americans could have moved the Steinstuecken residents into West Berlin and justified it as yet another episode in the massive dislocation of Europeans post World War II. But they didn't.

The Americans' reward for standing firm over Steinstuecken was a healthy dose of positive press coverage. Triumphant language crept into some of the wire service reports on the Communists' initial retreat from around the exclave (i.e., before the police visit incident). The AP said that the Vopos had "retreated" from the village and that the Soviet occupation authorities in Berlin had "bowed to the demands of American authorities." It said Mathewson told the Russians that "he would not tolerate the aggressive move into the village. He proposed that the Russians get the East German police out of there and then meet with the Americans 'like gentlemen' to decide who owns it."[24] UPI called the Communist pullback "the most humiliating public backdown by the Soviets in Berlin since they lifted their starvation blockade of the city in May 1949."[25]

The headlines were even more triumphant. "Reds Retreat from Germany Fire" (*Los Angeles Times*); "Reds Back Down in Zone Dispute" (*Pittsburgh Press*); "Reds Quit Village Seized in Reich" (*Philadelphia Inquirer*); "Reds Bow to US on Disputed Sector" (Anniston *Star,* Anniston, Alabama); "Red German Police Back Down: Leave Border Village" (*Free Press,* Burlington, Vermont); "East Germans Bow to US, Leave Disputed Town" (*Decatur Herald,* Decatur, Illinois); "Soviets Fearful of Reprisals, Return Berlin District to US" (*Asheville Citizen-Times,* Asheville, North Carolina). Newspaper readers across America read about this American victory in the Cold War. The Western Allies did have to deal with a few uncomfortable headlines over the West Berlin police incident: "Armed Russ Re-Enter US Berlin Area" (*Honolulu Star-Advertiser*); "Soviets Renege" (*New Mexican,* Santa Fe, New Mexico); "Commies Act Rough Over Berlin Suburb" (*Gazette-Times,* Corvallis, Oregon). Overall, though, the Steinstuecken affair was a public relations success for the Western Allies.

A small item in the *Miami News* on October 22 showed how much interest the Steinstuecken story generated in the American media. The *News* ran a section called "Say It Right." It told readers how to pronounce difficult names in current news reports. The "Say It Right" section of October 22 covered these names: Khartoum (the capital of Sudan), Port Said (an Egyptian city), and "Steinstuecken (German community): Stine'-stick-en." The *News* gets points for effort here but loses points for execution. The correct pronunciation is "Stine'-stook-en."

The *Miami News* also covered the story for its Spanish language readers. "Rojos Abandonan Pueblo Aleman" was its headline for a story on the exclave on October 28. "Los sovieticos abandonanron ocho kilometros cuadrados del territorio occidental, ocupados pro su policia comunista, y las autoridades occidentales acogieron la medida como la mayor victoria aliada desde que las rojos levantaron el bloqueo a Berlin."

Press reporting did raise one uncomfortable issue for the Americans. The HICOG records contain a copy of a UPI report on October 24, titled "U.S. Officials said to have Recognized Steinstuecken as part of Soviet Zone":

> An official of the Zehlendorf borough office, which administers Steinstuecken, told United Press Wednesday that the Office is in possession of a copy of a letter in which American authorities in Berlin admitted in 1948 that Steinstuecken belongs to the Soviet Zone.
>
> Until 1948 the storage depot of an American unit had been located in Steinstuecken, but it had to be closed at the request of the Soviets. [Note from the author: The documents prepared for HICOG leadership at the beginning of the Steinstuecken crisis, which summarized the village's key history, make no mention of an American facility actually in the village].
>
> On this occasion, the then American Commandant in Berlin, Colonel Babcock, notified the Soviet Sector Commandant in

> writing that the American authorities regarded Steinstuecken as part of the Soviet Zone.
>
> Confirmation from American sources could not be obtained.[26]

Another UPI story the following day reported that an "official American spokesman denied Thursday that the West Berlin suburb of Steinstuecken had at any time been recognized as part of the Soviet Zone. The spokesman said Colonel Babcock "had never informed Soviet officials that Steinstuecken was to be regarded as part of the Soviet Zone."[27]

A week later, though, the West German newsmagazine *Der Spiegel* ran a story. It reported that a Zehlendorf official had in his files not one but two letters from Babcock to the Soviets. Those letters clearly showed that Babcock wanted Steinstuecken to be absorbed into the Soviet Zone. What happened to the letters? On Thursday October 24—the day the first UPI article appeared—an American official came to the Zehlendorf government offices to collect the letters, so the Americans could examine them.[28] They were never seen again.

The German language is full of wonderful words. One of those is *schadenfreude.* It basically means "taking pleasure in watching someone else's discomfort." The Steinstuecken affair gave the Western Allies a chance to engage in a bit of *schadenfreude* with the West Berlin and West German governments.

On October 24, the Allied High Commissioners (HICOM) met with the West German economic minister to discuss East-West trade under the new Interzonal Trade (IZT) agreement. West German and West Berlin officials had signed the IZT with the GDR the previous month. West Berlin and West German officials had asserted that, once the IZT went into effect, the East Germans would remove or relax many of the restrictions they'd placed on trade to West Berlin.

As the HICOMs saw it, though, things weren't going well for the Western Allies. "We feel that while some action has been taken by Eastern authorities to reduce harassment of Berlin's external trade," reported HICOG Berlin on September 29, "Eastern authorities certainly did not take prompt and effective action to carry out their commitments."[29] The HICOMs pressed this point home in their October 24 meeting.

> [The British High Commissioner] opened the meeting by detailing ways in which the situation with regard to...parcel post, road tax, ship lift, barge traffic, etc.... had deteriorated since the signature of IZT agreements. He said the West Germans had given the Allies the impression that, if they left the West Germans to deal with the East Zone on trade matters, greater progress could be made. However, in two recent cases of friction with the East Zone and the Soviets over Steinstuecken and East-West trade, the Allied commandants appeared to have achieved results with the GDR on Steinstuecken, whereas under the Federal Government there had been continued deterioration in the trade situation.[30]

The State Department's records of the meeting make it clear that the West German economic minister was embarrassed. Those records don't tell us if the Allied negotiators suppressed subtle "I told you so" smiles at the same time.

In early November, the Americans and Soviets met to discuss Steinstuecken's status. Both sides stuck to their previous legal positions. The Russians asserted that Steinstuecken belonged to the state of Brandenburg; the Americans retorted that it was part of the Zehlendorf *Bezirk* of West Berlin. When the Americans refused to drop or relax their claim to the exclave, the Soviets let the whole Steinstuecken matter drop. That left the exclave *de facto* in American hands.

De facto but not *de jure* (legally). An article in Britain's *Guardian* newspaper on November 6 said that, in the US-Soviet discussions, the Americans "intended to press for recognition that Steinstuecken is legally part of Berlin and for free and unimpeded access for the villagers to the city."[31] They achieved neither goal. The Soviets didn't agree to recognize Steinstuecken as part of the US Sector or make it easier for exclave residents to travel to Berlin.

The West Berlin government proposed a solution to the "free and unimpeded access" problem. It offered to trade some other small West Berlin exclaves for a right-of-way to Steinstuecken. The *Philadelphia Inquirer* ran an AP wire story on October 27, under the headline "Deal with Reds Asked." "West Berlin officials suggested that the Allies purchase a corridor to Soviet-surrounded Steinstuecken by surrendering two other 'island' districts to the Russians. They proposed the cession of Wueste Mark and Nuthewiesen, two small plots of land without occupants or buildings, in return for free passage to US-administered Steinstuecken."

The Soviets didn't agree. Steinstuecken would remain an exclave. The only land route to it would remain through Soviet Zone territory. That was a setback for the West. Steinstuecken would remain severed from the rest of West Berlin, with no American soldiers or West Berlin police "corporal's guard" on hand or on call to protect it.

West Berlin did take one step to underline its claim to the hamlet. It designated an official city representative for Steinstuecken. "West Berlin today appointed a governing magistrate for the disputed village of Steinstuecken," wrote the AP on October 28. "The borough of Zehlendorf chose Albert Neumann, a resident of the village, as the administrative head for its affairs. The action was taken with the support of the western allies who claimed the little island town of 50 families belongs to West Berlin by tradition."[32] Now Steinstuecken had a semi-official "mayor," recognized by West Berlin.

By mid-November 1951, life in Steinstuecken had returned to normal. It was an uncomfortable and uneasy normal, to be sure. "Steinstuecken is still in a state of semi-siege," wrote the *Guardian* on October 31. "The road is closed to all motor traffic and food has to be brought in by bicycle or small handcart. The inhabitants are allowed to pass to and fro across this strip of the Soviet zone, but no West Berlin police may do so."[33] Village residents had to accept that the neighborhoods and woods surrounding their hamlet were, technically, hostile territory.

Catudal writes that Steinstueckeners, and West Berliners in general, had a term for the overall feeling of uncertainty that pervaded the Western sectors of Berlin during the Cold War: *Alles blieb beim alten,* "everything remains the same." You knew that, at any moment, world events could disrupt (if not destroy) your life. But, until then, your life, in its normal pattern and routine, went on.[34]

For the Americans and the Western Allies, October 1951 was a defining moment in the West's relationship with Steinstuecken. General Mathewson had said it himself, in one of his communiques during the early hours of the crisis, that "from a practical point of view," the little neighborhood "might well be absorbed by the Soviets." Mathewson was right. On a continent with millions of refugees, creating a few hundred more could have been justified. (The Zehlendorf government, in fact, had prepared housing for Steinstuecken residents in case they had to flee).[35] The Americans could have backed away from Steinstuecken if they'd really wanted to.

But they didn't abandon the village. Instead, they laid claim to it. They figuratively (but firmly) planted the Stars and Stripes in Steinstuecken. In so doing, they put American prestige and credibility at risk. From then on, Steinstuecken was an "American" village for as long as US troops occupied and protected West Berlin. It became a Yankee "advanced hedgehog position" in the midst of Soviet Zone territory. A long, often tense, and always intriguing relationship between a small group of German villagers and one of the world's two major superpowers had begun.

CHAPTER FIVE

When I want the West to scream, I squeeze on Berlin
— Soviet Premier Nikita Khrushchev

In the summer of 1952, the National Security Council (NSC) issued a policy paper on Berlin. Its title was imposing: "U.S. Policy and Courses of Action to Counter Possible Soviet or Satellite Action Against Berlin." It contained this frank assessment:

> As long as Germany remains divided and Berlin is a land island within the Soviet Zone, the maintenance of our position in the city will not be easy. On the contrary, it is likely to be as nerve-wracking as it is important, and there is no way to make it otherwise.

"We must expect continuing harassing measures of greater or lesser severity," the NSC paper warned.[1] The events of the 1950s proved them right. Throughout that decade, the Soviets and East Germans harassed West Berliners and the Western Allies. They blocked the *autobahns* to West Germany, then unblocked them, then blocked them again. They levied taxes on trucks and barges. Soviet aircraft buzzed (and occasionally fired at) Allied aircraft. Soviet and East German authorities routinely imposed fresh travel restrictions on West Berliners, West Germans, and Allied personnel. The Communists missed no opportunity to wrack Allied nerves as America tried to maintain its position in West Berlin.

By the end of October 1951, that position included Steinstuecken. Official American records, along with the letters and recollections of Steinstuecken residents, describe how the Soviets and East Germans applied pressure to the village throughout the 1950s. Time and time again, the American occupation authorities had to intercede on its behalf. Meanwhile, the people of Steinstuecken struggled to cope with the many challenges arising from their isolation from the rest of Free Berlin.

Seven months after its rescue from the GDR, Steinstuecken was embroiled in crisis again—as was the rest of West Berlin. On May 26, 1952, the FRG signed a series of agreements with the United States, Great Britain, and France. They were called the "Contractual Arrangements." Their purpose, according to a HICOG Information Bulletin in June 1952, was "to include the Federal Republic in the community of free nations as an equal partner."[2]

The Contractual Arrangements covered an array of subjects—settling Nazi debts, outlining the privileges of foreign troops stationed in West Germany, spelling out the FRG's support responsibilities for Berlin, etc. Once the agreements went into force, the Allied occupation of West Germany would officially end. The Occupation Statute would be abolished, ambassadors would replace the High Commissioners, and West Germany would be an equal among Western nations again.

Two weeks before the signing, an Undersecretary of the Army attended a conference with John J. McCloy on May 8. There, wrote the undersecretary, McCloy "stated his deep concern for Berlin. There are firm indications that the Soviets are planning a number of moves and related demonstrations to terrorize the West Germans and embarrass the Allies in order to prevent the signature of, or if signed, the ratification of" the agreements.[3]

The Soviets didn't wait for the signing ceremony. On April 29, two Russian fighters attacked an Air France airliner as it flew in one of the approved Berlin air corridors. Two passengers were wounded. At the beginning of May, Soviet authorities at the Babelsberg *autobahn* checkpoint outside Berlin blocked American and British MP patrols for several days.[4]

Once the Contractual Agreements were signed, the Communists swung into high gear. They stopped Western Allied MP patrols again. Most of the telephone lines between East Berlin and the West were cut. And in the most dramatic move of all, the Communists moved to choke off travel and commerce between West Berlin and East Germany. They closed most of the border crossing points from West Berlin into the Soviet Zone. At those crossing points that stayed open, now

West Berliners needed special GDR travel documents to enter the Soviet Zone.

The GDR enacted regulations that drastically curtailed the ability of East German citizens and stores to do business with Western merchants. Shops in Steinstuecken had always served customers from Babelsberg and Potsdam. Walter Steinweg described his East German neighbors as the "prime clients" for his small store, with ten customers from the Soviet Zone to every one customer from Steinstuecken. The GDR crackdown ended that. The drop in customers caused Steinweg's store to be "no longer economically viable over the years."[5]

West Berliners were especially disturbed by new GDR regulations on who could own property in East Germany. Many West Berliners had cottages, small farms, plots of land, or other property in the Soviet Zone. In many cases, their families had owned that property for generations.

In June 1952, the GDR press published an announcement "which suggests," wrote General Mathewson in a protest note to the Soviets on June 2, "that West Berliners who have property or business in the Soviet Zone will not be permitted in the future to visit that property or attend to their business unless they definitely cease to reside in West Berlin."[6] A HICOG Berlin message of June 12 said that the "cutting off of access to the Soviet Zone, where many West Berliners have relatives, farms, etc.. which they could previously visit without hindrance," was one of the few Communist harassments "which appear to have aroused any concern among the local population."[7]

The GDR "suggestion" wasn't an empty threat. Thousands of West Berliners who didn't move permanently to the Soviet Zone lost their property there. The Western Allies protested, but did nothing more. As Catudal put it, the Allies didn't put the same value on a West Berliner's vacation cottage or garden plots as they placed on his home and neighborhood. "These land holdings, it was thought, involved an entirely different relationship, i.e., a personal one between West Berlin citizens and Soviet Zone authorities."[8] This caused much anguish in the Western sectors of the city.

The GDR also began to physically separate East from West. GDR construction crews created a 100-meter wide strip of bare earth along the boundary between West Berlin and East Germany. A State Department report described it as a "devastated area along the border."

Observers reported that "trees had been uprooted, brush cleared and designated areas plowed."[9] "Trenches were dug, barricades were set up and machine gun posts were established, and clearings were cut through the woods to provide an uninterrupted field of fire," wrote Catudal. Residents whom the GDR didn't consider politically reliable were evicted.[10]

Steinstuecken felt the new Communist squeeze, too. On June 1, Soviet authorities had trees cut down and laid across the *Waldweg*. Armed Soviet soldiers began patrolling the pathway and forest in between the exclave and Wannsee.

Initially, Steinstuecken residents could still walk to and from Wannsee, over the *Waldweg*. However, Vopos told them that, soon, they would have to obtain GDR travel passes if they wanted to continue using the *Waldweg*.[11] This new requirement wasn't unique to Steinstuecken. As mentioned earlier, all West Berliners now needed East German passes to go into the Soviet Zone. But most West Berliners lived and worked in the Western sectors. They didn't need East German permission to *get to their own homes!*

A HICOG information paper said that, as of June 1952, the "Soviet authorities had" in private conversations with the Americans, "conceded that Steinstucken belongs to West Berlin rather than the Soviet Zone."[12] However, the *Waldweg*—the one connection Steinstuecken had to the rest of West Berlin—ran through the Soviet Zone. In the seven months in between the failed attempt to annex Steinstuecken and the new crisis over the Contractual Arrangements, the Soviets and Americans hadn't reached any agreement on an approved accessway to the exclave.[13] So, when this new crisis arose, village residents still needed the Communists to allow them to go to and from home. By June 3, Soviet and GDR border guards started to prevent Steinstueckeners who lacked the new GDR passes from going to Wannsee.[14] Essentially, they were trapped in their village.

The Vopos tried to get the Steinstueckeners to accept the new GDR passes willingly. Johannes Niemeyer was a college professor who taught in Berlin. He owned a home in Steinstuecken. Throughout the 1950s, Professor Niemeyer wrote a steady stream of letters to newspapers, American occupation authorities, and the West Berlin and West German governments. He detailed, often in colorful language, the ongoing problems the isolated Steinstuecken residents faced. His memory lives on in modern-day Steinstuecken in a street named "Johannes-Niemeyer Weg."

One of Professor Niemeyer's documents described the GDR's attempts to charm the exclave's residents into accepting GDR travel passes. "The Vopos offered us, as a special case, long-term entry passes with photographs, free of charge. They politely requested that we all get the passes within two days." They even arranged for a photographer to take the travel pass photos for free.

Niemeyer recalled "the question a Vopo asked an old Steinstuecken resident. The Vopo asked her whether he could obtain an official list of all residents. The commander of the Potsdam *Volkspolizei* detachment even paid us a visit."[15] The residents didn't like the idea of the East Germans having a list of all of them. Soviet Zone authorities could use it to make it hard (or impossible) for new people to move into the village.

American occupation officials undoubtedly feared the Communists were up to their 'salami slicing' tricks again. Allowing the GDR to impose travel document requirements on American Sector residents would set a bad precedent. It might encourage the Communists to slice the Berlin salami some more. The Americans urged the exclave residents to refuse the GDR request. "On the recommendation of the American military government," wrote Niemeyer, "we all together rejected the Vopo's offer." HICOG records report that "the great majority" of exclave residents "failed to apply for GDR passes, and reportedly are unwilling to do so."[16]

On June 4, Cecil Lyon lodged a protest with the Soviets. He also went to the Western press. In a UPI report from June 6, Lyon called the new restrictions a "hunger blockade" on Steinstuecken.[17]

The Communists backed down. "Later in the same day" as Lyon's protest, "the physical barriers were removed" from the *Waldweg.*[18] Trucks could once again reach the exclave. The GDR abandoned its attempts to make residents obtain GDR travel documents. Also, the Soviets evacuated the houses they'd taken from Steinstuecken residents several years earlier.[19]

The Western press reported on this latest Western "victory." "Less than 24 hours after a strong American protest," wrote the UPI on June 6, "Red troops removed felled trees blocking access to isolated Steinstuecken."[20] "Russ Yield in Berlin Dispute" was the headline for a UPI story in the *Minneapolis Star* on the same day.

The Western sectors of the city also weathered this newest of Cold War storms. "The Commie campaign of harassment against West Berlin, initiated in reprisal for signing of the Contractual Agreements" … "now appears" not to have "had any appreciable effect on the status and security of the city or on the determination of West Berliners to stand fast in face of Commie pressure," reported the HICOG's Berlin element on June 12, 1952. "Communist-inspired demonstrations have been unimpressive in scope." In the few cases where Communist demonstrators did try "to penetrate West Berlin, mobs have been broken up quickly and without undue difficulty by the normal West Berlin police force." "In balance," reported HICOG Berlin, "morale of West Berliners seems not only generally unimpaired, but, if anything, higher than before. Berliners tend to thrive when in the limelight".[21]

By the end of 1952, Steinstuecken was no stranger to the Cold War limelight. Twice within the past year, the village's name had appeared in headlines across the world and commanded the attention of the Cold War's two prime antagonists, the US and the Soviet Union. Impressive for a place no larger than a college football stadium.

A section of railway track split the village into eastern and western sections. Only one major street, Bernhard-Beyer Strasse, ran within the exclave itself. Three other streets—Stahnsdorfer Strasse to the north, Rote-Kreuz Strasse to the west, and Steinstrasse to the south—bordered the village.

Calling those three streets on the edges of the exclave "borders" wasn't just a figure of speech; they really were borders. If a Steinstueckener crossed one of those streets, he/she actually went from the American Occupation Sector of West Berlin into the Soviet Occupation Zone of Germany. "On this side is the West, on that side is the East," wrote Niemeyer. "Over there, Vopos stand."[22]

In the fall of 1952, Steinstuecken had about 160 residents. That's about the same number that lived there in October 1951, when the GDR tried to seize the exclave. Since then, though, some new neighbors had moved in. The GDR assigned an entire company of border police to watch the little village. They established a permanent checkpoint, with twenty-four-hour manning, in Kohlhasenbrueck on the border between the US Sector and the Soviet Zone.[23] Smaller guard posts were established at the entrance to Steinstuecken and along the *Waldweg*. Professor Niemeyer described it as "a surveillance ring around Steinstuecken. This surveillance employs an estimated 20 personnel at all times. For our paltry 160 Steinstueckeners!?"[24]

Anytime an exclave resident went to West Berlin to go to work or attend school or visit family, they had to go through GDR checkpoints. The Vopos checked residents as they left the exclave and at the Kohlhasenbrueck border post as they entered West Berlin. On the way home, they had to clear the same checkpoints again. "They timed you," recalled Magrit Wiese, who grew up in Steinstuecken. "They knew exactly when you left the first checkpoint."[25] If you took too long to traverse the *Waldweg*, the Vopos might react. The guards recorded the full name of each traveler.[26] Steinstuecken residents still refused to accept Communist travel papers. They used West Berlin identity cards instead, which the Vopos accepted.

If you were to "depart from the *Waldweg*—to call it a street or even an access way is a joke—you run the risk of arrest or other 'difficulties,'" wrote Niemeyer. "Because, if you're caught off the *Waldweg*, now you lack a valid travel pass in the 'DDR.' The same applies if you cross the road in front of our houses"[27] on the edges of the exclave. The woods around the *Waldweg*, where Steinstuecken children had always played, or the streets around the village, which residents had always crossed to visit their neighbors or run a quick errand in Babelsberg, were now foreign territory.

In the early 1950s, the Vopos didn't always inflict "difficulties" on Steinstueckeners who strayed outside the village. A lot depended on the attitude of the Vopos on duty. Some guards allowed children, and even adults, to cross into the Soviet Zone neighborhoods or woods. Wilfried Hammer recalls that "during the early 1950s, all the people in Steinstucken used to have both currencies, Ostmarks and Deutsche Marks. Since there was no wall between [Steinstuecken and Babelsberg], the only [border] control were some Vopos who patrolled along the border, mainly on the roads. At first, everybody just had to ask permission to visit anybody. Our aunt and uncle even could [still] go by car to Steinstücken. As the Cold War progressed, things got more and more difficult. [Access to the exclave] sometimes depended on who was on duty at the border."[28]

Children had an easier time than adults. "Some soldiers were quite human at first," recalled Wilfried Hammer. "Most of them didn't care whether children from either side played together in Babelsberg or

Steinstücken territory. My brother Michael had a good friend living just across the border and they met almost every day." "The young folks found ways through the bush, avoiding contact with the Vopos stationed around the village, and went to the movies or the bakery," said Elke Hammer, Wilfried's wife.[29] When Vopos caught Steinstuecken kids in this kind of "prohibited trespassing," said Elke Hammer, usually they "were not punished harshly. Mostly the Vopos escorted them back to Steinstuecken, warning them not to do that again, especially when they were young."[30]

Wilfried Hammer told this story to Leland McCaslin for McCaslin's book *Secrets of the Cold War: Exposed*. In the fall of 1958, Wilfried and his friend Dieter Gertz were playing soccer on a meadow outside of Steinstuecken. Two Vopos approached and asked them why they didn't stay inside their village. The boys replied that Steinstuecken didn't have a good soccer field. The Vopos then arrested the boys and took them to the East German police barracks. There the Vopos lectured them, telling them they had no right to trespass into the GDR.

Dieter was three years older that Wilfried, and apparently the Vopos thought he might be old enough "to take political advice," as Elke Hammer recalls it. "They asked him about his (and his mother's') attitudes toward Communism and tried to influence him." Perhaps the Vopos wanted to recruit Dieter for the East German security services. "At last, after about an hour of investigation, they let them go home—a little frightened, but no injuries."[31]

For adults who wanted to visit Steinstuecken, the Vopos created many more "difficulties," as Herr Niemeyer would have put it. When the GDR imposed its harsher border controls in the summer of 1952, any adult who wanted to visit Steinstuecken but wasn't a resident needed a GDR travel pass. Less than one kilometer of Soviet Zone territory separated Steinstuecken from Zehlendorf, but no matter. You still needed a pass.

"The Eastern 'Volkspolizei' allows neither residents of West Berlin or West Germany, nor East Berlin or the Eastern Zone to use the trail that goes through the Soviet-occupied woodlands," wrote Niemeyer in a September 1952 letter to the US High Commissioner. "Only persons whose ID card indicates that they are a resident of Steinstuecken may pass."[32] Two years later, Professor Niemeyer complained again about access for visitors from West Berlin, this time to the USCOB. "West Berliners can only enter after cumbersome appointment procedures."[33]

Prospective visitors often had to wait several days while the East Germans processed their pass applications. They denied many. The Western Allies weren't always helpful. "For the most part, West German and West Berlin citizens were discouraged from obtaining East Zone permits to visit Steinstuecken," wrote Catudal. "Western officials did not want to take any step which might be interpreted as some sort of recognition of the Communist regime."[34]

The Vopos didn't just block family and friends. They stopped commercial and official traffic, too. Any delivery truck carrying coal or food, or the mailman, doctor, or clergyman in a car or on foot—all had to have GDR passes. "Neither any West Berliner, not even the postman, nor any inhabitant of the eastern zone, can get legally to us," complained Niemeyer in the summer of 1952. "No delivery person, no craftsman, no relative and no vehicle."[35]

Throughout the 1950s, it was common for the GDR to impose fresh traffic restrictions on Steinstuecken. The National Archives contain documents that detail one episode in the spring of 1953. On March 30, the HICOG Protocol Branch in Berlin wrote a report on a meeting with the Soviets about one car and its owner. Apparently, at that time in Steinstuecken, only one resident owned a car. The Vopos were creating "difficulties" (the HICOG's words, not Professor Niemeyer's) for this motorist.[35]

The HICOG representative reported that, at the meeting, there had been "no disagreement between Soviet and United States authorities on the right of Steinstuecken residents to travel freely between Steinstucken and Zehlendorf." However:

> Unfortunately this principle of free access to Steinstuecken is evidently incorrectly understood by the members of the People's Police, who have recently prevented a Steinstuecken resident from driving his West Berlin registered car to and from Steinstuecken, and informed him that in order to do this he must have a special permit.
>
> Furthermore, it has been brought to our attention that several members of the People's Police have threatened Steinstuecken residents with some sort of inspection, including weighing, of the parcels which these people necessarily carry back and forth between Zehlendorf and Steinstuecken. I stated that we considered such

> action by the Eastern police to constitute an unreasonable interference and quite contrary to the agreement concerning this subject.[37]

The Soviet officials were extremely polite, but apparently they didn't fix the problems. Less than a month later, a HICOG staffer paid the Russians another visit. The Americans made the following complaints:

1. The Steinstuecken resident who owns an automobile was still being prevented from driving his car to and from Steinstuecken.
2. The People's Police were continuing to examine packages which Steinstucken residents carried between Steinstuecken and Zehlendorf.
3. Moreover, the People's Police had begun to interfere with the delivery of coal to Steinstuecken and had informed a truck driver that he must give them 48 hours' notice [before any future deliveries. Also, coal trucks would have to use an alternate, longer, and less efficient road to reach the exclave instead of the more direct *Waldweg*.]
4. The People's Police have been stopping the woman who has been bringing mail from Zehlendorf for Steinstuecken residents and examining the mail.[38]

In regards to complaint #4, a week earlier, on April 9, West Berlin police had told the Americans that Communist border troops had detained and harassed Frau Luise Schultze, a Steinstuecken resident, as she carried mail from the exclave to West Berlin. A translation of the police report is in the National Archives.

Frau Schulze "was stopped by two Vopos and three Russians at the barrier in Kohlhasenbrueck. Then she was ordered to show the contents of the mailbag." When she "refused to open the mailbag, she was taken to the guard house, where she should remain until she would open the bag. After some minutes, Frau Schulze unlocked the bag," and the Vopos searched it. They made her open some of the parcels in the bag. They also unwrapped some of the Western newspapers she was carrying and "read them superficially." As they "read" the papers, the Vopos mocked her. They shouted "slogans, such as 'America, the strongest power in the world'" at Frau Schmidt." Fifteen minutes later, they allowed her to proceed to Zehlendorf.[39]

Steinstuecken's mail delivery problems made the Western press. The *Minneapolis Star Tribune* ran an article from Reuters on June 28. It explained why Steinstuecken residents had to carry their own mail in the first place. Its headline: "The Postman Doesn't Even Ring." "Because their west Berlin postman has been twice barred and once arrested by East German police, the 150 people of Steinstuecken have arranged to collect and distribute their mail themselves. Friday the village postman, recently barred and arrested for 'encroaching' on East German territory, delivered his mail bag to a Steinstuecken citizen at the western end of the track."[40]

The continued American pressure paid off. One day after the second American visit to the Soviets, the Vopos contacted the Steinstuecken mayor. Two weeks later, the mayor met with the local border police commander, and received the following list of access procedures:

a. Henceforth, vehicles owned by Steinstuecken residents could move freely between Steinstuecken and the main body of the American sector between 4AM and 10PM. If emergencies arose during the remaining hours, a special permit would be required.
b. West Berlin craftsmen may enter Steinstuecken to work, provided that [a Steinstuecken representative] gives the border police a day's notice of their intended entry. This also applies to deliverymen, doctors and West Berlin officials who desire to enter Steinstuecken on business.
c. The regular postman from Berlin/Wannsee (American Sector) will again be allowed to deliver mail in Steinstuecken.
d. The dirt road leading directly from Zehlendorf to the Steinstuecken exclave may be repaired by West Berlin workers.
e. The border police will not closely control hand bags and packages carried into Steinstuecken, though spot checks will continue since the packages technically enter the GDR.
f. Friends and relatives from West Berlin will not yet be permitted to visit Steinstuecken.
g. The pastor from Wannsee who has been holding services in Steinstuecken will not be permitted to enter. (This apparently stems from the fact that the pastor in question recently thoroughly irritated the border police.)

h. Persons who desire to move to or from Steinstuecken, particularly anyone who intends to move furniture, must have appropriate papers approved by 'the four Allied commandants.'[41]

Take a second look at that last paragraph. To do something as simple as bring your new sofa or kitchen table home from the store, the GDR wanted Steinstueckeners to comply with travel directives approved by *all four* occupying powers.

The forest path to Wannsee had no lights. In the summer of 1952, Steinstuecken residents asked the occupying powers to erect streetlights. In any other suburb in the modern world, the neighborhood association would approach the city council. But Steinstuecken wasn't like any other suburb. Its residents had to appeal to higher authorities than City Hall. Much higher.

"American and Soviet representatives in Berlin were able to get together in November on two projects along the border of the US Sector and the Soviet Zone," according to an article in the HICOG Information Bulletin for December 1952. One of those projects was an effort to "place electric lights along the road leading to the US Sector exclave of Steinstuecken." According to the article, titled "Cooperation in Berlin," the American and Soviet occupation authorities had been notified of "the inadequate illumination of the several hundred yards of the road crossing Soviet Zone territory, and Soviet agreement was asked to the construction of a row of street lights. Agreement was contained in a letter dated Nov. 4."[42] The approving authority for that agreement was none other than Sergei Dengin, the head of the Soviet Control Commission—the highest-ranking Soviet official in Berlin. Here is the text of that letter from Dengin to General Mathewson:

> Dear General.
>
> In connection with your request, stated during a discussion on 21 October 1952, concerning the illumination at night of the road leading from Steinstuecken into the US Sector of Berlin, I wish to state that the Soviet authorities have no objection to the putting up of electric lights along the abovementioned road.[43]

Mathewson thanked Dengin,[44] East Berlin employees of the West Berlin electric utility erected the street lamps,[45] and Steinstueckeners got their lights.

As you read the HICOG records and the letters and recollections of Steinstuecken residents, you'll notice that the Americans never dealt directly with the East Germans. Exclave residents would meet with the Vopos, and West Berlin officials dealt with their counterparts in East Berlin and *Land* Brandenburg. But American occupation officials only talked to the Soviets. They refused to work officially with any East German officials. Why? As far as the Western Allies were concerned, there was no officially recognized East German government in the first place.

"It is the position of the United States," said a State Department report in the spring of 1959, "that, under international law, the international entity known as Germany remains in existence, notwithstanding what has happened since 1945 as an incident of Four Power occupation." As the Western Allies saw it, World War II wasn't officially over. There was still no final peace treaty between the wartime allies and "Germany." "The Government of the United States does not consider, and will not admit, that Germany as an international entity is permanently divided into new and separate states."[46]

What did that have to do with Steinstuecken? The Vopos guarded the borders, checked the resident's West Berlin identity cards, and mocked the West Berlin newspapers under their authority as representatives of the German Democratic Republic. But the Western Allies didn't recognize the GDR. The Americans didn't see the *Waldweg* as a path through the territory of a new country. To them, it crossed the Soviet Occupation Zone in a defeated-but-still-united Germany.

The Americans feared that, if the Western Allies met or worked officially with the Vopos or any East German officials, it could create the impression that the Western Powers accepted the existence of the GDR. That would undermine the West's argument about Germany's status. It also might discourage millions of Germans who hoped their country could reunite soon. If West Germans (and the rest of the world) saw the Allies treat the GDR as a real country, people might start to accept that Germany was divided in two forever. Hence the Western Powers dealt with the Soviets, their fellow occupying power, instead of the GDR.

This explains why the Western Allies discouraged West Berliners from applying for GDR travel permits to go to Steinstuecken. As the Americans saw it, Steinstuecken should be treated the same way as any other part of the US Sector of Berlin. West Berliners didn't need a pass to visit Zehlendorf, so they shouldn't need one for Steinstuecken, which was part of Zehlendorf. The GDR had no right to demand that travelers get East passes because the "GDR" itself had no rights at all.

At the end of March 1953, at the same time that the Vopos were harassing Steinstuecken motorists and mail carriers, West Berlin Mayor Reuter met with senior State Department representatives in Washington. According to the Memorandum of Conversation from that meeting, Reuter said it was "difficult to say what the Soviets intend to do in, or to, Berlin in the near future. Pressures are imposed, then removed just as suddenly, without any clear pattern emerging." Reuter speculated the Soviets applied restrictions then relaxed them in order "to keep us perplexed and in a state of tension."[47]

The Soviets and their East German surrogates frequently squeezed on West Berlin during the 1950s. A favorite trick was imposing new taxes on commercial traffic traveling through the Soviet Zone to West Germany. For example, the GDR tried to increase toll rates on non-GDR vehicles using the *autobahns* in March 1955. The West Berlin government estimated the new rates would raise truck tolls *eight-fold!* For very large trucks—the ones that moved much of West Berlin's products and foodstuffs—the new rates were *fourteen times* higher. "Many small independent truckers could not afford to pay these increases out of their own pockets," reported HICOG Berlin on March 31, 1955. Officials feared shortages could 'develop in some fresh food, such as milk."[48]

Three years later in May 1958, the Communists raised taxes on barge traffic, supposedly to pay for a new dam.[49] A 1958 newsreel titled "German Cold War: Reds Hike Tariff on Berlin Supplies" described the situation, in colorful language backed by the ominous music you often hear in newsreels:

> An ominous new development in the Cold War that is still grim, and near to West Berlin. Traffic on the rivers and waterways that carry nearly a third of the city's staple supplies has been subjected to a new toll by Red-ruled East Germany. A tariff that could total upwards of a million dollars annually.

> Whether it is merely what it seems, or the first in a new series of economic harassments remains to be seen. West Berlin plans to retaliate, with a tax on East German traffic.
>
> This uneasily recalls the days of the blockade and the airlift. Troublesome memories renewed by pressure on a civic artery.[50]

(A million dollars in 1958 would be worth more than $8 million in 2018). A State Department report said that, despite what the newscaster had said, "the FRG declined to give serious consideration to economic countermeasures, and decided to reimburse the carriers to cover the toll increase."[51]

The Communists didn't just tax Western civilian traffic; they blocked and harassed it, too. In October 1957, to facilitate a currency conversion in East Germany, the GDR stopped all West German surface traffic for one day. "At the same time," reported the State Department, "the East Germans detained, examined and in some cases confiscated West German parcel post shipments."[52] Three years later, in November 1960, the State Department's *Bulletin* carried excerpts of a protest note the US government sent to the Soviets over East German actions that previous August:

> East German spokesmen made a 'declaration,' in which they threatened interference with normal civilian access between the FRG and Berlin. Thereafter, East German authorities carried out this threat by harassing persons in transit to Berlin by prolonged delays in rail and road traffic, subjection to frivolous police interrogation, and in many cases outright denial of passage. More than one thousand individuals were thus, without cause, denied use of rail and road.[53]

The Western Allies got their fair share of grief, too. In February 1957, the US comprised this list of Soviet harassment attempts on official US travel to West Berlin, within the past ninety days:

- Inspection of ID cards or passports of passengers on US Berlin passenger trains.
- Seizure of Russian translations of travel orders on any of the passengers they considered objectionable.

- Insistence that a 'Certificate of Status' stamp entry be in the passports of personnel traveling on US orders by either train or autobahn
- Failure to clear a US truck convoy unless Soviet inspection of truck interiors was permitted. [The convoy turned back]
- Refusal to clear US military vehicle convoys without inspection of ID cards of enlisted personnel.
- Threats to occasionally enter Allied passenger trains to check travelers against [manifests.][54]

"Chronic Communist harassment," wrote the State Department in September 1958, "continued to be one of the prices of maintaining Berlin as an outpost of freedom."[55]

US military and State Department records contain many reports of Soviet and GDR harassment at railway and *autobahn* checkpoints. Some are amusing. This happened when the Soviets detained an American train on March 26, 1960:

> Marked in dust on one of the cars was a series of straight lines forming a square with a long nose, which the Soviets claimed represented a swastika. Train held [for three hours] awaiting arrival of a Soviet colonel.... Inspection of train then revealed a swastika one foot high marked in the dust on the car, in addition to previous markings. This marking was not on the car at the time of the original inspection. A Soviet soldier had been observed loitering alongside of car by a member of the train crew.[56]

Throughout the 1950s and early 1960s, Steinstuecken often felt GDR pressure. In 1954, the Soviets demanded a list of all people who wanted to travel from West Berlin to Steinstuecken on official business—postmen, chimney sweeps, firemen, coal deliverymen, etc. "U.S. officials," wrote Catudal, "hoping that access procedures would run more smoothly in the future, decided to comply. They gave a list to the East German border guards."[57] People on the list could go to and from Steinstuecken without a GDR travel pass.

Then, in August 1955, writes Catudal, "Communist authorities unilaterally tried to change the rules related to access. In a letter addressed to the Governing Mayor of West Berlin, the East German regime stated that, beginning the following month, all West Berliners, technical persons included, would be required to obtain travel documents in order to visit Steinstuecken." A permit would be valid for four months, after which the permit holder would have to go to East Berlin and renew it. When some West Berlin deliverymen and technical workers refused to renew their passes, the Vopos blocked their entry to Steinstuecken. However, in October, as the weather turned colder, the GDR did relent a bit. They gave some coal deliverymen permission to deliver coal without a pass.[58]

Western officials decided to test the GDR's willingness to block emergency personnel who had no passes. They sent the Zehlendorf fire brigade to Steinstuecken. "Previously," writes Catudal, "the brigade had been let through unhindered. This time, however, it was turned back." That spurred American officials to get involved. Americans-Soviet negotiations led to the fire brigade receiving permission to go to Steinstuecken without GDR passes in January 1956. One month later, the East Germans (presumably urged on by the Soviets) temporarily suspended—but did not rescind—the pass requirement for other technical workers.[59]

The GDR was willing to risk bad publicity in order to stick to its bans. In April 1956, Steinstuecken's only refrigerator failed. The Vopos refused to let a West Berlin electrician come repair it. West Berlin newspapers had a field day, so much so that two Soviet officers actually went to Steinstuecken to inspect the refrigerator and verify that, yes, indeed, this one important electrical appliance didn't work.[60] No matter—the GDR still blocked the electrician.

Finally, at the end of April, the mayor of Berlin himself, accompanied by an entourage of reporters and other onlookers, went to the Kohlhasenbreck checkpoint. He told the Vopos on duty that, as the mayor of Berlin, he wanted to visit Steinstuecken, where some of his constituents lived. The Vopos refused, In response, wrote Catudal, "the entire community" walked up the *Waldweg* and greeted the mayor at the checkpoint. Reporters' cameras clicked away, recording this show of determination and defiance by the exclave residents.[61]

The Vopos didn't budge. The mayor left without visiting the exclave.[62] "West Berlin Mayor Blocked by Reds" was the headline for a *New York Times* news service report on the event.[63] More American-Soviet negotiations followed, which led to more modifications to access procedures. Finally, in May, Steinstuecken received a brand-new refrigerator.[64]

"Alfred and Emma Morawietz celebrated their golden wedding anniversary on the eastern side of a barrier that cuts the main street of their town in two," wrote the UPI on September 11, 1958. "Emil Meyer, Deputy Mayor of the West Berlin borough of Zehlendorf, stood on the western size of a red and white colored pole and handed a bouquet of flowers over the pole to Frau Morawietz." The deputy mayor "was refused passage to the village by East German police."

In the summer of 1956, the GDR did allow the mayor of Zehlendorf and other West Berlin officials to travel to Steinstuecken. The mayor of West Berlin even visited once in August. However, that November, the East Germans changed their minds again. They demanded that West Berlin officials now obtain special GDR passes. After that, no more West Berlin government leaders went to Steinstuecken in the 1950s.[65] As for the West Berlin police, they hadn't been allowed into the exclave since late October 1951, when three policemen had been trapped overnight there.

Life in Steinstuecken lacked some of the basic benefits of normal city living. There was no bus or light rail service, and taxis couldn't reach the exclave. If you wanted to take a taxi, the bus, or the light rail, you had to walk through the *Waldweg* to Kohlhasenbrueck. Professor Niemeyer often complained about the lack of public transportation. "Are people with luggage, the old and sick expected to go, in every type of weather, on a half-hour long trek over the forest," he asked in July 1952.[66]

Undoubtedly the professor knew that West Berlin would be, to put it mildly, reluctant to extend its bus lines into the Soviet Zone. He had a novel suggestion, though: Have the Western Allies claim the *Waldweg* as West Berlin territory! For years Steinstueckeners had begged the Western Allies to establish a travel corridor from Wannsee to the village, a corridor that West Berlin police (and American troops) could control.

Niemeyer proposed a way to do it. He claimed the *Waldweg* "was West Berlin property and had been managed for a long time by Wannsee, until Zehlendorf handed over management of it to the GDR Forest Service without cause." The professor proposed that, "in the international negotiations" necessary to create a travel corridor, "it could be said that a 'throughway' from Steinstucken to West Berlin exists and persists."[67] Apparently, he couldn't sway the occupying powers.

No Western-controlled corridor was established; no buses or taxis appeared. Steinstueckeners, regardless of their age or health or how much luggage they had, still had to trek over the *Waldweg* and through the GDR checkpoints.

If you had a house in Steinstuecken that you wanted to sell or rent, it could be difficult. It's hard to attract prospective buyers or tenants if machine-gun-toting Vopos are in their way. Also, who wants to live in a city neighborhood with no buses or taxis? "For our apartments we find no renters, for our houses we find no buyers," lamented Professor Niemeyer. "Several renters pay virtually no rent at all, because the owners are happy to have someone in the houses."[68] Rents in Steinstuecken, not surprisingly, could be quite low. Wilfried Hammer's family moved to Berlin in late 1949, when his father found work in the city. "His mother's long-time friend lived in Babelsberg," recalled his wife Elke, "and told them of a cheap flat to rent in Steinstücken. Now we know why it was cheap."[69]

Isolation had its perks. Several exclave residents told a West Berlin newspaper reporter that they never saw city tax collectors.[70] Isolation also made Steinstuecken a quiet, peaceful place to live. One benefit of having armed police all around the town and along the *Waldweg*—it deterred crime. "We feel as if we're in Abraham's castle," remarked Professor Niemeyer. "We are so well watched and observed!"[71] "Steinstuecken was great," recalled Magrit Wiese. "It was peaceful, it was quaint." In the 1950s, "it was just a nice place to be and live."[72]

Despite all the tensions, there was no mass exodus of residents. In fact, some people moved in. After one letter in which he listed many of Steinstuecken's challenges, Professor Niemeyer remarked: "And yet, no one moves away, for this was home. There are certainly few corners so idyllic as this one near Berlin."[73] For the most part, Steinstuecken residents learned to get along with the Vopos. They tried not to antagonize them. And in most cases, the Vopos didn't bother the residents. They checked their passes and waved them on their way. For the exclave's residents, day-to-day life was often surprisingly routine.

The residents took a few steps of their own to improve their situation. At the end of 1952, Steinstuecken citizens worked with the West Berlin government to improve the road surface on the *Waldweg*. "West Berlin authorities agreed to supply 500 cubic yards of rubble and the tools for the job," wrote a Reuters wire reporter on December

21. "Trucks drove up and dumped rubble and shovels at the road block which marks the end of West Berlin and the beginning of the path to the village." Villagers used the rubble to improve the road. "This is the first project of the Steinstueckian Five Year Plan," a village resident told the watching Vopos.[74]

According to that same Reuters report, the hamlet complained when the GDR cut power to the village near Christmastime. Power cuts in Soviet Zone countries were commonplace. But the Steinstueckeners claimed that, because they paid their electricity bill to the GDR in West marks, which were worth four times the value of East marks, they deserved uninterrupted service. "Shortly afterwards," wrote Reuters, "power was restored to Steinstuecken, and the lights went on again"… "standing out against the surrounding blackness of the Soviet zone."[75]

Magrit Wiese shared another less tranquil memory of her childhood in Steinstuecken—the time her parents smuggled a refugee to West Berlin. Just as Steinstueckeners could cross the street into the Soviet Zone, East Germans could cross into the exclave. Occasionally, East Germans would sneak into Steinstuecken, hoping to escape into West Berlin. The Steinstueckeners still alive today were children during the Cold War, so they remember little about refugee smuggling. Their parents didn't talk much about it, undoubtedly because they feared reprisals. But exclave residents did occasionally run the risk to harbor and transport refugees.

"At one point, I remember there was a New Years' Eve party," said Magrit Wiese. "And, I asked my mother, who is that? It was all family at the party, I knew everybody, but who is that?" *That* was a refugee. Years later, Magrit's family told her the whole story. "He knocked on the window, scared, and my parents took him in." They did more than that. "My father smuggled him out. My aunt and my mother was sitting in the back seat [of their car], and he was laying in between, and they had a blanket over him. I mean, of course, they were scared to death. But they got him out."[76]

Magrit's relatives were right to be scared. The Vopos could look into Steinstuecken from the surrounding neighborhoods. They could see which households let refugees in. Steinstuecken had no security fences or West Berlin police to keep the Vopos from visiting those households and dragging their residents into the Soviet Zone. And what would have happened if the checkpoint guards had lifted that blanket in the backseat of Herr Wiese's car? Magrit didn't hear these stories until years later. "I was way too small" in the 1950s to get mixed up in something as dangerous as helping refugees.

Everyone in Steinstuecken got mixed up in those dangers in August 1958. At 5 a.m. on August 7, residents heard gunfire. An East German Army deserter rushed into the exclave. He knocked on the doors of several houses, looking for refuge. No one let him inside, undoubtedly in fear of the Vopos who were surely chasing the man. Eventually he hid in a haystack.[77] Soon, a Vopo detachment entered Steinstuecken and searched for him. When exclave residents warned the Vopos they were on West Berlin territory, the East Germans withdrew. But soon hundreds of Vopos surrounded the hamlet.[78]

In Catudal's account of the incident, a teenage Steinstuecken resident saw the deserter hide in the haystack and went over to talk to him. East German border troops, now watching the exclave intently, saw the boy "walk up to and seemingly converse with a haystack." A Vopo detachment rushed back into Steinstuecken—violating West Berlin territory for a *second* time—grabbed the deserter and dragged him back into the Soviet Zone.[79]

The episode "touched off a frenzy of protests in West Berlin," wrote Catudal. "The three Western Powers, the United States in particular, were criticized for not intervening. From the time the first shots had been heard in the exclave, until the deserter had been captured, almost four full hours had elapsed. Outraged citizens demanded to know why nothing had been done in that time."[80] "The West German and West Berlin press," wrote the State Department, "apparently inspired in part by exaggerated accounts of the incident and confused by a lack of understanding of the isolation of and situation in the exclave, not only violently denounced the Soviets but also sharply criticized the U.S. authorities for not taking more effective action. Concern about the situation was also expressed by the Berlin Senat and the Federal German Foreign Office."[81]

The UPI and AP wire services reported the Germans' anger. "The West Berlin paper *Der Tag* said that only a show of force such as the stationing of US military police in Steinstuecken could prevent a repetition of" the GDR's incursion, said a UPI wire report.[82] The next day, *Baltimore Sun* reporter Bynum Shaw wrote an article headlined "US

Berlin Move Weak, West Germans Say." "An American refusal to intervene with more than paper in a Berlin border violation is raising doubts here as to the United States' willingness to back up its repeated pledges to guarantee the security of the beleaguered city," Shaw wrote. He relayed more West German press reactions. The *Allgemeine Zeitung* thought the US Army chief of staff didn't react sharply enough to the invasion. "His utterances, it said, were 'in accordance with the laxity with which the United States forces in Berlin handled the incident.' The paper declared American authorities 'should have intervened energetically and promptly under the four-power statute.'" There was more:

> The socialist *Frankfurter Rundschau* said the American protest was worthless. 'Who believes seriously in the effectiveness of such protests which actually have degenerated into political gestures?' it asks.
>
> Hamburg's independent *Die Welt*, which recently has been sharply critical of American action in many fields, entitled its latest complaint 'The Americans Disappointed Berlin.'
>
> In Duesseldorf, the right-center *Der Mittag* declared that, if the US is unwilling to take risks, its guarantees become valueless.[83]

The criticism raised concerns at the US Embassy. "We will not be able to endure another invasion of Steinstuecken without taking more positive and forceful action" in the future, it wrote in a telegram to Washington on August 28, "unless we are willing to accept a sharp and perhaps vital blow to our position in Berlin and West Germany."[84] West Berlin's mayor felt compelled to reassure his citizens. "West Berlin Mayor Willy Brandt said in a radio address Sunday the Western Allies will protect the city against Communist encroachments. He said the Western powers have given the city security guarantees and will live up to them." That appeared in a UPI wire report on August 25 in the *Palm Beach Post.* The headline: "West Berlin Sure of Aid of Allies."

Once again, Steinstuecken caused colorful headlines in American newspapers. "800 East German Police Raid Village in US Sector of Berlin" (Louisville *Courier Journal*); "East Germans Raid Enclave in US Hands" (*Chicago Tribune*); "Reds Capture Man in US Sector" (*Great Falls Tribune*, Great Falls, Montana); "Red Horde Hunts Down Fleeing Man" (*Fort Lauderdale News*); "Bold Red Move" (*Cincinnati*

Photo credit: U.S. State Department

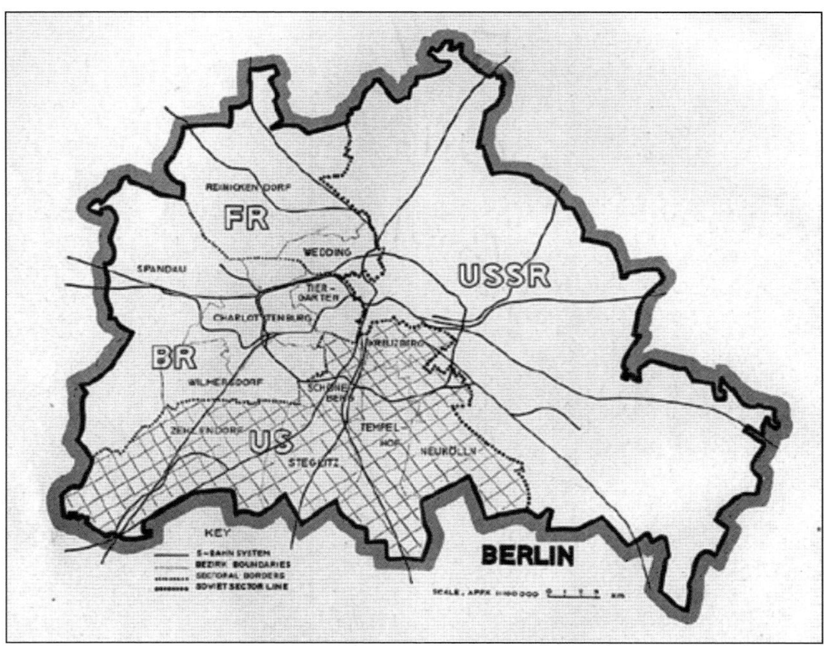

The top map was prepared by the U.S. State Department prior to the occupation of Berlin. The bottom map came from the U.S. occupation government, four years later. Neither one showed Steinstuecken, which lies just outside the southwestern corner of Berlin. Photo credit: HICOG

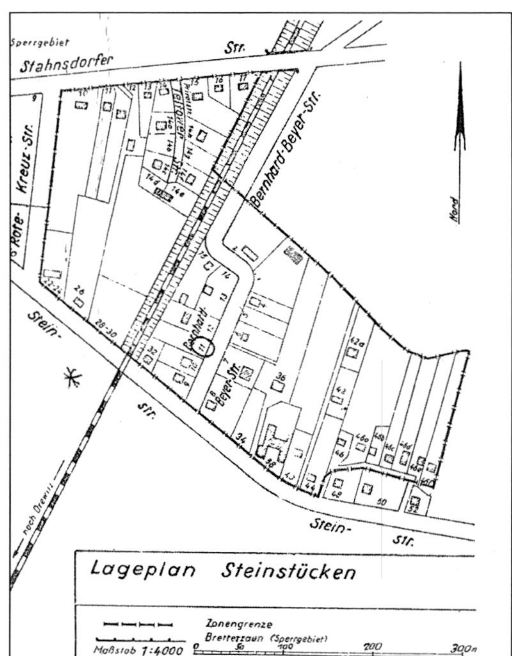

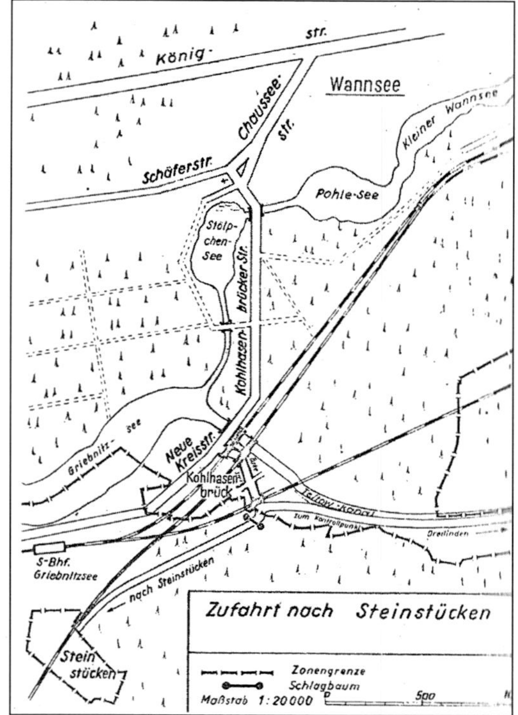

Top: map of Steinstuecken. Bottom: a map of the area around Steinstuecken. Photo credit: City of Berlin

In the bottom map, Berlin is north of the hatched line, which shows the boundary (Zonengrenze) *between the city and the neighboring state* (Land) *of Brandenburg. The West Berlin city government prepared these maps ca. 1951.*

Children play in the bombed out streets of Berlin, summer 1945. Photo credit: U.S. State Department

A devastated Berlin during the spring and summer of 1945. Photo credit: OMGUS

One-room shacks were often visible in the bomb-shattered wrecks of once-huge buildings. Photo credit: OMGUS

Wrecked weapon systems—or parts of them—littered the city. Photo credit: OMGUS

Photo credit: OMGUS

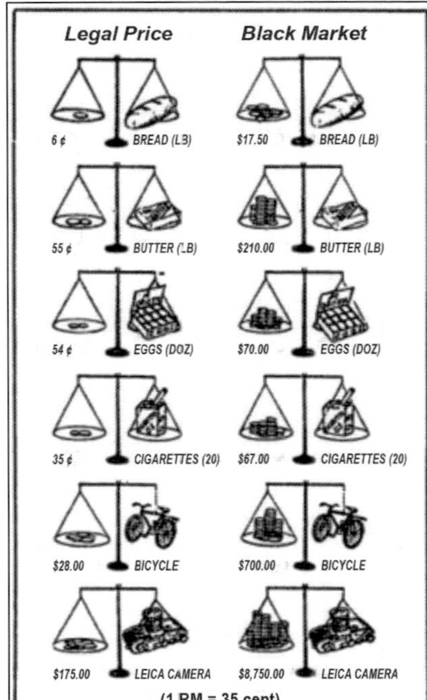

These graphics from OMGUS publications demonstrate the extent of Berlin's devastation. The image above shows the Victory Column (Siegessaule), *which commemorates Prussian victories in the 19th century. In the summer of 1945, Berliners were reduced to plowing the land around the monument—which had been a major city park—to grow more food. At left, a comparison of official versus black-market prices in the city. Photo credit: OMGUS*

The senior British, American, Russian, and French officials on the Kommandantura. The graphic is undated, but it is from the early years of the occupation. Photo credit: OMGUS

American (on the left) and Russian (on the right) officers at a Kommandantura meeting. Standing behind them are American and Russian translators. Photo credit: OMGUS

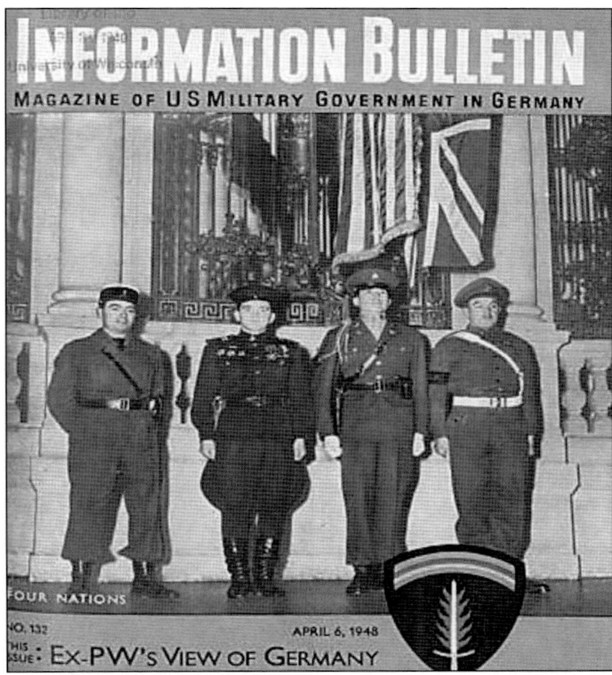

Photo credit: OMGUS

Photo credit: OMGUS

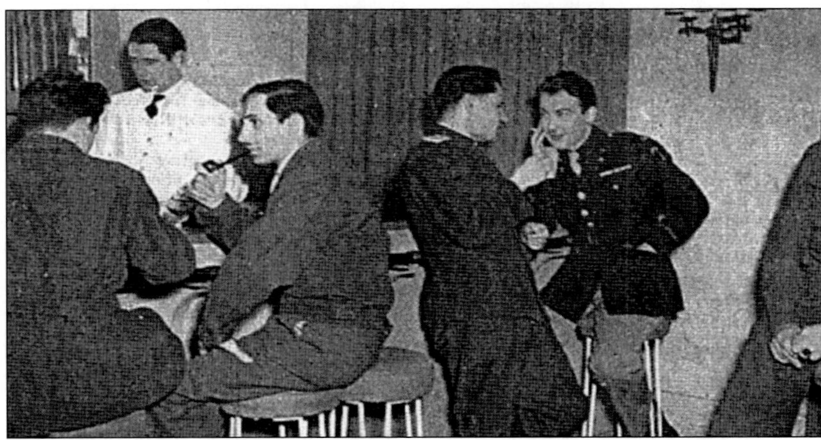

Above: French, Soviet, American, and British guards at the Allied Control Authority (ACA) headquarters in Berlin. Below: an American officer socializes with a Soviet colleague at the ACA bar. Photo credit: OMGUS

Photo credit: OMGUS

Photo credit: OMGUS

Scenes from the early years of occupation, when American authority over Germans was almost absolute. American occupiers ran the criminal courts (top), parole boards (center), and news broadcasts (bottom). The uniformed officials with triangles on their collars are civilian employees of OMGUS. Photo credit: OMGUS

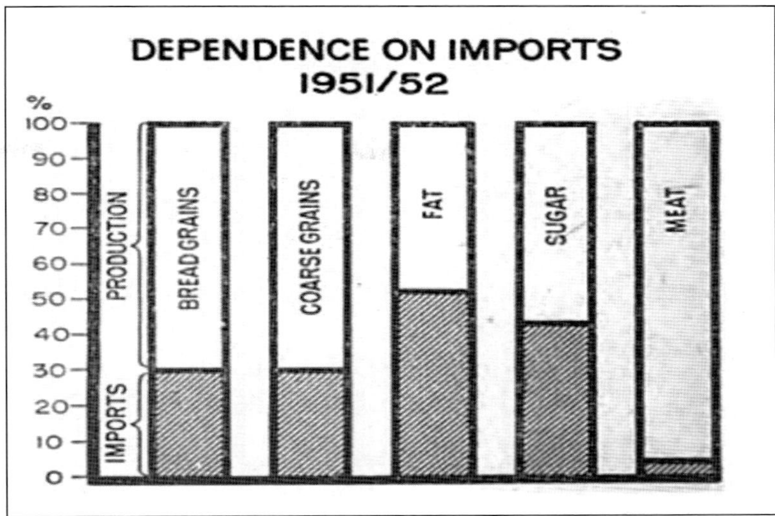

1951 was the sixth year of the occupation. Despite the Wirtschaftwuender, *West Germany's postwar economic miracle, West Germany still relied heavily on US imports for its food supply, as this OMGUS chart shows. Photo credit: HICOG*

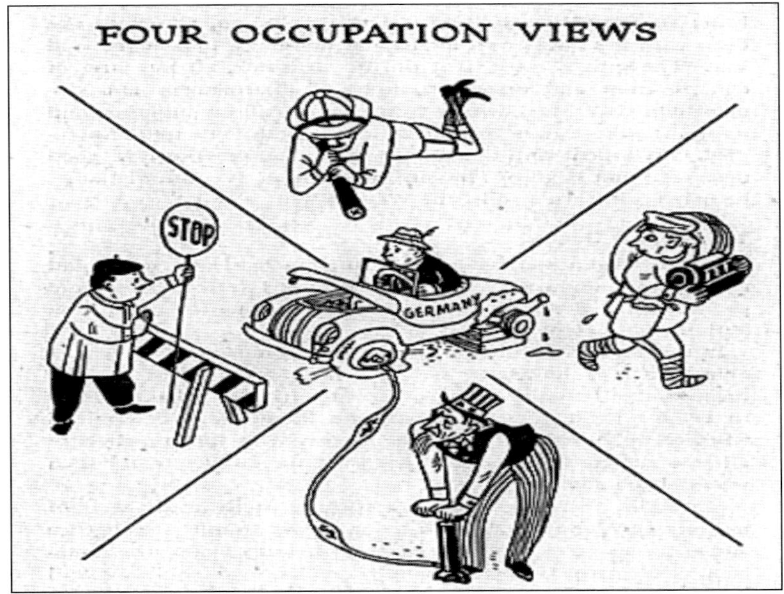

An cartoon from Foreign Policy *magazine in 1950 illustrates the different ways each of the wartime Allies was handling Germany. The Russians took as much from Germany as they could, the French wanted to block it from becoming a continental power again, and the British watched it warily. The U.S., by contrast, was working the hardest of all four of the wartime allies to prop up Germany, and then revive it. Photo credit:* Foreign Policy *Magazine*

East German political cartoons from 1951, urging West Germans to NOT align themselves with the Western Allies. This magazine cover shows a caricature American soldier, urging a West German to take up arms and fight in a third World War. "Ohne mich" ("without me") was a rallying cry for pacifists. Many West Germans feared being caught in the middle of a war between the U.S and USSR. Photo credit: Donald Smith

Germans on opposite sides of a divided table—symbolizing eastern and western Germany—struggle to reunite their divided country. The German word for table is "tisch." A common Communist propaganda slogan was "Deutsche an einem Tisch" (All Germans around one table.) A stereotype American soldier, the spirit of Adolf Hitler and a caricature of West German chancellor Konrad Adenauer (standing on top of an "industrialist") try to block them. Communist propaganda accused the U.S. of using NATO and the Cold War to prevent the reunification of Germany. Photo credit: Donald Smith

Photo credit: OMGUS

Photo credit: Wikimedia Commons

As I See America

By ERNST REUTER
Governing Mayor of Berlin

This article on his impressions of the United States was written by the governing mayor of Berlin at the special request of the Information Bulletin. Mayor Reuter's most recent visit to America, from Feb. 22 to March 8, was a tour sponsored by the Americans for Democratic Action.

Ernst Reuter was West Berlin's mayor during the Steinstuecken crisis of 1951. Top left: Reuter addressing a crowd. "RIAS" stands for "Radio in the American Sector," the radio station OMGUS created to counter the Soviet-dominated Radio Berlin. Top right: a postage stamp the U.S. Post Office issued in 1952 to honor Reuter. Bottom: the first page of Reuter's "As I See America" article in the HICOG Information Bulletin of May 1951. Photo credit: HICOG

General Lemuel Mathewson, US Commander of Berlin (USCOB) during the Steinstuecken crisis of 1951. Photo credit: U.S. Army

The Soviet Tanker's Memorial in West Berlin, "protected" by Mathewson's chicken wire fence. Photo credit: OMGUS

The Berlin Anzeiger *newspaper ran this cartoon on October 24th, after the Americans convinced the GDR and Soviets to release their grip on Steinstuecken. The title is "Little Red Riding Hood, 1951." Mathewson, the hunter, has slain the Soviet wolf. Next to him, a woman symbolizing Berlin holds the now rescued "Red Riding Hood," Steinsuecken. Photo credit: Family of Hans Bierbrauer*

In 1952, the Soviets and East Germans sealed off West Berlin from the Soviet Zone. Here East German workmen build a wall across a street just north of Steinstuecken. Photo credit: Berlin State Archives, F Rep. 290 No. 0046749. Photographer: Gert Schütz.

Photo credit: OMGUS

The 1946 Berlin city elections caused an extraordinary confrontation: the Soviet-supported Socialist Unity Party (SED) competed against Western-leaning parties for control of the city government. The banner in the top photograph says "The Soviet Union is Germany's Best Friend." The bottom photograph shows the Brandenburg Gate in election mode. Photo credit: OMGUS

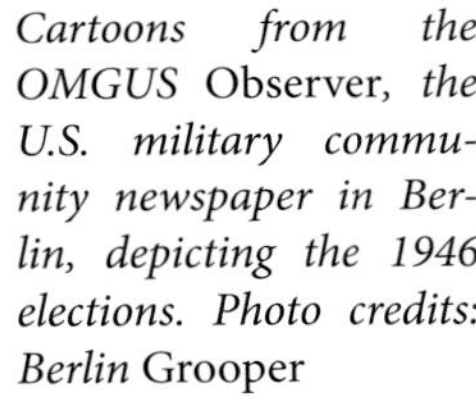
Cartoons from the OMGUS Observer, *the U.S. military community newspaper in Berlin, depicting the 1946 elections. Photo credits: Berlin* Grooper

Photo credit: OMGUS

Election day in Berlin, October 1946. Each political party offered its own slate, or "list," of candidates; voters then picked the list of the party they wanted. The woman with the sandwich board is urging voters to choose List 1, the West-backed Social Democrats Party (SPD). The kiosk is covered with posters for List 2, the Communist-backed Socialist Unity Party (SED). Bottom photos credit: Berlin Grooper

Photo credit: Berlin Grooper

Berliners cast their votes in the 1946 city elections. The polling place shown at top has the flags of all four occupying powers, plus the bear symbol of Greater Berlin. Notice the triumphant caption OMGUS writers placed on the bottom photograph. Photo credit: OMGUS

Photo credit: Berlin State Archives, F Rep. 290 No. 0046749. Photographer: Gert Schütz.

The "refrigerator incident" of April 1956. The Governing Mayor of Berlin, Otto Suhr, tries to visit Steinstuecken. Top: an overview of the scene at the Kohlasenbrueck checkpoint. The dirt road leads to the exclave. Below: Mayor Suhr and a crowd of reporters are blocked by GDR border guards. Photo credit: Berlin State Archives, F Rep. 290 No. 0046749. Photographer: Gert Schütz.

Photo credit: Berlin State Archives, F Rep. 290 No. 0046749. Photographer: Gert Schütz.

The people of Steinstuecken came to see the mayor. Top: a young resident of the exclave gives the mayor flowers. Bottom: residents and reporters listen to the mayor at the checkpoint. Photo credit: Berlin State Archives, F Rep. 290 No. 0046749. Photographer: Gert Schütz.

Occasionally in the 1950s, West Berlin officials—but not Americans—could walk to Steinstuecken. Here, the mayor of Zehlendorf Bezirk*, Dr. Willy Stiewe (far right) escorts some city officials past the GDR border checkpoint on a visit to the exclave. Photo credit: Berlin State Archives, F Rep. 290 No. 0046749. Photographer: Gert Schütz.*

When the Berlin Wall was erected, the GDR encircled Steinstuecken with a barbed wire fence. Neighbors were now sealed off from each other. This boy, who lived in the Soviet Zone, looks through the wire into Steinstuecken. Photo credit: National Archives

TIME

THE WEEKLY NEWSMAGAZINE

GENERAL CLAY

"I will not be bluffed."

Above: General Lucius D. Clay, taken when he was the U.S. Military Governor of Germany. Photo credit: U.S. Army

Below: the cover of TIME *magazine for July 12, 1948, in the midst of the Berlin Airlift. General Clay became an international hero for leading Western Allied resistance to the Soviets during the Berlin Blockade. Photo credit: Wikimedia Commons*

September 21, 1961: Lucius Clay, Der Vater der Lueftbruecke *(The Father of the Airlift) and now the personal representative of President Kennedy in Berlin, lands unannounced in Steinstuecken. Top: Clay exits the helicopter. Bottom: exclave children and parents greet him with flowers. Photo credits: Kurt Behrendt*

Photo credit: Kurt Behrendt

Above: Clay's helicopter in the little field that served as a helipad that day. Heike Behrendt is the small girl in the foreground. Below: as Clay toured the exclave and met with its residents, other exclave residents toured the helicopters. Photo credit: Kurt Behrendt

Clay's two Army pilots meet the villagers. On the left is Captain Jeff Hastings; on the right is Lieutenant Tom Clark. Photo credit: Kurt Behrendt

Clay's helicopter departs for Berlin. Photo credit: Kurt Behrendt

Exclave residents waving goodbye. The photograph captures the poignancy and sadness of Steinstuecken's unique situation. The caption reads: "In the immediate vicinity of the helicopter as it takes off are the Steinstueckeners who waved goodbye. In the background are residents of Babelsberg and excited Vopos – [East German] officers almost shoulder-to-shoulder with the inhabitants of the exclave, but still separted by mines and the barved-wire border." That barbed-wire border fence, less than a month old at the time of this photograph, separated people who'd been neighbors and friends for years. Photo credit: Kurt Behrendt

Photo credit: Kurt Behrendt

Clay visited Steinstuecken three more times in 1961 and 1962. Above: Clay looks at a collection of photographs of the exclave, taken by Kurt Behrendt, seated to Clay's left. The man on Clay's immediate right is Friederich Reichow, the unofficial "mayor" of Steinstuecken at the time. Below: Reichow and a group of exclave children accompany Clay on a walk around the village. Photo credit: Kurt Behrendt

Photo credit: Kurt Behrendt

W.R. Smyser, a State Department official stationed in Berlin, often accompanied Clay on his trips to the village. Here, Clay and Smyser listen to Friederich Reichow and share a glass of wine at Walter Steinweg's "Restaurant Steinstuecken," the only restaurant in the village at the time of the Cold War. Photo credit: Kurt Behrendt

Photo credit: Kurt Behrendt

Clay tours the perimeter fence with Zehlendorf Bezirk mayor Willy Stiewe. Steinstuecken residents often asked the general for his autograph, and he obliged them whenever he could. Photo credit: Kurt Behrendt

Photo credit: Kurt Behrendt

September 23, 1961: The Americans put "boots on the ground" in Steinstuecken. Above: members of the 287th MP Company test radios while Mayor Reichow looks on. Below: a resident greets the MPs with flowers. Photo credit: Kurt Behrendt

Members of the 287th MP Company on duty in Steinstuecken. The MPs were lightly-armed. The machine pistol carried by the MP on the right, commonly refered to as a "grease gun," was the largest machine gun the MPs normally had in the exclave. Photo credits: Kurt Behrendt

Top: East German workers perform maintenance on their side of the border. Bottom: as a GDR border guard watches the workers, two American MPs in Steinstuecken watch all of them. Photo credits: Kurt Behrendt

This electronic billboard was in West Berlin. Its messages were visible throughout much of East Berlin. West Berlin press used the billboard to broadcast uncensored news into Communist-controlled territory. In English, the logo on the billboard says "The Free Berlin Press Announces." Photo credit: HICOG

A section of the wire fencing around Steinstuecken in October 1961. Photo credit: Kurt Behrendt

Enquirer); "East German Raiders Trigger US Protest—Toted Machine Guns Across Border" (*Springfield News-Leader*, Springfield, Missouri); "US Raps Red Raid" (*Philadelphia Inquirer*).

To be fair, the Western Powers and West Berlin authorities couldn't have done much without risking a major incident. If West Berlin police had tried to drive to the exclave, the Vopos at the Kohlhasenbrueck checkpoint certainly would have stopped them. (What could the West Berlin police have done in response? Storm the Vopo checkpoint?) As for the Americans, it beggars belief that the Soviets would have sat by quietly if a US Army column had tried to drive to the exclave. A State Department report in September 1958 said, "the key problem is how to get West Berlin police or American troops across the 100 yards of well-guarded Soviet Zone territory which separate the US Sector proper from the Steinstuecken exclave."[85] (The report gets the distance wrong; more than a kilometer separated the exclave from West Berlin).

By the end of the 1950s, American authority over the exclave was no longer in dispute. Whenever the Vopos squeezed on Steinstuecken, American officials held firm, pushed back on the Soviets, and the pressures usually relaxed. But there was always tension in the little village. What might happen next? What provocation would the Vopos try next time? What could happen to this "idyllic corner near Berlin", as Professor Niemeyer described it, if the Cold War heated up?

As the 1960s began, the Cold War had heated up. Soviet Premier Nikita Khrushchev was squeezing West Berlin again. In the fall of 1958, he threatened to toss aside the Potsdam Agreements, which said World War II would end when the Allied powers signed a peace treaty with a reunited Germany. Khrushchev said he was ready to sign a separate peace agreement with the GDR. That would end the war as far as the USSR was concerned. The Western Allies' rights in West Berlin as occupying powers would also end. If the Western Allies wanted to stay, they would have to negotiate with the GDR.

This "Berlin Ultimatum" touched off another period of high tension between the Soviets and the West. Khrushchev's penchant for public outbursts heightened tensions further. At a meeting of the UN General Assembly in October 1960, Khrushchev became angry. He pulled off his shoe and pounded the table with it. He bullied President Kennedy at their summit meeting in Vienna in 1961. In a speech in East Berlin in the summer of 1961, West German journalists started to mock him.

Khrushchev turned, pointed at them, and said, "We buried you at Stalingrad, and we will bury you again!"[86]

Frequently he boasted of improved Soviet nuclear weapons and hinted that he might use them. "We do not want to frighten anyone," Khrushchev told Soviet journalists in November 1958, "but we can tell the truth … now we have such a stock of rockets, such an amount of atomic and hydrogen warheads, that if they attack us we could wipe our potential enemies off the face of the earth." If these weapons were "exploded over some country there will be nothing left at all."[87] Khrushchev often preceded major foreign trips with a rocket launch to rattle his hosts and demonstrate Soviet might.[88] His obituary in the *New York Times* recalled a story of Khrushchev "telling an envoy from a Mediterranean country, 'Get out of NATO or we will drop a nuclear bomb on you.' When the ambassador protested that 'you are such a big country and we are such a small country.' Mr. Khrushchev replied, 'That's all right. For you we will use only a teeny tiny nuclear bomb.'"[89] Russia's successful launch of Sputnik in 1957 made Khrushchev's threats seem much more plausible. If the Soviets could launch a satellite that circled the globe, Western leaders feared they could launch a warhead into orbit, too. Western nerves were on edge.

As the summer of 1961 drew to a close, the situation in and around Berlin remained unsettled and tense. The Kennedy administration was trying to sort out what to do, as was the rest of the West. Some State Department officials urged Kennedy to hold a tough line with the Soviets; others called for negotiation and compromise. During that summer, former Ambassador to West Germany David Bruce, then serving at the US Embassy in London, offered to participate in future talks on Berlin and the German question. "I should be happy to" come to Washington "to participate in such a study, preferably in August or September, since the situation should be somewhat clearer then."[90]

Ambassador Bruce had no idea how prophetic his words would be. On August 13, 1961, the East Germans and Soviets clarified the situation in Berlin for everybody.

CHAPTER SIX

The President decided that the following course of action shall be taken with respect to Steinstuecken.
National Security Action Memorandum, subject "Steinstucken and Friedrichstrasse Crossing Point," September 14, 1961.

Before dawn on Sunday, August 13, 1961, thousands of East German soldiers and workers fanned out along the twenty-seven-mile-long boundary between East and West Berlin. They tore up streets and strung barbed wire across the roads and pathways between the Soviet and Western Sectors. Armed guards took up posts along the border. When the sun rose, East Berliners saw they were trapped.

"To put an end to the hostile activities of the revanchist and militarist forces of Western Germany and West Berlin," the GDR announced, "such control is to be introduced on the borders of the GDR, including the border with the Western sectors of West Berlin, which is usually introduced along the borders of every sovereign state. Reliable safeguards and effective control must be insured on the West Berlin borders in order to block the way to the subversive activities."[1]

For more than sixteen years, East Germans had used Berlin as an escape hatch from communism. Millions had gone west. In July 1961, over *30,000* East Germans had crossed into West Berlin, the highest total in one month since 1953.[2] Five thousand escaped on August 11 and 12 alone.[3] The Soviets and East Germans had had enough. Many of the refugees were young or skilled workers—the kinds of citizens the GDR couldn't afford to lose. The GDR was bleeding to death. The barbed wire, torn-up streets and armed guards—the precursors to the Berlin Wall—were the tourniquet.

West Berliners were stunned. The occupying powers were supposed to treat all Berlin as one undivided city. Supposedly, Berliners could enter any of the four occupation sectors. Many West Berliners, fearing Communist harassment, avoided East Berlin. But thousands of East Berliners worked at jobs in the Western sectors. Thousands of East Germans visited West Berlin daily, to shop, go to the movies, etc. Many West Berliners had family and friends in the Soviet Sector. Even though *de facto* four power city government had ended more than a decade earlier, Berliners had still been able to move (for the most part) throughout their city, even as the Cold War ground on. The events of August 13 literally and finally chopped the city in half.

The Western Allies protested vigorously to the Soviets. They insisted the GDR wasn't a sovereign country, and East German authorities had no right to block travel within the city. The Soviets disagreed. "As has already been emphasized, the Soviet garrison in Berlin does not interfere with the affairs of the capital of the German Democratic Republic," said the Soviets as they rejected the American protest. The Soviets said the matter laid "entirely within the competence" of the GDR, "in the fulfillment of the normal rights of each sovereign nation to protect its national interests."[4] West Berliners waited to see what the Western Allies would do.

They didn't do much. "Relief was the dominant emotion in Washington for the 24 hours following the border closing," wrote CIA historian Donald Steury. "The refugee problem had become acute, leading to concern that more drastic actions were in the offing."[5] That June, the U.S. Ambassador to Moscow had told Washington that Khrushchev's "principal objectives" for Berlin and the German question included "stabiliz[ing] the regime in East Germany" and "neutraliz[ing] Berlin as a first step [toward] its eventual takeover by the GDR."[6] The Soviets couldn't stabilize the GDR or neutralize Berlin until the refugee flow stopped.

Washington recognized and accepted that. "Closing the borders defused what had seemed to be an increasingly critical situation," observed Dr. Steury.[7] Western diplomats drove through the GDR checkpoints into East Berlin to verify that the *Western Allies* could still move back and forth freely between the Soviet and Western Sectors. (They could—GDR border guards allowed them to pass). But American, British, and French forces did nothing to tear down the barbed wire barricades or otherwise reopen East Berliners' access to West Berlin.

"Berliners and West Germans reacted to this seeming complacency" by the Allies "with fury," wrote Dr. Steury. "Hundreds of thousands of West Berliners demonstrated at the Brandenburg Gate." Mayor

Willy Brandt "angrily demanded some action from Kennedy." Steury describes how Brandt's press secretary recalled the "frustration felt in Berlin" by the Western Allies' unwillingness to stop the GDR:

> It took hours (Dr. Bahr recalled) to convince the [Allied] commandants to give orders that [would put] at least some armed, uniformed people in jeeps patrolling the line. It took more than 24 hours before the commandants got permission to transmit a small, weak protest to their Soviet colleagues on the other side in East Berlin. It took more than 48 hours before the first protests came from Washington, Paris and London to Moscow. This was the reality. After three days, when it was absolutely clear for the Eastern side and the Communists that no major tough reaction could be expected from the Western side, they started to build up the Wall.[8]

Washington soon realized it had badly underestimated the anger in West Berlin and West Germany. Six days after the GDR closed the borders, Vice President Johnson flew to West Berlin to reassure Western sector citizens (and the rest of the Free World) that the US still stood behind West Berlin. To emphasize that, the Kennedy administration ordered an American infantry battle group to road-march from West Germany, across East Germany, into West Berlin. Hundreds of thousands of West Berliners cheered Johnson's visit and the military reinforcements. For a while, rattled nerves in the city settled down.

But the Communists weren't finished. Vice President Johnson left West Berlin on August 21. The next day, the East Germans issued new, stricter travel guidelines. West Berliners could now enter East Berlin at only four crossing points—and they had to pay! "West Berlin citizens now require a permit to visit East Berlin," said a GDR proclamation. "A fee of one West mark will be charged for a permit."[9] "New measures over the past week," reported the CIA in its weekly intelligence summary for August 24, "involve controls that might be encountered at a recognized international frontier—including replacement of the barbed-wire barricades erected along the East-West Berlin sector border on 13 August with concrete barriers, the strengthening of barbed-wire fences along the zonal border adjoining West Berlin on three sides, and various types of personal checks on those desiring to cross the border."[10]

The East Germans also warned Berliners, "in the interests of their own safety, to keep 100 meters away from both sides of the sector border."[11] *Both* sides of the sector border? Many West Berlin streets, homes, and businesses were within 100 meters of the border—were they now in a potential danger zone? The GDR promptly made the danger seem quite real. In the days following the border closure, West Berliners frequently massed to protest, sometimes just a few yards from the lines of Vopo guards and wire barriers. On August 25, East German police threw tear gas at two groups of protesters. They even fired warning shots over another group in the French Sector.[12]

The Soviets also ratcheted up the pressure on West Berlin. On August 23 the Soviets accused the Western Allies of improperly allowing West German officials and citizens to travel through the designated air corridors between West Germany and West Berlin. The Soviets said West Germany was using West Berlin as a base from which to destabilize East Berlin and East Germany.

"All kinds of revanchists, extremists, saboteurs and spies are being transferred from the German Federal Republic to West Berlin," the Soviets claimed in their protest note. "In this way, the United States, Britain and France are plainly abusing their position in West Berlin." In 1945, claimed the Soviets, the "air corridors were set aside for the three Western powers on a temporary basis to insure the needs of their military garrisons, not for the subversive and revanchist purposes of West German militarism."[13]

The East Germans joined in a few days later. In its weekly intelligence summary for August 31, the CIA wrote the following: "Echoing the allegations contained in the Soviet note that the Western powers are conniving in the use of the Berlin air corridors by West German 'revanchists' and 'militarists,'" the GDR's deputy foreign minister protested the use of the corridors by Western civilian airlines. The East German diplomat charged that the "profitable business of American, British and French airlines in the air corridors is illegal." Moreover, "there is no single agreement in which the Western powers were granted the right to use the air corridors for civilian flights."[14] (In 1961, no West German airlines could fly to West Berlin; only carriers from the Western Allies could.)

"US Mission officials in Berlin believe that the Soviet note of 23 August has caused further apprehension among West Berliners, who regard unrestricted air access as an essential element of their freedom," the CIA reported at the end of August. West Berliners traveling by rail or the *autobahn* were always subject to harassment; airline passengers didn't have that worry.

"Mayor Brandt and other SPD leaders believe that, despite the temporary improvement of morale resulting from the visit of VP Johnson and reinforcement of the Berlin garrison, a feeling of frustration and hopelessness is already beginning to spread through the West Berlin population."[15] The new border restrictions depressed morale even more. The West German ambassador to the US met with Secretary of State Dean Rusk on August 26. The ambassador warned that, in the eyes of many West Berliners, the Allies' unwillingness to force open the Berlin Wall hinted that the Western Powers might tolerate other, more painful Communist encroachments on the city. "West Berliners could not distinguish between Western acceptance of the closing of sector borders and other rights" which the West had repeatedly pledged to protect[16]—namely, the rights of West Berliners to live as free people.

The Kennedy administration wasn't willing to risk a confrontation with the Soviets just so Berliners could travel anywhere in the city they wanted. The administration was determined to maintain *Allied* access into the Soviet Sector. But even then, there were limits to how far the Americans were willing to go. This is an excerpt of a telegram from the Joint Chiefs of Staff to General Lauris Norstad, the US Commander in Chief in Europe, on August 25:

> The objective of insisting on our access to East Berlin by the US Command, Berlin, is to demonstrate our determination to maintain our legal right of entry to East Berlin. Concurrently we desire to give political and psychological evidence of US attitude in regard to developments in the Berlin situation.
>
> A clear distinction must be made, however, between US right of access to East Berlin and West Berlin. While we consider the US right of access to East Berlin to be important, we do not consider it so vital that it must be maintained by the use of force which entails combat, except that required for self-defense if our forces are fired upon in the implementation of measures indicated below. U.S. forces so fired upon in East Berlin should defend themselves and withdraw to West Berlin, forces fired upon in

> West Berlin should return fire only so long as they are under fire. No line of action should be initiated to maintain the U.S. right of access to East Berlin, therefore, which would result in serious loss of U.S. prestige if U.S. forces involved should have to withdraw.
>
> However, U.S. right of access to West Berlin from FRG is of such importance as to require, if necessary, the use of force entailing combat.[17]

The Kennedy administration focused on safeguarding West Berlin and access to it by rail, air, and road. As long as the Soviets and East Germans didn't threaten those rights, Washington would let the East Germans keep walling off East Berlin. West Berliners and their officials protested, often in anguish, but the White House held firm. It wasn't willing to risk war so that Berliners could circulate freely throughout the city or East Germans could flee to the West. President Kennedy told a New York Times reporter that, if the East Germans had wanted to flee, they'd had fifteen years in which to do it.

But the Kennedy administration didn't want to see West Berlin shrivel and slip into decline, either. Soviet General Chuikov wasn't exaggerating when he'd said the Russians found it "intolerable" for the West to be in Berlin. West Berlin was a Western showcase in the middle of Communist Europe. Before the Wall, East Berliners and East Germans could visit West Berlin. They could compare Communist propaganda to the sights and experiences of West Berlin and come to their own conclusions about which way of life (East versus West) was best. "West Berlin is the cheapest atom bomb in the heart of the eastern empire," remarked Ernst Reuter, and for good reason.[18]

West Berlin was an invaluable Cold War asset for the West—as long as it stayed vibrant and healthy. What if the Berlin Wall crisis soured young people and talented workers on life in West Berlin? If workers concluded that the city's Western sectors didn't offer them a prosperous, stable, and safe future, they'd leave for West Germany. If companies feared that East German rolling blockades would make it impossible to do business with the West, they'd leave the city too. West Berlin's economy and society would shrivel—what kind of beacon would it be then?

Famed journalist Edward R. Murrow entered US government service in January 1961, as head of the US Information Agency (USIA). He was in Berlin when the Wall crisis broke out. Its impact on West

Berliners' morale alarmed him. On August 16 he cabled Washington that there was "real danger that Berliners will conclude they should take themselves, their bank accounts and movable assets to some other place. What is in danger of being destroyed here is that perishable commodity called hope."[19]

That same day, West Berlin Mayor Willy Brandt handed US diplomats a letter for President Kennedy. It said that, if Communist pressure on Berlin wasn't checked, "Berlin would be like a ghetto, which has not only lost its function as a refuge of freedom and symbol of hope for reunification, but which would also be severed from the free part of Germany. Instead of flight to Berlin, we might then experience the beginning of flight from Berlin."[20]

West Berlin was more than a "symbol of hope," as Mayor Brandt put it. It was a symbol of victory, the site of past Cold War successes. Some of the West's earliest triumphs over Communism had occurred in Berlin. That made the morale and public relations stakes for the Western Allies even higher. If West Berlin were to now wither and decay, and become a failed city, Western (and especially American) prestige would suffer.

The Berlin Airlift was the West's most smashing victory over Communism to date. The Soviets had been confident that the Allies couldn't fly in the thousands of tons of food and coal West Berlin needed each day to survive. The Russians "assumed comfortably that we couldn't do it for the large German population,"[21] recalled General Frank Howley, the US Commandant in Berlin (USCOB) during the blockade.

Many Western Allied leaders felt the same way. "A Four Year Report" is an OMGUS report on the first four years of the Allied occupation of Germany—a period that included the Berlin Blockade. According to the report, some of the Western Allied leaders "felt that the population of Berlin could not be maintained by air."[22] They also feared that West Berliners wouldn't tolerate prolonged hardship. Howley, in his memoir *Berlin Command,* said that the British commandant "expected the Berliners to start rioting, due to short rations." He "predicted that the Russians would drive us out of Berlin by October."[23] (The blockade started in June). Some Allied leaders feared "that the population would desert their newly-acquired democratic ideas and would, for the sake of avoiding personal privations, swing their loyalties to the East."[24] They "believed that the people would rise up in their suffering and ask us to leave so that they might live."[25]

Western pilots and logisticians soon proved the doubters wrong. The Berlin Airlift was a triumph. For almost an entire year, it ferried in enough supplies to keep West Berlin alive. After ten months the Soviets quit. They reopened the road and rail links to the city in May 1949. Allied leaders took to the airwaves and newsreels to crow about beating back the Russians. "The Soviet planners failed to recognize our strength in the air," said General Lucius Clay, the US Military Governor in Germany at the time. "They did not understand our determination to fulfil our obligations to the people under our charge."[26] "I hope that the Communists, who have spent so much time insulting us," said Howley in a post-blockade press conference, "will realize that we really aren't such a 'soft' democracy."[27]

The Allies weren't the only ones to show that they weren't soft. The people of West Berlin proved to be tough as well. Berliners not only endured eleven months of short rations; they also stayed solidly by the Allies' side.

The Soviets offered hungry West Berliners a deal: Shop for food in the Soviet Sector of the city and receive enhanced rations. All the West Berliners had to do was trade in their Western sector ration cards for Soviet Sector cards. The Russian gambit failed. As Howley proudly recalled in *Berlin Command*, "It is a matter of record that, when we had our full provisioning plan in place, less than one hundred thousand Germans in the three Western sectors succumbed to the blandishments of the Russians and obtained food in the Russian sector."[28] (More than two million Berliners lived in the Western sectors at the time.) An OMGUS public opinion survey in September 1948, three months into the blockade, asked West Berliners if they would "prefer continuing the present situation in Berlin or bringing it to an end by uniting Berlin" under a Soviet-controlled East German government. 88% of respondents preferred to endure the blockade.[29]

The airlift's success and West Berlin's defiance gave the Allies plenty of chances to gloat and rub their success in the Russians' faces. Here's an excerpt from an American newsreel, released four months into the blockade:

> The 100th day of Russian blockade. But Moscow hadn't counted on the determination of the Western Allies. Nor had Moscow counted on the will of the Berlin people.

> The Russian blockade slashed transportation. The people walked.
>
> The Russian blockade cut gas supplies. The people got used to cooking slowly.
>
> The Russian blockade brought darkness to the city. The people got used to candlelight.[30]

The airlift wasn't the first time that West Berliners had displayed courage and determination in the face of Soviet threats. Since the early years of Allied occupation, West Berlin citizens had vocally and forcefully opposed several attempts by the Soviets and their German Communist allies to grab political and economic control of all of Berlin. From early 1946 on, the Western occupying forces were surprised (and overjoyed) as they watched West Berliners defy the Communists. By the spring of 1948, when the Soviets finally resorted to the blockade, the West Berliners had already dealt the Communists several political and public relations setbacks. These were important victories for the free world in the early stages of the Cold War.

In October 1946 Berlin held city-wide elections. When the Western Allies first took over their occupation sectors in July 1945, they had agreed to keep the city and *Bezirke* government officials the Russians had installed throughout all of Berlin. The Western Allies quickly discovered that many of the officials in their own occupation sectors were more loyal to the Soviets than to them. This made it hard for the Allies to govern their sectors as they wished or to push back against Russian efforts to influence all aspects of Berlin life. The impending elections, though, could change that. Western sector voters could oust pro-Soviet government officials.

The election was also a *de facto* referendum on the Soviets. It gave Berliners an opportunity "to pass judgment on the government the Russians had given them since 1945,"[31] wrote Howley. An OMGUS report elaborated on the election's potential impact:

> Berlin becomes a sounding board for the response of the German people to the differing concepts of democracy and government presented by the four jointly occupying powers when the citizens of Berlin go to the polls on Sunday, 20 October in their first municipal election in 14 years.

> Only in Berlin have the citizens of one city of Germany had actual experience with the different kinds of democracy and the kinds of government for which the various Allied powers stand. It is reasonable to draw the conclusions that when Berliners go to the polls, many of them will not necessarily be voting for or against any party, but consciously and seriously for one particular concept of democracy.
>
> Germany will ultimately make this same decision, and the Berlin vote, establishing upon such a decision, will have a great influence upon the ultimate destiny of Germany and therefore upon the political destiny of Europe. Berliners will go to the polls on 20 October to give democratic self-government to their city, but, with the counting of the ballots, it will become known what kind of democracy they have chosen and into what pattern the future may fall.[32]

The October 1946 elections would test all four of the occupying powers. Berlin was the one place in occupied Germany where the Soviets and the Western Allies lived in close contact. By late 1946, it was obvious that the Soviets and the West had very different goals for the postwar world. Berliners had had a chance to compare how the Communists and the Western democracies actually behaved, governed, and treated their people. They could now indicate, with their votes, which way of life they preferred. "The press of Germany and the whole world is avidly discussing" the upcoming election, wrote OMGUS. "[N]ewspapers and periodicals all over the world are devoting a great deal of speculation and space as to the results."[33]

The Soviets badly wanted to do well at the polls. "The Russians made no secret of their determination to get their men elected, by hook or by crook," wrote Howley, "because if they didn't Communist control of the city would be lost forever."[34] At first they tried normal politics, appealing to Berliners for support. "In addition to rallies and meetings," wrote Howley in *Berlin Command,* "the Reds neglected no form of approach, even the German version of political baby kissing. Quite a few pre-election food parties were held"... "At the schools they distributed cakes, cookies and notebooks 'with the compliments of the SED' [the Soviet-backed German political party]."[35] Banners at pro-Communist election rallies read: "The Soviet Union is Germany's Best Friend."

However, "when blandishments failed," wrote Howley, "the Russians wielded the big stick on their opponents, breaking up meetings, obstructing normal electioneering activities, and playing the role of political bullies and thugs."[36] The Russians spread rumors that the Allies planned to leave Berlin soon after the elections. This frightened many West Berliners. Howley was forced to publicly reassure citizens that the Americans would "stay there twenty years, if necessary."[37] Intimidation was more open and brutal in the Soviet Sector, but West Berlin was not immune.

Berliners who displeased the Communists tended to disappear from city streets and homes. Soviet secret police could reach anywhere in the Western sectors. In the spring of 1946 the *New York Times* reported an increase in the "kidnappings of politically strategic individuals" in Berlin.[38] On February 26, 1946, the Western Powers formally requested that the four-power Berlin occupation government, the *Kommandantura*, investigate "the arrests of three Berlin judges and one senior court officer in various Berlin sectors and their subsequent disappearance."[39] From the State Department's report on the matter:

> There has been during several months a series of arrests and disappearances of Germans in the western sectors of Berlin. There is some evidence that these arrests have been effected either by Russian officers and officials, or by German police of the city magistrature acting—it is commonly believed—on Russian suggestion. Recently there have also been incidents of the removal by Russian officials of certain Germans travelling on the American train from Berlin to Frankfurt on American military permits and orders.[40]

Frank Howley wrote that the situation got so bad in West Berlin that "I had to issue a public warning to residents in the American Sector, telling them what to do in the case of a kidnapping." Howley described one incident.[41]

> A car would run down the street, men in civilian clothes would jump out and grab their victim, then race over the Russian border. In one case German agents looking for a certain woman on political charges first seized her sister in the Russian sector and got from her where the "criminal" could be found in our sector. They picked her up on the street and her screams, as the car raced for Russian territory, were the last heard of her.[42]

"It was," as Karl Mautner put it, "a dirty cold war at the time."[43]

Imagine going to the polls under such conditions. Imagine a situation where simply showing up to vote might land you on a Communist list of suspected "reactionaries." Who would have blamed you for just staying home on Election Day?

The election results were devastating for the Communists. Turnout was huge, with 89% of eligible voters casting ballots. The Social Democrats (SPD) and the Christian Democrats (CDU), the two most popular parties in West Germany, received over 70% of the vote citywide. The SED got less than 20%.[44] "The latest German elections, particularly those in Berlin, have undoubtedly been a great disappointment to the Soviets," cabled State Department official Robert Murphy on October 23, three days after the elections. Russian officials "were downcast," crowed Howley. "It was a great a personal defeat in a campaign they had directed with such devious fervor."[45]

West German press had a field day with the election results. "Extensive editorial comment in the licensed newspapers of the US Zone acclaimed the results of the municipal election in Berlin on 20 October as a victory of democratic forces," said an OMGUS review of German press coverage. "The citizens of Berlin, as a rule widely disliked by South Germans, were hailed as the standard-bearers of the new democracy." The *Schwaebische Landeszeitung*, a southern German newspaper, said all of Germany owed thanks to the Berlin voters "who have to live under incomparably more difficult conditions than" the people in West Germany.[46]

Two years later, Berliners went to the polls again. The city held elections on December 5, 1948, during both the Berlin winter and the Berlin Blockade! The city had now split into two *de facto* camps, with the Communists running the Soviet sector and the Western Allies running West Berlin. The Soviets knew the SED had no chance of winning at the ballot box in the Western sectors. Instead, they tried to play on West Berliners' fears. They hoped worried West Berliners would use the election as a vote of "no confidence" in the Western Allies.

The Communists tried to scare West Berliners away from voting. "Immediately preceding the election," wrote Dr. Harry Franklin, chief of the Political Affairs Branch of OMGUS Berlin, "there were widespread rumors—doubtless SED-inspired—that severe disorder would occur in many polling places in the western sectors. Another was to the effect that the Soviet Zone police surrounding Berlin were in a high state of alarm."

"A whispering campaign, again SED-inspired, was launched saying the polling lists with voters' names checked off would come into Soviet hands upon the early western Allied evacuation of Berlin and then the voters would be subject to severe reprisals. In an attempt to make the whispering campaign more plausible, the [Soviet Army's German language newspaper], on the Saturday morning preceding election day carried an ADN [Soviet-licensed news agency] dispatch under a big front-page headline: 'The Western Allies will Leave Berlin In January.'"[47]

The SED called the election in the Western sectors an "illegal and terroristic" act. They implied that the Western Allies and their West Berlin lackeys would force reluctant West Berliners to go to the polls. The Communists urged voters to "spoil" their ballots. A ballot which was "spoiled"—mismarked, defaced, or otherwise damaged to the point that it was not valid—should be viewed as a silent protest against the West, the SED said.[48]

Nothing the Soviets or the SED tried worked. "Communism—at least that of the Soviet totalitarian type—received its most smashing defeat in postwar Germany on Sunday, December 5," wrote Dr. Franklin triumphantly. 86.3% of eligible West Berlin voters cast ballots. Less than 3% of the ballots were spoiled—the amount of spoilage seen in a normal election. "To all those veiled threats and intimidations interspersed with certain Soviet-SED blandishments," Dr. Franklin wrote, "West Berliners responded by going to the polls in a most orderly but determined fashion and indicating unmistakably their stand. There were no disorders at the polls and only a few minor incidents."[49]

The free world's press celebrated again. "Western world press reaction to the Berlin election results was highly laudatory for the courageous stand taken by the electorate," said an OMGUS press review. "Berlin democratic press comment stressed that Germans in the Soviet Sector and in the Soviet Zone look to West Berlin after the December 5 election as a rampart of political and social freedom and the outcome of that election as really speaking for them, the disenfranchised. As to West Berlin proper, a German newspaper editorial headed 'Berlin Chooses Freedom' aptly characterizes the result."[50]

An OMGUS Information Bulletin for January 1949 reported that the "Berlin municipal elections in December have evoked widespread editorial comment in US newspapers. The editorials generally agreed that the vote was a resounding repudiation of communism and that it topped a record of rejection wherever men have been free to express their real preferences." The *New York Herald Tribune* characterized the elections as being "almost the first time in which the issue between communism and western democracy was fairly and fully joined in men's minds.... The Berliners knew what was at stake; they knew what freedom and the franchise meant, and from out of their ruins, they have returned an answer which, because of its very sources, is perhaps the greatest moral defeat that the Soviet Union has ever suffered."[51]

That same OMUGS bulletin listed several examples of West German press reaction to the December 1948 elections:

> 'They (Berlin voters) have shamed any inhabitant of the western zones ... who is afraid to express his opinion publicly because the Russians may come some day.... The Berliners expressed the will of all Germans under no circumstances to remain passive and neutral in the fight between East and West.... This obligates us all.... The elections also proved irrefutably how the people in the East really think, while they have to keep silent under terror. ... All Eastern Europe would vote like the Berliners—if they got the chance."(*Darmstadter Echo*)
>
> '[W]hatever the jarring note which may have been connoted south of the Main by the name Berlin, it now shines in fullest glory.... The moral greatness of Berlin should lead us to overcome group and provincial differences and to feel ourselves as members of a nation which has once more won the right to live. Young German democracy has withstood its baptism of fire, not in Munich or Bonn, but in Berlin." (*Heidenheimer Zeitung*)

If, at the end of the 1950s, anyone doubted whether West Berlin was still an important symbol of Western and Free World success, Department of the Army Pamphlet 355-200-2, dated 19 January 1959, dispelled those doubts. Its title: "West Berlin: Free World Outpost." "The Western Allies are acutely aware of the importance of maintaining a free West Berlin," the pamphlet said. "The progress and reconstruction that have taken place in West Berlin since World War II have been universally admired, for this was accomplished in an area totally behind the Iron Curtain." … "The progress West Berlin has made in reconstruction and economic development under freedom is in sharp contrast to the drab conditions in Communist-controlled East Berlin. There, rebuilding lags, shops have little to offer and freedom is a luxury not permitted. So brightly does West Berlin shine as a haven of freedom to the East Germans living under Communist rule that it has become the gateway through which hundreds of thousands of them have fled, and continue to flee, from Soviet dictatorship. In West Berlin they can see the meaning of freedom in action."

Imagine the humiliation and the loss of prestige and confidence the Kennedy administration, the Americans, and the Western Allies would suffer if the city where they achieved so much was now to wither and decay.

The anguish the Wall caused wasn't confined to Berlin. Morale in West Germany suffered, too. That was bad news for the Americans. America needed West Germany to stay firm with the West. On August 29, the West German ambassador delivered a letter from Adenauer to the White House. In it, the West German chancellor warned of rising "trends toward neutralism in Europe." The ambassador assured the president "that there was no fundamental reversal of mood in the FRG." For "the most part," calls for neutralism "were on the part of small splinter parties which had been quiet for the past couple of years, but were now speaking up again." Nevertheless, there "was some latent neutralism around, some doubt about how far the West would go" in making concessions to the Soviets "and some question about whether the Chancellor's Atlantic policy had been right."[52]

The Chancellor's Atlantic policy. That was a reference to Adenauer's staunch support for West Germany's alignment with the Western European community and a strong alliance with the United States. Adenauer's opponents often derided him for it. Kurt Schumacher, leader of the SPD during the early 1950s, once called him "Chancellor of the Allies." Throughout the 1950s, though, West Germans had followed Adenauer's lead and supported strong defense and economic ties with the West.

However, the West Germans expected US support and protection in return. If they sensed that American will in Berlin was weakening, the West Germans' faith in the Atlantic alliance might erode. Cold

War historian Jean Edward Smith writes that, in that letter, Adenauer warned Kennedy that "if the United States did not begin to defend its position in Berlin, a desire for accommodation with the Soviet Union, perhaps even a neutral role between East and West, could become a serious factor in West German politics."[53]

The fall of 1961 was an especially bad time for Adenauer to have a Berlin crisis. West Germany was in the middle of a national election, and Adenauer had a battle on his hands. His main opponent was … Willy Brandt! The West Berlin mayor's political star rose through the Berlin Ultimatum crisis. Brandt was now a prominent politician in West Germany. He led the SPD list as its candidate for Chancellor. If West German voters perceived an American collapse of will in Berlin, the chancellor's Christian Democrats could suffer at the polls. Adenauer worried he might lose power.

The Americans still needed West Germany's allegiance to the West, just as they had since the Cold War began. In 1961, though, they had another, more specific need—West German troops joining NATO. "We were keen to have the Germans rearm as part of NATO," recalled the State Department's Jack Sulser. "The other member countries of NATO were not doing as much as we thought was necessary. They thought they were doing as much as they could, since their economies were still recovering from the war. From the beginning the US saw German entrance in NATO and German rearmament as the main source of additional conventional strength to offset the Soviets and other Warsaw Pact countries."[54]

Sulser had a point—many NATO nations were not ponying up troops. They cited a host of reasons—the cost of raising, training, and sustaining armies; the perception among some Western Europeans that nuclear weapons rendered conventional ground forces obsolete; a sense that the Soviets were unlikely to attack Western Europe. Some NATO nations had overseas colonies they had to protect. Britain needed troops in Malaysia and Kenya; the French had a major insurgency to fight in Algeria. As a result, NATO relied heavily on American forces. The Americans wanted West German troops to help them.

In the early years of the occupation, rearming the Germans was the farthest thing from the Western Allies' mind. In 1950, McCloy recalled conversations with Adenauer about German armed forces. The chancellor told McCloy that, because the Allies had disarmed the Germans, the Allied had "incurred an obligation to defend them. Mr. McCloy replied by reminding Adenauer that Germany had been disarmed because she could not be trusted with arms."[55] Ten years later, the Americans were not only willing but eager to trust West German troops with weapons again. "[W]e had to keep the Federal Republic hospitable to the NATO military establishment,"[56] recalled State Department political officer Joseph Green Jr.

The West Germans were not willing to simply defer to the Western Allies' wishes. The West Germany of the late 1950s and early 1960s was no longer a shattered nation of smashed factories and despondent people. West Germans were prosperous, and they knew it. Their location on the European continent made them vital to NATO; they knew that, too.

The Contractural Agreements ended the Western Allies' occupation rights. That meant they had to negotiate a "Status of Forces Agreement," or "SOFA," with the West Germans. SOFAs determine matters like the amount of money the host country (West Germany, in this case) would pay to support the foreign forces on their soil, the extent to which German law would apply to Allied personnel, etc. The Americans found the Germans to be hard negotiators. "It was rough going," recalled Joseph Green Jr. "The Germans didn't feel defeated anymore.[57]

In 1955 the West Germans formally reconstituted a national military. It was (and still is) called the *Bundeswehr*. The West Germans raised the number of divisions they'd promised to contribute to NATO. The process didn't always go smoothly, though.

British Army Major Edgar O'Ballance wrote an article on the new Germany Army for CGSC's *Military Review* in May 1960. ("CGSC" is the US Army's Command and General Staff College). "After the initial impetus" for West Germans to join their new army, "volunteers came in very slowly and early recruiting figures were disappointing. By October 1956 only 53,000 of the 90,000 desired for the period had enrolled. Appalled by the heavy loss of life and property in the war, the Western German people viewed the new military setup warily." The West Germans turned to conscription, which drew a fair amount of resistance from "some political parties and the trade unions."[58]

West German military and civilian leaders weren't ready to obediently put their new divisions where NATO wanted them nor do whatever NATO told them to do. "The Western Germans were not convinced that the NATO policy for defense necessarily was the right one," wrote Major O'Ballance. "The Germans had experienced fighting the Soviets in Russia and did not hesitate to let NATO know this."

NATO's primary strategy, he wrote, "was purely one of defense." One concept for defensive warfare is "fluid defense." The defenders fall back when attacked, surrendering ground until an opportunity opens up to counterattack. The West Germans had qualms about "fluid defense," for good reason. Any ground NATO surrendered, even temporarily, would be German ground. Eager "to prevent Western Germany from becoming a battleground," the *Bundeswehr* pushed for a more mobile defense philosophy, which would take any fight into Communist territory. The *Bundeswehr* also refused to just buy British, French, and American weapons for its forces; it developed its own tanks and fighting vehicles.[59]

Former State Department official Frederick Flott tells this amusing story. Planners from all the national militaries in NATO developed estimates for their military budgets.

> As you might expect, with the product of professionals who were good economists, the costing estimates were very close from all the interested countries, except when it came to the matter of field clothing, of uniforms. The German estimate was about four times what everybody else had put in. When we inquired why there was this unusual wide discrepancy, their answer was that the Germans were equipping them all to fight in Russia with polar, warm, clothing! They weren't going to get caught again like November, 1941.[60]

President Kennedy would've chuckled at Green's story, no doubt. But Adenauer's letter and the West German ambassador's warnings about falling West German spirits and rising doubts in the chancellor's Atlantic policy made it clear that morale in West Berlin and West Germany was once again in bad shape. That caused real concerns. Kennedy needed West Germany as a willing ally, politically and militarily. On September 4, Kennedy replied to Adenauer's letter. "If ever there was an illustration of the need for NATO and justification of the reasons why it was founded," the president wrote, "the issue of Berlin provides it."[61]

The East Germans increased their pressure on Steinstuecken. The Vopos severely limited access to the exclave. Many of the West Berlin workmen who'd gotten East German permission to go to and from Steinstuecken—often through long and painful negotiations—now couldn't get past the checkpoint guards. Access, writes Catudal, "was limited to Steinstuckeners and a few select personnel." Zehlendorf's mayor tried going to the exclave on official business; the border guards stopped him. Apparently the new GDR border crossing guidelines applied to travel to and from Steinstuecken, too. The Zehlendorf mayor—as with all West Berliners—now required an East German visa to visit the exclave.[62]

The East Germans extended the wire barricades running along the East/West Berlin border to the hamlet. "On 2 and 3 September, East German police built a barbed-wire fence along both sides of the road leading through East Germany from West Berlin to Steinstucken, an exclave of the U.S. Sector of Berlin," the CIA reported in its Intelligence Weekly Summary for September 7. (The "road" was the *Waldweg.*) The Vopos also fenced off portions of the residential areas in the exclave.

Steinstueckener Magrit Wiese was not yet a teenager when the new barriers appeared. "They came overnight," she recalls. "Nobody knew" about the Vopos' plans. "In the midst of the night, all of a sudden, we heard all these trucks." The next morning, Steinstueckeners and their East German neighbors watched in shock as the Vopos laid the wire. Ms. Wiese recalls "people crying on the other side, and people being pushed back" from the wire barriers. "It was devastating. I stood there myself crying, just crying."[63]

During the 1950s, from time to time the Vopos had thrown up wire barriers around the *Waldweg* or dug ditches across it to harass the exclave residents and West Berlin and American officials. But those were temporary. When the "crisis du jour" ended, the Vopos removed those barriers. These new wire barriers didn't disappear. Wooden crossbeams soon reinforced them to create a sturdy fence around the exclave. Steinstuecken was now truly sealed off from East Germany.

The new fences hit Steinstuecken's children especially hard. Many had friends in Babelsberg or Potsdam. "We used to play with those kids," said Magrit Wiese.[64] Soon, pictures appeared in Western newspapers of former playmates staring at each other through barbed wire.

The events of August and early September caused adults in Steinstuecken to worry about their future. When the East Germans sealed the borders, all accepted practices or understandings for how the Communists and West would co-exist in and around Greater Berlin either went out the window or were called into question. Thousands of East Berliners had worked in West Berlin, bringing much-needed income into East Germany. Nevertheless, the East Germans and Soviets willingly shut off that source of revenue. Free movement throughout Berlin for everyone had been accepted practice ever since the Allied occupation of Berlin began. The Western Allies considered it an important occupation right that the Soviets couldn't unilaterally take away. But the Soviets took it away. Closing the sector border was a public relations catastrophe for the Communists. Newspapers and television programs ran countless pictures of distraught families now separated by the Wall waving to each other in tears across the barbed wire. The Soviets and East Germans were willing to accept all of that.

Imagine you're a Steinstueckener in early September 1961. You see your neighborhood sealed off by barbed wire and guards. You recall the East German decree that all West Berliners should stay 100 meters away from the sector border. In Steinstuecken, the border lay literally right outside the front doors of some of the exclave's houses. If the East Germans ever enforced their 100 meter decree, many of Steinstuecken's homes would be at risk.

And, if the Soviets were willing to let the GDR cut Greater Berlin literally in half, why wouldn't they let it occupy Steinstuecken? The East Germans claimed they *had* to close the Berlin sector borders because of the threat from Western spies, saboteurs, and revanchists. Desperate times call for desperate measures, as the saying goes. Soviet and East German spokesmen had already accused the Americans and West Germans of using Steinstuecken as a base for subversive activity. Why wouldn't the Communists deal with the exclave once and for all? Steinstueckeners had good reasons to worry.

Fortunately for Steinstuecken, and for West Berlin, by the middle of September, Washington had finally realized it had to do more in Berlin. Kennedy decided to send a high-profile American representative. "I am appointing General Lucius Clay to be my personal representative in Berlin," the president announced in a news conference on August 30.[65] "The situation in Berlin is a serious one, and I wish to have the advantage of having on the scene a person of General Clay's outstanding capacity and experience." Calling Clay "an American in whom the Secretary of State and I have unusual confidence," Kennedy said Clay would "serve as long as the special arrangement seems desirable."[66] Kennedy's choice of Clay, the hero of the Berlin Airlift, thrilled Berliners.

In September 1961, the Americans had a thorough operations plan for any new Steinstuecken crisis. In September 1958, one month after the Vopos had barged into Steinstuecken to seize and carry away a defector, the US Ambassador to West Germany had urged Washington to develop plans to better handle any future East German incursions. "I feel strongly that we must have specific contingency plans that make it possible for the US Commander in Berlin [USCOB] to take prompt and decisive action if faced with another Communist action against Steinstucken." The ambassador said he was "firmly convinced, for political and morale reasons, that it was absolutely necessary we be in a position to take immediate action to deal with any future Communist incursions and deliberate violations of exclave borders."[67]

By the time General Clay arrived, the Berlin garrison had developed a plan for another Steinstuecken incident: Operations Plan, or "OPLAN" 3-3, dated April 18, 1961. Paragraph 3, the "Execution" portion of the OPLAN, laid out the specific actions the US Army would take if the Communists threatened Steinstuecken again:

> [Paragraph] 3. EXECUTION
>
> a. Concept of the Operation. ON ORDER of CINCUSAREUR [Commander-in-chief, U.S. Army in Europe] Berlin Command will dispatch military police patrols by vehicle or helicopter to gain access to STEINSTUCKEN, quell disorders and/or evacuate personnel seeking asylum. In the event of an incident the command will be alerted and a tank infantry force moved to the vicinity of Rose Range [a training area used by American forces]. If required this task force will be committed, using such force as required, to restore order in STEINSTUCKEN and/or to evacuate previously committed Military Police elements and personnel seeking asylum. This plan will be implemented in three separate course of actions, each of which requires prior approval by CINCUSAREUR.
>
> 1) Course of Action A. (Operation Access). A vehicular mounted or helicopter borne military police patrol will

be dispatched to STEINSTUCKEN to test the communist's intentions of blocking US access.

2) Course of Action B. (Operation Incident). In the event of an incident or civil disorder in STEINSTUCKEN the command will be alerted and a 3d Battle Group tank infantry force will be dispatched to an assembly area (744075) [presumably this is the grid coordinate for a geographic location] Southwest of Rose Range to provide psychological impact and to prepare to accomplish Operation Extricate using such force as required. When approval is received, a vehicular mounted or helicopter borne military police patrol will be dispatched to STEINSTUCKEN with instructions to proceed to the scene of the incident, capture or eject unauthorized persons in the area, restore order, and evacuate personnel seeking asylum.
3) Course of Action C (Operation Extricate). In the event the military police patrol is unable to control the situation or if they are detained by communist forces the 3rd Battle Group Task Force will be directed to proceed to STEINSTUCKEN, using such force as required to gain access, restore order and/or to extricate previously committed US personnel and persons seeking asylum.[68]

(All items in brackets were added by the author.)

Separate annexes covered the details for all three Courses of Action. And, they were quite detailed. The OPLAN spelled out how exactly how many military police (MPs) would go on the patrols, what ranks they would be and the number and types of weapons they would carry. For Course of Action A, the MPs would send "one officer and three enlisted men (one with the ability to speak and understand German) mounted in one radio-equipped jeep," and armed with ".45 caliber pistols, police clubs and one .45 caliber sub-machine gun." For Course of Action B the MP contingent was expanded by six more enlisted men, two more jeeps, two more .45 caliber submachine guns and "nine CN and nine CS grenades"—but no additional German speakers. The "tank infantry" task force was two companies of infantry, four tanks and an assault gun platoon. The MP and infantry task force commanders would even receive preprinted flyers to give to the GDR border guards, that spelled out (in Russian, English and German) the Americans' intentions to go to Steinstuecken.

If the GDR resisted, the American infantry task force commander was instructed to wait thirty minutes, to give the GDR border guards time to confer with their superiors. After thirty minutes, if the GDR still refused, the OPLAN did NOT tell the task force commander to retreat. Instead, he was to "direct his task force to proceed to Steinstuecken using the most direct route."

> "If, while or after passing through the Kohlhasenbruck Check Point, any of the following events occur: task force receives enemy fire, task force encounters mines or task force encounters any kind of resistance, task force commander will attempt to overcome resistance to the extent feasible. If overwhelming resistance is encountered, the task force will disengage, but will withdraw only on order of the Commanding General, Berlin Command."
>
> "The task force will not repeat not open fire until fired upon, and then only to the extent necessary to accomplish the mission of extracting US personnel and equipment, and personnel seeking asylum, in self-defense, or in restoring order in Steinstuecken."

Notice that the task force was NOT directed to abandon its mission, even if it encountered "overwhelming force." It was told instead to "disengage," presumably to wait for further instructions…including a possible order to resume the advance, perhaps with reinforcements. This wording indicates that US Berlin Command was ready to fight for Steinstuecken, at least to some degree.

This next portion of the order shows the detail and forethought that went into the Steinstuecken reaction plan: "Movement off the road to Steinstuecken is not authorized prior to coming under enemy fire, and then only to the extent necessary for self-defense, or to execute an orderly and timely withdrawal." Apparently someone on the Berlin Command operations staff feared the task force's leadership, in the midst of a tense situation, might leave the *Waldweg* and drive their tanks and armored personnel carriers over the fields and through the forests around the exclave.

Discussions on how to deal with the new Berlin crisis dominated the Kennedy White House in the first weeks of September. The president wanted detailed, well-thought-out plans for how to counter specific aggressions the Soviets and East Germans might launch. American diplomats and generals pondered, among other things, precisely how to react if the Communists tried to close one of the air corridors or blocked *autobahn* traffic to West Germany. Western leaders planned a significant troop buildup in Western Europe. They also pondered how to restart negotiations with the Soviet Union in hopes of finally reaching a lasting agreement over Berlin and "the German question." These were momentous times in Washington.

And in the midst of those critical times, the safety of a single West Berlin village captured the attention of some of the most powerful men on Earth. Steinstuecken, a neighborhood too small for its own school or a gas station, drew the personal attention of the President of the United States.

On September 14, President Kennedy and his key advisors gathered in the White House to discuss two potential flashpoints in Berlin: Steinstuecken, and the one point along the sector border where Allied personnel could still enter East Berlin—the checkpoint at Friedrichstrasse. The president was joined by the Secretary of State, the Secretary of Defense, the Attorney General (his brother Bobby), the Chairman of the Joint Chiefs of Staff (CJCS), and senior State Department officials.[69]

General Lyman Lemnitzer, the CJCS, took notes of the meeting; these notes are on file in the National Defense University in Washington. According to those notes, when the subject of Steinstuecken came up, Secretary of State Dean Rusk gave an overview of the Steinstuecken problem while General Lemnitzer showed President Kennedy a map of the area. Assistant Secretary of State Foy Kolher then gave an update of the current situation in and around the exclave. He pointed out that no incidents had occurred (presumably, this meant the Communists hadn't physically threatened the exclave) and that there was "no indication there will be" any direct threats.

Secretary of Defense Robert McNamara then reviewed options for coming to Steinstuecken's aid in a crisis. The notes indicate that McNamara raised three options: "air, or ground, or both." (That appears to mean a helicopter incursion, a ground probe, or a combination of both). Lemnitzer's notes then say, "Go with A, then to Russians." That seems to mean that McNamara recommended using helicopters ("A") to reach the exclave. Then, if that failed, approach the Soviets and ask for their help. A note in the margin mentions that "we have not maintained patrol access for many years." This must refer to the fact that US personnel had not sent patrols or otherwise visited Steinstuecken by ground since the Berlin Airlift. Arguably this set a precedent: By not exercising their rights to go by ground to the exclave in the past, it made it harder for the Americans to assert that right now.

President Kennedy seemed to agree. Lemnitzer's notes say "P—approve A—put onus on Russians. Do not assemble in B until touch base with Washington." That appears to mean that President Kennedy approved an air mission to Steinstuecken. If that failed, the US should reach out to the Russians, who, as an occupying power, had the responsibility (or "onus") to deal with East German authorities in the Soviet Zone.

Troops were not to assemble for a ground operation ("B") without checking with Washington first. Lemnitzer's notes contain this comment: "Do not launch without an incident (quell disorders and/or people seeking asylum.)" These appear to be further instructions from the president that US forces should not move on Steinstuecken unless some event occurred (e.g., a confrontation between exclave residents and Vopos, GDR threats to enter the exclave to recapture refugees) that forced the Americans' hand.[70]

After the meeting, the White House issued National Security Action Memorandum (NSAM) number 94, subject: Steinstuecken and Friedrichstrasse Crossing Point. Here is the portion of that NSAM that pertained to Steinstuecken.

> The President decided that the following course of action shall be taken with respect to Steinstuecken. These decisions were taken at a meeting at the White House at 10 a.m. on September 14 attended by the President, Rusk, McNamara, Lemnitzer, Taylor, Nitze, Cabell, Rostow, and Attorney General Kennedy.
>
> In case of an apparent blocking of access to Steinstuecken or other interference with U.S. rights there, USCOB is authorized to establish the Communists' intention and other pertinent facts by sending to Steinstuecken a vehicular mounted or helicopter borne M.P. patrol. This patrol will not use force in discharging its mission.
>
> If force is considered necessary to reestablish access or other rights, General Norstad will seek authority from Washington.

> Helicopter supply of Steinstuecken is authorized, if necessary.
>
> No special overt measures should be taken before the event, without referral to Washington.[71]

Washington's concerns about provoking an incident that could spiral out of control are obvious in this NSAM and other guidance messages the White House issued. Where possible, the Kennedy administration wanted US officials in Berlin to seek guidance from Washington before doing anything risky. "The US does not want to go from a repulsed jeep probe on the autobahn to all out nuclear war in one move," Secretary of State Rusk quipped in a cable to the American Embassy in London.[72] Caution, in some cases excessive caution, was the *modus operandi* of the Kennedy administration when it came to Berlin.

That caution is evident in the records of a meeting Secretary Rusk had with the British and French foreign ministers in Washington, a few hours after President Kennedy gave his guidance on Steinstuecken. The foreign ministers discussed Steinstuecken; here is a summary from the State Department's minutes of that meeting:

> The American Exclave of Steinstucken. The Secretary said he knew the Ambassadors and possibly the Ministers were familiar with the problem of Steinstucken, an exclave of the American sector of Berlin.
>
> While it is not yet clear that access to Steinstucken is to be blocked, we have developed some plans for this contingency. At present these are limited to a military police jeep probe or a helicopter mission to Steinstucken to test the Communist intentions. Should these be rebuffed, the military are under orders to request further instruction from Washington. In any event, we propose to take no initiative at Steinstucken.[73]

"We propose to take no initiative in Steinstucken." Someone forgot to tell General Lucius Dubignon Clay.

CHAPTER SEVEN

"Wir danken dem Bewahrer unserer Freiheit."
(We thank the Preserver of our Freedom.)
—Inscription on the footstone at the grave of General Lucius Clay, placed by the citizens of Berlin, US Military Academy, West Point, New York

"It seemed essential to me when I arrived to take a few measures to demonstrate American intent to be firm on the ground in Berlin. It would not have occurred to me that I would have been sent here for any other purpose".[1]

General Clay wrote those words in a cable to Secretary of State Dean Rusk at the end of January 1962. This cable, plus many other messages Clay sent while he was President Kennedy's representative in Berlin, is preserved in *Foreign Relations of the United States*. These messages show Clay's thinking about Steinstuecken and its impact on the US position in Berlin. They also lay out Clay's reasons for what he did concerning the exclave.

In the cable, Clay reviewed some of his key actions since he returned to Berlin the previous September. "At the time of my arrival West Berlin morale was still low, although definitely recovering from the extreme low point. Confidence in Allied determination, rightly or wrongly, was badly shattered by the wall."[2] In an earlier cable, in mid-October, Clay warned Kennedy that, if West Berliners lost faith in the West, the Western sectors might fall into decline. Allied diplomats feared West Berliners would pull their money out of city banks and migrate to West Germany. Clay told the president that "underneath the outward signs of a normal, prosperous city there is a very real tension. It is not a personal fear of an immediate danger but rather a doubt as to the future of the city as a desirable place to live and to raise a family."[3]

Clay knew West Berliners, West Germans, and Western Europeans expected him to show strength. General Lucius Clay symbolized America's commitment to West Berlin. During the Berlin Airlift—which many Western Allies had expected to fail—Clay's determination to hang tough lifted the city's spirits and stiffened its spine. West Berliners revered him. They called him "*Der Vater der Luftbruecke*" (The Father of the Airbridge"). When Vice President Johnson went to Berlin, Kennedy sent Clay with him to boost West Berliners' morale. Wikipedia's page on the Berlin Wall Crisis calls Clay's appointment as Kennedy's representative "an unambiguous sign that Kennedy would not compromise on the status of West Berlin."[4]

Clay's welcome in September was tumultuous. "General Lucius D. Clay came back to Berlin today to tell weeping, cheering, flower-throwing thousands that 'Berlin and its people always will be free,'" wrote the UPI. The *Bend Bulletin,* of Bend, Oregon, ran that UPI report, under this headline: "Tears, Cheers Greet General on His Arrival." "After an exchange of welcomes with West Berlin mayor Willy Brandt and receiving a 19-gun salute" from US Army tanks, "Clay rode into the city to a roaring welcome. West Berlin police estimated that up to 100,000 persons lined the streets for 10 miles to see Clay ride by." Another UPI wire report said that Berliners "dodged through the motorcycle escort to shove bouquets into Clay's hands."[5] An AP report said, "Berliners turned out by the thousands to give him a rousing and emotional welcome."[6]

Clay's presence was a double-edged sword for the Americans. "I can assure you," Clay told Kennedy in his mid-October message, "that here in West Berlin any failure to act positively and determinedly with me here in this capacity will be assumed to have your direct approval. Moreover, each time we fail to act, my value as a symbol of American determination will diminish and, in fact, will result in greater loss of confidence than otherwise."[7] With Clay back in Berlin, West Berliners expected the Western Allies, especially the Americans, to push back against the Communists. "Unfortunately the West Berliner is concerned only with what we do," Clay wrote Kennedy. "The failure of the British or French to react promptly when incidents occur does not disturb the West Berliner; if we fail, he is dismayed."[8]

Clay felt the East Germans were testing the Western Allies to see how much they could get away with. Slashing the number of crossing points, declaring a 100-meter wide no-go zone *that stretched into West Berlin*, stopping American military vehicles on the *autobahn* to West Germany—all seemed to be parts of a GDR campaign to challenge the city's quadripartite status and the rights of the Western Powers as occupiers.

"Unfortunately, the East German police, apprehensive initially in exercising authority over Allied personnel, are emboldened by success and trying now to increase their authority," Clay wrote to Secretary of State Rusk at the end of September.[9] Jean Edward Smith, in his biography of Clay, wrote that "in West Berlin, Allied inaction was seen as weakness in the face of a continuing East German assault, and Berliners anticipated that the encroachment would continue until the Allies forcefully brought it to a halt."[10]

Clay needed an opportunity to show West Berlin (and the rest of the world) that America's commitment to West Berlin remained firm. But he couldn't spark a crisis that might escalate. Fortunately for Clay, an opportunity quickly appeared.

On Clay's first day in Berlin, he toured the growing East German border fortifications. There, he met Willy Stiewe, Zehlendorf's District Mayor. Mayor Stiewe briefed Clay on Steinstuecken's history as an exclave and the increased pressures on it since the Berlin Wall crisis started. "Clay immediately went to the entrance of the *Waldweg*" and observed the overall situation there, wrote Catudal.[11] Because Steinstuecken was "within the area in which I have a responsibility," Clay told the State Department in a cable on September 28, "I considered it my immediate duty to pay it a visit."[12] Later that day, Clay went to US Army headquarters in Berlin and informed the USCOB, Major General Albert Watson, that he planned to drive to Steinstuecken the following day, September 20.[13]

A visit by Clay would help the Americans in several ways. It would reassert American occupation rights to Steinstuecken and emphasize the exclave's status as a neighborhood of West Berlin, not Brandenburg. Over and over, as you read the interviews of State Department veterans of Berlin, they talk about the efforts they made and the imperative they felt to continually and openly exercise American prerogatives as an occupying power. The fear was, if the US didn't assert those rights, the Soviets would try to slice them away. Steinstuecken would be easy to slice off. The Vopos could just lock the checkpoint gates on the *Waldweg*.

Clay's visit would let the Americans regain the initiative in Berlin, at least in a small way. Ever since the GDR had divided the city, the West had been in "react" mode. The Western Allies had been forced to react to whatever the GDR and the Soviets chose to do. React when the East Germans tore up Berlin streets and blocked them with barbed wire. React when the number of crossing points was slashed. React when East German water cannons sprayed West Berlin protesters.

A Clay visit would turn the tables. The West would do something that the Communists would have to react to. It would be a bold move in a time of high tensions. Probably not the kind of move the State Department would have suggested. ("*We propose to take no initiative in Steinstucken.*") But it would push the East Germans and the Soviets back on *their* heels a bit, for a change.

Clay planned to surprise the GDR border guards at the Kohlhasenbrueck checkpoint and get past them and into the exclave before the local Vopo headquarters could react and block him. Clay, writes Catudal, "was convinced that he could force the border guards stationed along the *Waldweg*" to open the gates for him.[14] Apparently the general thought the element of surprise, plus his celebrity status, would be enough to momentarily befuddle the Vopos on duty in the early morning.

Clay told his plans to only a few people to minimize chances they would leak. Early on the morning of September 20, Clay and a small party got in their cars and drove to Kohlhasenbrueck.

There, Clay found the surprise was on him. The border guards were there—and they weren't alone. Clay "discovered the Berlin press corps, and a large number of jubilant citizens waiting for him," writes Catudal.[15] Richard Boehm, a State Department officer stationed in Berlin, described the scene. "Clay arrived at the checkpoint at 6AM, and there was the mayor" of the Zehlendorf neighborhood of Dahlem, "his wife, 300 West Berlin schoolchildren and about 500 East German cops."[16] Clay's plan had failed. He wasn't going to surprise anyone that morning. "Clay could instantly see that he had a loser on his hands," recalls Boehm. "He accepted the bouquets and turned around and went back to his headquarters. He didn't try to go through with the program. He saw that it was not going to work."[17]

How did Clay's plans leak? Two theories stand out. Richard Boehm hints that the mayor of Dahlem might have leaked them. According to Boehm, on September 19, Clay "said that nobody was to know" his plans for the next morning. "It was important that the East Germans not be prepared for this. He said, 'I want them to be taken by surprise, have no instructions, and not know what to do.' We said that we thought that was a good idea but that we would have to tell the mayor of Dahlem. He had been very cooperative, and his nose would be far out of joint, since it was his borough. We thought that we ought to tell him but swear him to secrecy. Clay was extremely reluctant to do this, but he finally agreed that we could tell the mayor. So we did."[18]

Catudal floats another theory, which stems from research by German journalists Hermann Zolling and Uwe Bahnson. According to that theory, an Army officer assigned to US Army Europe (USAREUR) headquarters in Heidelberg came to Berlin and leaked word of Clay's plans to the local media and citizens. The USAREUR commander, General Bruce C. Clarke, was unhappy that Clay was in Berlin with lots of independent authority. "Upon learning of General Clay's intention to drive to Steinstuecken," writes Catudal, "Clarke contrived a way to stop him."[19] If true, this would be just the first run-in Clay had with General Clarke and other American generals in Europe during the Berlin Wall crisis.

Clay wasn't ready to quit, though. The reasons that made his trip to Steinstuecken a good idea at 6 a.m. on September 20 were still good reasons after the attempt failed. Plus, the Berlin press was sure to report Clay's failure; that could dampen morale in the city. He also had a pressing new reason to go to Steinstuecken.

Some East Germans had broken through the wire fencing around Steinstuecken and were now hiding there. That news, Clay explained to President Kennedy in his message dated October 18, "had reached Berlin on the morning of my trip, and would soon have become public. A failure on our part to have rescued these refugees would have seriously damaged our position here."[20] Clay felt that, once East Germans refugees managed to escape "into the areas for which we are responsible, we must provide them protection. Otherwise I cannot see why we are in Berlin."[21]

In his biography, Clay said one of his first actions in Berlin was to send "American soldiers to patrol the sector boundary. There had been several incidents in which it was alleged that East Germans had crossed into our sector to pick up people who fled. I put patrols out with orders that if anyone [fled from the East and] came across into the American sector, no one was to be allowed to come and take them back." Clay felt this "would help show the Berliners that we were not going to give in."[22]

Steinstueckeners knew that, if GDR deserters appeared on their doorsteps, trouble would follow. Everyone remembered the summer of 1958 when Vopos stormed into Steinstuecken to capture and carry away a GDR deserter. West Berliners and West Germans wanted assurances from the Americans that Steinstuecken, arguably the most vulnerable spot in West Berlin, wouldn't be left to fend for itself. Clay wanted to reassure them. The problem was Clay couldn't walk or drive to the exclave.

But he could fly.

Airliners and other high-altitude aircraft flying to and from Berlin had to stay within one of three narrow air corridors. Lower-altitude aircraft didn't have that problem. The four wartime allies had established an airspace zone known as the "Berlin Control Zone," or BCZ. The zone's maximum altitude was 10,000 feet. It covered all of Berlin and included all the city's exclaves. British, French, Russian, and American aircraft could fly much more freely within the BCZ.[23] Clay took advantage of that.

At approximately 11 a.m. on September 21, three US Army helicopters lifted off from the US Sector and headed toward the city border. Two of them were escorts; the third carried General Clay and his interpreter. They crossed into the Soviet Zone, then General Clay's helicopter turned toward Steinstuecken. It landed in a grassy field. For the first time in more than a decade, a representative of the US government had come to visit.

Here is how Catudal describes Clay's arrival:

> Immediately after putting down, the general stepped out to greet a middle-aged lady who, before Clay's unheralded landing had been occupied in her garden nearby. Recovering from her initial shock, she ran to embrace him. Like most Berliners, she recognized him almost at once. As if this were a signal, a large crowd of enthusiastic citizens promptly converged on the general. Each wanted to shake his hand and extend a warm, personal greeting.[24]

Kurt Behrendt, a Steinstuecken resident, described Clay's arrival: "Together with a liaison officer and two pilots wearing officer's rank, the general, in a dark blue suit, a gray Homburg hat in his hand, landed in a meadow and came out of the U.S. Army Sikorsky helicopter."[25]

Lt. Tom Clark was one of the pilots. In a letter to his wife, Clark said that the exclave's residents "were quite impressed with the helicopter and were overjoyed to see General Clay." Not only had it been years since Steinstueckeners had seen American visitors, but it was also the first time a helicopter had ever landed there.[26] In fact, according to the Berlin Brigade's daily intelligence summary, it was the first time the Americans had ever flown helicopters outside the boundaries of the Western occupation sectors.[27] "Until the time that Clay returned to the helicopter landing pad," said Kurt Behrendt, "the residents of Steinstuecken, especially the children, had an extensive opportunity to inspect the helicopters." Residents gawked at the helicopters and children crawled through them while Clay toured the exclave.

Clay made his way to Restaurant Steinstuecken, the combination grocery and bar owned by Walter Steinweg. Residents crowded in after him. They gave him bouquets of flowers and offered him wine. For forty-five minutes the general spoke with them and fielded their questions, He drank some of their wine and signed the village guestbook. Most important of all, he reassured them that the US remained committed to protecting them.

Clay then returned to his helicopter, followed by many residents. "Waving a last good-bye," writes Catudal, "General Clay held up two figures in the shape of a 'V for victory.' 'I'll be back,' he said. Then he climbed back into his helicopter and was gone."[28]

Clay's visit thrilled the Steinstueckeners. But it didn't change the realities of their situation. They lived in a little pocket of free territory surrounded by the Soviet Zone. The residents behaved accordingly. "Steinstuecken residents, who didn't have jobs in the city, hurriedly gathered together on the meadow near the border," wrote the *Berliner Morgenpost* in its article on Clay's flight. "They recognized their important guest. But their enthusiasm was not excessive, their rejoicing remained restrained. The people in Steinstuecken saw Vopos hidden in the bushes. They saw a truck fully loaded with weapons come from the direction of Babelsberg. So they shook the general's hand in silence."[29]

Kurt Behrendt took many pictures of Clay's visit. One shows exclave residents waving goodbye to Clay. It, along with its caption, captures the poignancy and sadness of Steinstuecken's unique situation. The caption reads: "In the immediate vicinity of the helicopter as it takes off are the Steinstueckeners as they waved goodbye." Visible in the distance, less than a hundred yards away from the landing pad is another group of people, obviously watching Clay's departure. They, said Behrendt, were "residents of Babelsberg and excited Vopos—[East German] officers almost shoulder-to-shoulder with the inhabitants of the exclave, but still separated by mines and the barbed-wire border." That barbed wire border fence, less than a month old at the time of that photograph, separated people who'd been neighbors and friends for years.

Clay wanted his visit to grab people's attention. It did. "Clay Flies to Pocket in U.S. Zone" was the headline for a *Stars and Stripes* article the following day. A United Press International story under that headline described the general's visit in dramatic, even inspiring, language: "General Lucius Clay flew over Communist territory Thursday to the tiny American Zone enclave of Steinstuecken, in a demonstration of western allied rights to go anywhere in Berlin."[30] "During his second day on the job as President Kennedy's special representative in Berlin, Gen. Lucius D. Clay made a morale-building visit to an old Berlin trouble spot," wrote the AP.[31]

Clay's trip put Steinstuecken back in American newspaper headlines. "Clay Pays Surprise Visit to Red-Surrounded Town" (*Philadelphia Inquirer*); "Clay Drops in on Western 'Isle' In Sea of Reds" (*Chicago Tribune*); "German Town Heartened by Clay's Surprise" (*Indianapolis Star*); "Gen. Clay Defies Reds, Flies over Russ Zone. Demonstrates Firmness by Taking Copter To Village in American Sector" (*Los Angeles Times*); "Clay Proves US Firm on Berlin" (*Cincinnati Enquirer*).

Some headlines were downright triumphant. "Clay Astounds Commie Police by 'Copter Trip" (*Palm Beach Post,* West Palm Beach, Florida); "Gen. Clay Braves Red Guns to Visit Village" (*Waco News-Tribune*, Waco, Texas); "Clay Visits Town Ringed By Reds. US Means to Defend Every Foot, Copter Trip Shows" (Louisville *Courier-Journal*); "Gen. Clay Uses Copter, Challenges Red Police" (*Great Falls Tribune,* Great Falls, Montana); "Clay Shows US Firmness by Flying into Soviet Zone" (*Pensacola News Journal,* Pensacola, Florida); "Defiance Flight Made by Clay" (*Philadelphia Daily News*); "Clay Tosses Challenge At Commies" (*Santa Fe New Mexican*); "Gen Clay Flies to Prove Right" (*The Daily Interlake*, Kalispell, Montana).

"The German newspapers played it up 'real big front page stuff,' with headlines and all," Lt. Tom Clark wrote to his fiancée.[32] Here is the lead for the *Berliner Morgenpost* article on Clay's flight:

> *Clay came out of the air. In a helicopter to Steinstuecken. Vopos were surprised*
>
> Yesterday the residents of the little exclave of Steinstuecken had their great hour. General Lucius Clay visited in the company of an American liaison officer that tiny piece of West Berlin, which is surrounded by armed Vopos. For almost an hour the Special Ambassador to the American President stayed there. He shook the hands of the residents, he spoke with them about their concerns and issues, and he visited the only store in Steinstuecken.[33]

Clay's flight angered the Communists. "The East Germans immediately attacked Clay's flight as provocative," wrote Jean Edward Smith in *The Defense of Berlin*. The Communist press called it "a warlike move in an otherwise calm situation." The East Germans accused Clay of violating the sovereign airspace of the GDR[34]—a sovereignty that neither Clay nor the Americans recognized.

Their reaction on the ground as Clay flew to the exclave was more restrained. The general didn't announce his flight beforehand, so the Vopos around Steinstuecken were probably caught by surprise. Jean Edward Smith, in his biography of Clay, says that some East German guards aimed their weapons at the American helicopters but did not fire.[35] Lt Tom Clark's account is more lighthearted. "The Vopos didn't know what to do and were quite amazed at the whole deal. Of course they weren't in the area, but they were right across the street from where we landed."[36] (As Kurt Behrendt's photograph of Clay's farewell shows, Clark wasn't exaggerating.) The *Berliner Morgenpost* poked a little fun at the GDR border guards: "The Vopos ran horrified from the barbed wire border."[37]

The East Germans weren't the only ones unhappy with Clay's flight. The British objected strenuously. They thought Clay was reckless. Smith quotes journalist George Bailey, who wrote that the British told Washington that they "affirmed their support of the United States in all major issues, but questioned the wisdom of risking an incident over such a trifling matter."[38] The British thus joined a growing number of

Western Allied officials, military and civilian, who would find Clay's boldness in Berlin troubling.

On September 28th, one week after his trip to Steinstuecken, Clay cabled Secretary of State Rusk. In that cable, which has already been referenced several times in this chapter, Clay lays out some of his reasons for going to the exclave. "Steinstuecken is a recognized part of our responsibility and if we fail to meet this responsibility the repercussion in Berlin would be serious indeed." Clay acknowledged that the Americans' options for defending the exclave were limited. "We can argue with some validity that since we cannot protect Steinstuecken by force we must not endanger its people." Having said that, though, Clay held firm: "The same argument applies to our entire responsibility." (Here, presumably, Clay means the Americans' responsibility to all West Berlin.) "The right to use the air and our responsibility to protect the people in our sector are the basic rights to which we are committed."[39]

"There is no longer time for either caution or timidity when our basic rights are threatened," Clay told Rusk. "The Russians are not going to war to stop us from taking refugees out of Steinstuecken. They may well take the acts which would cause war if we fail to exercise our rights at Steinstuecken, in the belief that we have given up these rights. I know of no better opportunity that we have had to have shown our determination" than Steinstuecken, "and unfortunately we do not have enough such opportunities to fail to utilize those which do arise."[40]

Clay's point was spot-on. In the fall of 1961, the Western Allies really hadn't had many opportunities to demonstrate their resolve in Berlin or push back against the East Germans and Soviets without a real risk of combat. If the American, British, or French forces had tried to breach the Berlin Wall or sent troops into East Berlin to push back the water cannons dousing West Berlin protesters, the East Germans might have started shooting. No one wanted to chance that.

Going to Steinstuecken, however, was largely risk-free. Despite the GDR (and British) grumbling, Clay had the authority recognized by the Four Powers to fly there. Going by helicopter avoided a face-to-face confrontation with the Communists. Had Clay persisted in trying to drive or walk to Steinstuecken, a confrontation would have been unavoidable. Because he could fly, though, he could avoid one. Clay was able to publicly demonstrate American resolve to stick by its promises to defend West Berlin, boost morale, and push back on the Communists—and do it in a way that minimized the risk of inflaming tensions.

Steinstuecken, therefore, turned out to be a blessing in disguise for the Americans. Ever since Mathewson had laid claim to the exclave in October 1951, Steinstuecken had been a burden for the American occupation forces. For ten years, American officials had had to grapple with a never-ending stream of GDR and Soviet harassments of the little village. While Khrushchev could squeeze on Berlin to make the Western world scream, the Soviets and GDR could squeeze on Steinstuecken to give the Americans headaches.

And what did the Americans get in return? At first glance, nothing. They couldn't use Steinstuecken to base troops or erect radio antennas. Steinstuecken didn't have a major power facility or water pumping station or some other utility or natural resource that West Berlin could use. It was just a quaint collection of houses and small fields—and a real pain in the neck for the Americans.

Until late September 1961, that is. Steinstuecken gave Lucius Clay the opportunity he needed to demonstrate that America meant business in West Berlin. Clay needed to be bold. He felt it necessary to show the Russians and East Germans, in no uncertain terms, that the US would not back down. At the same time, though, he couldn't risk a war. Berlin was a powder keg, and the world was on edge. Clay needed to achieve the maximum impact possible with the minimum amount of risk. Steinstuecken gave him that unique, even invaluable, opportunity.

Clay's flight did create a fresh problem. By going to Steinstuecken, Lucius Clay reasserted America's commitment to the exclave and its status as part of the US Sector. Clay didn't plant the Stars and Stripes in Steinstuecken; Mathewson had already done that ten years earlier. But Clay's trip brandished the flag. It blared the message that the US could be trusted in West Berlin, even in the most exposed parts of the American Sector. Now, the American forces in Berlin would have to back that up. Clay's flight had *de facto* increased America's immediate burden in West Berlin.

What if the Communists upped the ante? What if a Vopo patrol entered Steinstuecken and camped out on the field that Clay had just used as a helipad? What if Soviet troops replaced Vopos at the Kohlhasenbrueck checkpoint? What if a Russian tank entered the hamlet? The West would have found itself in quite a pickle.

Look back at President Kennedy's and the Army's plans for sending soldiers to defend Steinstuecken. At each step, they required go-ahead orders from the highest levels of American national command. (Most likely, President Kennedy himself.) What if the "go" orders never came? The Western troops in Berlin might have responded to a Communist provocation by doing … nothing. How would West Berlin—and the world—react then?

Clay understood that. In his September 26 cable to Rusk, Clay said "we must convince the Russians on the ground what our rights are, and not let them lapse one by one. We cannot expect them to believe us otherwise." But he also said that "I recognize that the use of force in Berlin is not an answer to our problem." In Berlin, America was "fighting a political battle, not a war." Clay was confident the US could "win the political battle." But he also said, "Of course, we cannot win a war in Berlin."[41] In his October letter to the president, Clay admitted that again. "Of course, we cannot solve the Berlin problem by using force in Berlin. We can lose Berlin if we are unwilling to take some risk in using force to bring about Soviet confrontation *even if we withdraw immediately when confronted with superior force*."[42] (Emphasis added). Clay understood that, if push really came to shove, the US might let the Communists slice Steinstuecken away. He knew his actions came with risks.

But Lucius Clay wasn't finished with taking risks with Steinstuecken.

No American personnel had driven or walked to the village since the time of the Berlin Airlift. Clay wanted to remedy that. He'd already set one precedent by flying to Steinstuecken. Now he wanted to set another—the right for Americans to travel to and from the exclave by ground. Neither the US Army nor the State Department had asserted that right during the Allied occupation of Berlin. Even President Kennedy's advisors acknowledged that. The history of Lucius Clay's actions in Berlin shows he firmly believed that, if the Americans asserted commonsense occupation rights (e.g., driving to and from a portion of one's occupation sector), the Soviets would relent. And as Mathewson's tough stance in October 1951 showed, they would make the East Germans relent, too. Accordingly, Clay set out to send Americans by vehicle to Steinstuecken.

According to several biographies and histories that cover the Berlin Wall crisis, Clay directed General Albert Watson, the USCOB, to send a ground force to Steinstuecken. Watson arranged to assemble two companies of infantry for the operation. That corresponds to the Courses of Action laid out in the Steinstuecken reaction plan in OPLAN 3-3: send a Jeep patrol to the exclave, but have an infantry/tank task force on standby if trouble occurred. However, on the day of the probe, General Clarke, the USAREUR commander, got wind of the plan and stopped it, just hours before it was supposed to launch.

The two main antagonists in this matter were General Clay (who ordered the probe) and General Clarke (who stopped it). In their biographies, both men paint polite pictures of how the other reacted. In *Clarke of St. Vith: the Sergeant's General*, General Clarke says he had decided to travel to Berlin because he wanted to be of help to General Clay. Clarke had received instructions that, as USAREUR commander, he was to help General Clay "with transportation, office, space, clerical help, quarters, etc."[43] Accordingly, Clarke reasoned that "he'd better get up to Berlin and see what General and Mrs. Clay would be needing."[44]

General Clarke arrived by rail on Sunday morning, September 24, three days after Clay's flight to Steinstuecken. General Watson met him at the train station, and both generals had breakfast. Watson told Clarke that Clay had ordered a probe to Steinstuecken. It was scheduled to launch at 10:30 that morning. Clarke, according to his biographers, "found that General Clay had organized a party of two companies to punch a hole in the route to exclave Steinstuecken." Clarke canceled the operation. He then met Clay and told him of his decision.

Clarke, according to his biographers, "was a great admirer of Clay. He had been a student of Clay's at West Point and later they were lieutenants together in the Corps of Engineers on civil works activities."[45] However, the general was sick of "post-war administrations sending vaguely high-ranking people over from Washington to have a say-so in the European Army." Obviously, Clarke saw Clay as one of those vaguely high-ranking people. His presence and actions in Berlin complicated Clarke's command of his troops there. Moreover, Clay's probe threatened to spark a shooting fight with the Russians. If Clarke's troops were to be sent to confront the East Germans, thus "potentially blowing the peace wide open—Clarke wanted the orders for that to go through channels, and if there were new channels, he wanted to know what those channels were."[46] Clarke must have feared those "channels" didn't include him.

Clarke's biography describes his meeting with Clay this way:

> He went to see General Clay. After cordial greetings, Clarke said, "Lucius, I don't know for sure what your job is here. But I have to tell you, my commanders are under instruction to execute only orders which come from my headquarters. If you don't agree, I guess you'll have to call the President."
>
> General Clay understood. He was too good a soldier to disagree.[47]

In his biography, Clay expressed sympathy for Clarke's predicament in Berlin. Clarke didn't have to deal with just General Clay. He also had another general in Europe to answer to—Gen. Lauris Norstad, the NATO commander. While General Clarke supervised Army troops in Europe, General Norstad commanded *all* American forces on the continent. When interviewed for his biography, Clay said that Clarke actually stepped back from the decision-making chain for Berlin matters. "Clarke, to his credit, recognized that he was just an additional cog in the machine. He couldn't make any decision without getting Norstad's approval. And it made him mad as hell that he couldn't make any decisions. So he got out. He told [General Watson, the USCOB] to report directly to Norstad."[48]

If Honore M. Catudal Jr. is correct, though, Clay and Clarke didn't get along as swimmingly as their biographies indicate. Their Sunday morning meeting wasn't warm and friendly. For another one of his books, *Kennedy and the Berlin Wall Crisis*, Catudal interviewed Clarke. When told by General Watson of the impending ground probe, Clarke said that he responded, "Al, don't you know who you work for?" In his meeting with Clay, Clarke claims he told Clay to "keep your cotton-picking hands off my troops." Clay reportedly replied that he could see that the two men were not going to get along well together.[49]

Searches of the National Archives failed to uncover any after-action reports or other records of this specific operation that Clay directed. Not all records from this time period have been declassified. Nevertheless, unless several histories and biographies are all wrong, the US Army was all set to send infantrymen, presumably armed and supported by combat vehicles, into territory defended by the Soviet Army in the midst of the Berlin Wall crisis. On Clay's own initiative. Without Washington's direction or approval. (*Foreign Records of the United States* shows no record of Clay notifying Washington of his plan, much less getting approval for it). Astonishing.

"I don't believe it," said William Richard (W. R.) Smyser. Smyser was a career State Department official. In 1961 he was General Clay's assistant in Berlin. In an interview for this book, the author asked Smyser if he'd heard of this incident. Smyser said that he had heard stories of it. But he couldn't imagine Lucius Clay ever doing something as shattering as sending a column of combat troops to Steinstuecken without the East Germans or Soviets having provoked the Americans first. "Clay was not interested in creating an incident. He did not want a crisis. He wanted things to move smoothly," Smyser said. "So, I have always regarded that story with a certain amount of skepticism."[50]

Clay "wanted to do things at the outer edge of his authority" said Smyser. He "wanted to make a point of the American presence in Steinstuecken and in Berlin." But he also "wanted to create a climate of confidence in Berlin. He did not want to create an incident from which he would have to retreat." Marching a column of infantry into Steinstuecken "would have created a sensation in the press."

The author asked Smyser how he thinks the Russians would have reacted. "They would have reacted very sharply," Smyser replied. "Clay would have known that. He would have known that what he was doing would create a crisis." A crisis from which he might have had to back down. "He was there to be a positive force for the Berliners. And being a positive force doesn't mean losing a battle."[51]

"Steinstuecken was something that was *sui generis*"—a unique, one-of-a-kind place. "We knew it was there, we took care of it, we did what was necessary to make sure that people there had the authorities that they needed, we knew that there were Berliners there, all that was fine. There was no particular reason for us to go in there and make a big point of it."[52] Or roil the waters surrounding this little island of West Berlin.

"He knew that [Steinstuecken] was an area of particular sensitivity. And, if there is one thing to put in your mind about Clay, it's that he understood sensitive areas, he understood sensitive problems. He handled them very, very carefully. Clay was not an idiot. He hadn't got to be a four-star general by doing stupid things. Everybody knew there was a limit to how far they could go in in Berlin. He knew that Steinstuecken was a sensitive place. But he also knew that it was a place for which we had a responsibility. And if we had a responsibility for something, then we would have to demonstrate that responsibility. And that was why we went there."[53]

When researching this incident, the author wondered why it wasn't mentioned more often in Cold War histories of Berlin. Surely the soldiers who'd been tasked to conduct this operation to go (and perhaps even fight their way) into Steinstuecken would have talked about it. Especially after the Berlin Wall fell.

Was it possible that the soldiers who were assembled to go to Steinstuecken were never told the details about the operation? Details like their objective? At first thought, that seems very unlikely. Good ground combat operations require planning and rehearsal. They're not thrown together at the last minute. It seems inconceivable that upwards of two companies of infantry would have rolled into Soviet Zone territory without some serious preparation. Surely all the soldiers would have known about it at least a few hours beforehand. (And almost as surely they would have talked about it in the years following the Berlin Crisis and the end of the Cold War). At the very least, their officer and sergeants should have known a day beforehand, so they could plan their operations.

It's possible that the junior soldiers might not have known. The author did some sophisticated research—he asked some questions on the Berlin Brigade's Facebook page! Several Berlin veterans from 1961 replied that during the Berlin Wall crisis, Army units constantly rolled out on alert to local assembly areas only to return to their barracks a few hours later. These veterans' recollections make it sound possible that soldiers mobilized for a Steinstuecken push might never have learned what their objective was before the mission was canceled. To a soldier in the ranks, it might have seemed like just one more alert.

As the National Archives puts more Berlin archives out for public review or more veterans share their recollections, perhaps historians can paint a clearer picture of what General Watson and Lucius Clay really had in mind for the Steinstuecken ground probe. But in the meantime, we're left wondering what their plan for that Sunday really was. *Something* noteworthy must have been planned because General Clarke intervened personally to stop it and told historians about it years later.

Catudal interviewed Clay for the same book where Clarke shared his story about the ground probe. "When queried about Clarke's version of this incident," Catudal wrote, "General Clay took issue with it but could not remember any details."[54] If the incident never happened or Clarke was wildly exaggerating (or misremembering) the whole thing, Clay would certainly have told Catudal that. Presumably in very strong language.

Clay's response to Catudal's question, therefore, lends itself to certain conclusions. *Some* operation was planned that Sunday for Steinstuecken, but it wasn't a major one. Clay certainly would have remembered directing Berlin Brigade to make a major push into Soviet-held territory, one that carried serious risk of a confrontation with the Russians. A column of combat-ready infantry marching to Steinstuecken would have carried that level of risk. Yet Clay couldn't remember any details.

But what about a column of Jeeps or smaller vehicles? One of the first things Clay did when he arrived in Berlin was to challenge the GDR's assertion that the territory for 100 yards on *either* side of the Berlin Wall was now no-man's land. Clay sent Jeep patrols into the areas of the US Sector that were right next to the Wall. He did this to demonstrate that those areas were under the control (and protection) of the Western Allies.

What if Clay had planned to send Jeeps to Steinstuecken instead of infantry combat vehicles? That type of operation would fit with the evidence we do have about the canceled ground probe. Berlin Brigade soldiers were already conducting regular Jeep patrols in the disputed border sectors. The junior soldiers could easily have seen a Jeep patrol to Steinstuecken as just another routine mission in the crazy and hectic days following the appearance of the Berlin Wall. It would have required much less planning—and much fewer people with a prior need to know about it—than a probe by infantry vehicles under combat conditions. And a Jeep convoy would have been sufficient to reassert the Americans' right as occupiers to go to Steinstuecken by ground, a right that the Americans acknowledged they'd never asserted properly.

Berlin Brigade OPLAN 3-3 said that "a tank infantry force" would be mustered---but the preferred force to actually send toward the exclave would be a "vehicular mounted or helicopter borne military police patrol." Following President Kennedy's meeting on Steinstuecken, American officials told the British and French that their current plans for Steinstuecken were "limited to a military police jeep probe or a helicopter mission." This is speculation, to be sure. But a planned Jeep probe to Steinstuecken would fit the evidence we have.

As the Berlin Wall crisis stretched into the end of 1961, Lucius Clay continued to butt heads with American military and diplomatic officials. Many bristled at his direct, action-oriented style and his independent authority. Martin J. Hillenbrand directed the Office of German Affairs at the State Department from 1958 to 1962.[55] Hillenbrand, in his memoir *Fragments of our Time*, described Clay as "headstrong and self-confident."[56] Referring to the "inevitable conflict of authority" that Clay's independent position created for Clarke and Norstad, Hillebrand wrote that "No general likes to have his command authority usurped, and Clay's attempt to give orders to the Berlin commandant could only raise hackles in Heidelberg and Paris."[57] (NATO headquarters was in Paris at this time.)

Hillebrand, and many other American officials, feared Clay's bold nature didn't fit well with the situation in Berlin, where the threat of nuclear war hung over everything. "The drama of General Clay's days in Berlin produced both its pathetic and alarming moments. Our forebodings in the State Department turned out to be all too correct. This was a man with an almost overriding sense of mission, a disregard of orderly procedures, and no real sense of the caution that the nuclear age necessarily imposed on responsible leaders."[58]

The most famous event in Clay's tour in Berlin was the standoff at Checkpoint Charlie. The one crossing point between East and West Berlin that Allied personnel could use, on Friedrichstrasse, became known as "Checkpoint Charlie." (This crossing point is the same one referenced in National Security Action Memorandum 94, the directive that covered Steinstuecken.)

On October 22, a senior State Department official tried to enter East Berlin through the checkpoint. GDR guards stopped him and eventually US MPs went to his rescue. Tensions mounted. Clay, writes Hillenbrand, "requested General Watson to place U.S. forces in Berlin on alert and to deploy tanks near Checkpoint Charlie." The Soviets moved up tanks as well. Soon the world saw pictures of American and Soviet tanks facing each other, separated by only a few hundred yards. For a few tense days, the world wondered what would (and feared what might) happen. Eventually, tensions eased, and the tanks withdrew.

That, according to Hillenbrand, "was the beginning of the end for Clay." Generals Clarke and Norstad were upset at "Clay's intrusion into their command channels in a matter involving alerting of troops and deployment of tanks and their crews. Both of them expressed themselves vociferously on the subject. It seemed like a classic case of picking the wrong issue for a show of determination." After this incident, "White House and State Department concerns about Clay began to grow."[59]

"Gradually," writes Hillenbrand, Clay "began to appreciate that more and more he was being cut out of the essential policy-making process." Eventually Clay left Berlin in early May 1962. Many in Washington, Heidelberg, and Paris were glad to see him go. Hillenbrand credits Clay for leaving quietly. "He behaved as a gentleman in his departure and caused no real problem for the president."[60]

American diplomats and generals may not have thought much of Lucius Clay's tenure in Berlin in 1961 and 1962, but millions of West Berliners (and 180-odd Steinstueckeners) thought he'd been invaluable. He'd shown determination and boldness at a time when many Germans wondered if the Americans had the will to hang tough in Berlin. The city's gratitude and its appreciation for its hero is evident in the words inscribed on the stone marker at Clay's grave in West Point.

Clay made three other visits to Steinstuecken, once on Christmas Eve of 1961 and twice in 1962. He toured the border fence, met with residents, and shared a glass of wine in Restaurant Steinstuecken with town and Berlin officials. Every time Clay came, residents greeted him with flowers and signs of gratitude. Magrit Wiese remembers the general signing lots of autographs.

Before Clay left Berlin, he had brought a gift to the exclave's residents—a television set. It was the first one ever in the village. It quickly found a home in Herr Steinweg's taproom. The television came with a small plaque attached to it. The inscription read: "To my friends in Steinstuecken from *Mitburger* (fellow townsman) General Lucius D. Clay."[61] While the TV set is long gone, modern-day Steinstueckeners still keep the plaque. Berlin honored him by naming a street after him—Clayallee.

Clay may have failed to get American infantry into the village. But he did accomplish something else, something that proved to be long-lasting and significant. "Steinstuecken had on this day a sensation," wrote photographer Kurt Behrendt, as he remembered Clay's visit on

September 21. "It would not be the last one." Two days later on September 23, Steinstuecken's next sensation arrived. An Army helicopter landed in the exclave again. Out stepped four MPs, fully armed and carrying enough rations for several days. General Clay had decided to establish a detachment of American soldiers in the exclave.

The United States Army had just put "boots on the ground" in Steinstuecken. For good.

CHAPTER EIGHT

Asked if he would have believed such a thing as a completely walled-in village existed, Williams replied, "Not before I came here. But now I believe it."[1]

—US Army Lt. George Williams, 287th MP Company

"No other Army unit has comparable duties."

That's how AP reporter Hubert Erb started his story on the 287th Military Police (MP) Company, on August 15, 1967. The 287th was the MP contingent for the US Army's Berlin Brigade. As the name implies, "military police" are both law enforcement agents *and* soldiers. They investigate crimes and arrest criminals; they also guard Prisoners of War (POWs), manage traffic, and safeguard areas behind the front lines.

Berlin was a unique place, so it's not surprising that the 287th MP Company had some unique missions. "They lead military convoys" on the Berlin-Helmstedt *autobahn* and "help get stranded Americans out" when their cars broke down or GDR police stopped them, wrote Erb. MPs from the 287th guarded the Army duty trains that ran between West Berlin and West Germany. "Its soldiers man Checkpoint Charlie in the heart of Berlin, right on the Communist wall dividing the city."[2] And on September 23, 1961, the 287th MP Company began another unique Berlin mission—guarding the exclave of Steinstuecken, twenty-four hours a day, seven days a week. This mission lasted eleven years, until 1972.

Vern Pike is a retired Army colonel. During his career he commanded an MP brigade and an MP battalion in West Germany. When the Berlin Wall crisis erupted, he was a lieutenant in the 287th MP Company. Pike was in the midst of things when American troops first came to Steinstuecken. "General Clay had flown out there in a helicopter," he recalls. "He had received reports that the residents out there had been harassed by the Vopos, the Volkspolizei. When he finished his deliberations out there, he came back to HQ and said 'We've got to fix this.' He called the Provost Marshal, who was my boss, and he directed the Provost Marshal to establish an MP presence out there to secure the people, secure the village and protect its resources."[3]

That sounds like a normal MP tasking; they perform security missions all the time. But it wasn't normal. The MPs in Steinstuecken wouldn't just pull guard duty. They would be making a statement.

"Boots on the ground" is the term for putting soldiers in a place (a village, a city, a country) the US is determined to hold onto. Possession really is nine-tenths of the law. When you put American soldiers in a specific place on Earth, it demonstrates America's will to assert its authority over—and possibly defend—that place.

"Boots on the ground" doesn't require an army. Even two or three soldiers, a group too small to repel a serious attack, can be large enough for America to make its point and send a message: When you harm any American soldier on duty, you invite retaliation by all America's armed forces. American "boots on the ground" establish a tripwire around the place they protect. Menace that place or the soldiers inside it, and you risk the consequences. On September 23, 1961, the Berlin Brigade put a tripwire around Steinstuecken.

That morning, an Army helicopter appeared over the exclave. It touched down in the same meadow Clay used two days earlier. Out stepped Lieutenant Pike and three of his men. They wore the distinctive uniforms of US Army Military Police—helmets with the white letters "MP" and MP armbands with the Berlin Brigade patch. Any onlooker that Saturday morning—exclave residents, Vopos on patrol—knew who the visitors were.

The MPs established living quarters and an operations base in the basement of the house of the "mayor" —the Steinstuecken resident who served as Zehlendorf's official representative and spoke with East German officials when necessary. Many called him the "mayor." In September 1961 the "mayor" was Friederich Reichow. He was about to have guests.

"We ran a communications wire up the outside chimney of the house and set up an antenna," recalls Vern Pike. The MPs would have two ways to communicate with Berlin Brigade: radio and telephone. They would sleep in Herr Reichow's basement and maintain a radio watch there. For meals they would come up to the kitchen. The MPs brought food from the MP company mess hall, enough to last them for a few days.

The American press picked up on this immediately. "Three US soldiers were dropped by helicopter today into Steinstuecken, a tiny part of Berlin separated from it by a mile-wide strip of Communist territory," the AP reported on September 22. "A spokesman of the US Army's Berlin command said the action of dropping the soldiers was 'part of the regular patrol of all portions of the American sector border.' He declined to say how long the soldiers would stay, but inhabitants of the tiny community of less than 200, reached by telephone, said the soldiers had bedding and supplies for a long stay."[4]

"The United States unexpectedly established a military police patrol in a Communist-encircled West Berlin enclave which the American army has neglected for the past 10 years," wrote the *New York Herald Tribune* wire service in a special report for the *Minneapolis Star-Tribune*. "It was the second striking United States move at Berlin since General Lucius D. Clay arrived here three days earlier as President Kennedy's special representative. The military police detachment consisted of only three men. They reached the enclave, a tiny village called Steinstuecken, by helicopter. The aircraft had to fly across a mile of East German territory that separates the village from West Berlin."[5] Colorful headlines told readers that America had a new Cold War outpost. "3 GIs 'Occupy' Red-Encircled Town" (*Minneapolis Star-Tribune*); "US Soldiers Land in Area of Red Ring" (*Kansas City Times*).

The 287th MP Company, the unit whose duties were unlike any other company in the US Army, had added another unique duty to its task list—safeguarding a village the size of a college football stadium. "I had a city map, we all had to carry these city maps, and I could barely find [Steinstuecken] on the map," said MP Herbert Judd. "It was one of these big fold-out jobs, about a yard by a yard, and I could barely find it."

The exclave residents were thrilled to have American troops stationed in their village. "They were afraid, they were scared to death," recalls Pike. "The East Germans were harassing these people. The West Berlin police couldn't go out there, because it was in the Communist part of Germany."[6] West Berlin police still couldn't drive to Steinstuecken, and they couldn't fly there either. In 1961, the four WWII occupation powers were still the only ones allowed to operate aircraft around Berlin. The August 1958 incident, when Vopos invaded their town to recapture a deserter, had confirmed what Steinstuecken residents already knew—GDR troops could come into their streets, pound on their front doors at any time, take away whoever they wanted, and no one could stop it. In late September 1961, that all changed.

"I never had [any of the Steinstuecken residents] thank me directly," recalls Ed Hamborski, a former sergeant in the 287th MP Company who served multiple times in Steinstuecken. "But you could see it in their eyes. There's no doubt about that."[7] "'We are very, very glad to see them,' said a Steinsteucken inhabitant when asked by telephone his opinion on the soldiers' arriving," wrote an AP wire service reporter.[8]

The MPs weren't equipped for any sort of pitched battle with the Communists. "We knew that if something happened, we were dead meat, our troops there," recalls Hamborski.[9] "We each packed a pistol and a grease gun, and we had these little [tear] gas grenades," recalls Herbert Judd, another former 287th sergeant.[10] No machine guns, mortars or bazookas. On average, no more than four MPs were in the exclave at any one time. Their mission was security, not combat. Deter the Vopos from menacing the exclave and its residents. And if necessary, repel Communist forces trying to enter the hamlet or at least delay them until Berlin Brigade could send reinforcements. "Our mission there was to protect the property and defend the residents of the Steinstuecken enclave," recalls Ed Hamborski," and that's including any refugees that entered the enclave."[11]

One reason Clay went to Steinstuecken immediately after he arrived in West Berlin was a report that an East German refugee had entered Steinstuecken and was now hiding there. "A failure on our part to have rescued those refugees would have seriously damaged our position here," Clay wrote to President Kennedy in October.[12] One month earlier and just a few days after he flew to Steinstuecken, Clay wrote this to Secretary of State Rusk: "We would be irresponsible if we played any part in helping refugees get through the cordon. But, if the Soviet and German police cannot keep them from doing so and they come into the areas for which we are responsible we must provide them protection. Otherwise I cannot see why we are in Berlin. I am sure too that this issue is one which would be clearly understood by the people of West Berlin and by our people at home."[13]

Soon after they arrived, the MPs had to deal with East German refugees. The exclave "was one of the very few places where somebody could conceivably escape,"[14] says Vern Pike. For the first few months after the Berlin Wall appeared, the GDR barrier around Steinstuecken was only barbed wire nailed to "crossbucks" —crossed wooden poles. Vopos then erected two other fences, with taller vertical poles, on either side of the crossbuck barrier. They were daunting obstacles but not unbreachable.

During the first months of the Berlin Wall crisis, a few East Germans did breach them. The Berlin Command's G2 (Intelligence) Section added a new section to its periodic intelligence summaries: an activity report for the "Steinstuecken exclave." Those reports show a fair number of refugees entering the hamlet. The G2 Intelligence Summary for October 31 says that twenty-five East Germans had entered Steinstuecken since the MPs' arrival one month earlier.[15] A G2 Intelligence Summary for November contained this eye-catching item: "On 10 November 1961, 2 Border Security Police defectors from the [Vopo] Company which guards Steinstuecken walked into the exclave in full uniform with weapons."[16]

All these refugees made it to West Berlin—courtesy of the US Army. None had to endure the same kind of harrowing journey Magrit Wiese described: hidden under a blanket as Steinstueckeners tried to sneak them past the Vopos. After September 23, 1961, East Germans who made it through the wire fences had an easier, more secure route to West Berlin: by air. The MP detachment collected refugees as they arrived, sheltered them, and then put them on Berlin Brigade helicopters for the final leg of their journey to freedom.

The 287th developed a system for handling their "guests." The MP detachment would call headquarters on the telephone. "We had codewords we used," recalled Ed Hamborski. "I didn't say 'We had two refugees,' I said whatever the code was."[17] (The Americans assumed that the GDR had tapped the phone line to Berlin). Berlin Brigade then sent a helicopter to the exclave. The MPs would load the refugees onboard, and the helicopter would take them to Andrews Barracks, the MPs' *kaserne* (compound) in West Berlin.[18]

The Americans took pains to conceal the identities of the refugees; the Vopos closely watched each evacuation flight. The MPs "would take extra MP uniforms out to Steinstuecken with them and they would dress up any refugees"[19] to look like American soldiers, said John Mentor, a lieutenant in the company. "We put them in ponchos, and escorted them to the helicopter, so [the border guards] wouldn't know just who was who,"[20] recalled Ed Hamborski. The Americans even moved the helipad to a more secluded part of the exclave, so that helicopters could touch down and load as far from prying GDR eyes as possible.[21]

News reports about the refugee airlift started to appear in Western newspapers. These are excerpts of UPI wire stories from *Stars and Stripes*:

> American officials shrugged off a communist protest of the U.S. Army's helicopter-lift of seven refugees over a mile of East German territory from the isolated exclave of Steinstuecken to West Berlin. (October 1, 1961)[22]
>
> A US helicopter lifted five refugees across the Iron Curtain from the isolated U.S. enclave of Steinstuecken, in East Germany Tuesday, to the sound of communist gunfire. No shots were fired at the American helicopter, but machine pistols chattered at refugees fleeing by ground along Berlin's uneasy borders. . . . One [refugee's] nerves quavered and he was about to return to communist Germany before Steinstuecken residents persuaded him to stay (October 5, 1961)[23]
>
> The United States Army Tuesday airlifted three persons from the isolated Steinstuecken enclave in West Berlin, an Army spokesman said Tuesday. In line with standing U.S. policy here, the Army did not confirm or deny the persons were refugees from East Germany. (February 8, 1962)[24]

The American commercial press covered the refugee story, too. The *Los Angeles Times* ran an AP story on September 28, titled "US Flies Berlin Refugees Over Communist Territory." "Two US Army helicopters plucked seven refugees from communism out of the Red-encircled community of Steinstuecken Wednesday and ferried them across Communist territory to the broader security of West Berlin proper. There was no Red interference with the airlift." The *Springfield Leader* of Springfield, Missouri, ran the same AP story, under the headline "US 'Copters Pluck 7 Out of Steinstuecken." An airlift of five refugees in early October led to these headlines on October 4: "US 'Copter

Liberates 5 East Germans" (*Cincinnati Enquirer*); "Copter Whisks 5 E. Germans to West Berlin" (*Democrat and Chronicle*, Rochester, New York); "US Flies East Escapees to Safety. Rescue from Steinstuecken Enclave Duplicates Incident Protested By Reds" (*Los Angeles Times*).

The "Reds" did protest, loudly and colorfully. "The East German Foreign Ministry said Thursday night the lifting of seven refugees from Steinstuecken by U.S. Army helicopters was an 'act of organized kidnapping' and a violation of East German sovereignty," said an AP story in the *Montgomery Advertiser* on September 29. "'Only because of the utmost restraint shown by the organs of the GDR was a serious incident avoided, an East German Foreign Ministry spokesman said. 'The people who initiated this will have to bear full responsibility for such provocation.'"

The American press poked fun at the East German complaints. "East Germans Cry 'Kidnap' After Rescue of 7 Refugees," was the *Montgomery Advertiser's* headline for that AP report. The *Cincinnati Enquirer* ran the same AP wire report, under this spicy header: "Reds Rap Airlift of Refugees." A UPI reporter outright mocked the GDR. He wrote that, after the first refugee airlift, "Next day the foreign ministry of the Communist puppet East German government went up in the air without benefit of helicopters."[25]

The US authorities brushed off the Communist protests. This comes from a UPI wire report in the *Times Record* of Troy, New York, on October 4: "An East German objection last week to the flight of seven refugees from Steinstuecken was ignored by American officials on the ground that the US has no relations with East Germany and has four-power rights to fliy where it wants to within Berlin airspace."

Steinstuecken resident Dieter Gertz, Wilfried Hammer's friend, kept a diary. He shared this entry from it with author Leland McCaslin: "23 Mai (May) 1965: A Vopo who wanted to escape from the GDR knocked at our terrace window and asked for help. I didn't let him in but went to see the MPs. They decided it was not safe to let him walk on the streets of Steinstücken because the watchtower-guards might see him. So they escorted him—climbing through gardens to their 'office.' Later, he was flown out by helicopter wearing an American uniform."[26]

Most refugees snuck through the wire quietly. Most—but not all. This is a CIA report from November 27, 1961:

An East German bus driver and his assistant rammed their empty vehicle into a section of the barbed wire surrounding Steinstuecken and fled into the enclave. They were removed with another refugee by USCOB (US Command Berlin) helicopter the following day. East German police pulled the bus back into the zone.[27]

Vern Pike remembers the event clearly:

It was November 61, in the evening. A passenger bus crashed into the barbed wire coming from Babelsberg. There were six people on the bus, and they were trying to escape to the west. The Vopos came storming up, yelling "Halt Halt," and they started firing their weapons up in the air, because these refugees were scrambling out of the bus.

And our MP who was on perimeter patrol at that time was a specialist by the name of Bloski. Old Bloski followed his orders precisely. He took his burp gun, let off almost a full magazine and started screaming at the Vopos 'Raus, Raus, get the hell out!' While he was laying down this covering fire, the refugees came tumbling out the front end of the bus, which was in Steinstuecken, and he took them into the MP HQ in the basement of the burgermeister's house. They radioed back into the MP station, using the codeword, and the next day a helicopter flew out to Steinstuecken. In the helicopter, they had MP uniforms and barber shears. We snipped the hair off of them so they looked like soldiers, and dressed them like MPs, and we flew them out of Steinstuecken.[28]

Many former MPs still tell the story of Bloski and the bus. They also exchanged other stories about refugees who made their way into Steinstuecken. AP reporter Hubert Erb recounted one of those stories in his 1967 article on the 287th MP Company:

The troops like to tell of the young MP out in Steinstuecken who was awakened one night by a knock on the door. When he opened the door, clad only in his shorts, there stood an East German with a submachinegun.

> The GI slammed the door, went and got his own weapon and came back. '*Nichts* shoot,' the East German said. He had come to ask for asylum.[29]

The East Germans weren't the only ones irritated with US officials over the helicopter flights. General Clay complained to Washington that American officials were overly cautious, even timid, when approving or managing the flights. When Clay first asked for helicopters to remove refugees from Steinstuecken, the State Department immediately approved: "However, this approval asked that the removal be done as much as possible under cover." For subsequent flights, "the local commander was told to get permission each time a helicopter was sent into Steinstuecken." For one of those flights, "when permission was requested to remove [refugees] by helicopter it required discussion between three commands with a lapse of approximately twenty hours before any action was taken. When the refugees were brought out it was still done as much under cover as possible." "The right to use the air," Clay told Washington, was one of "the basic rights to which we are committed" in Berlin. "We should have moved our helicopters openly but not ostentatiously into Steinstuecken and brought out whoever we wanted to openly and proudly."[30]

The GDR bolstered the barriers around the exclave. The barbed wire fence was strengthened and expanded. By the end of the first week in October, it completely encircled the hamlet. The new fence ran along the railroad track bisecting Steinstuecken;[31] that hampered access between the eastern and western halves of the village. It also cut off access to the field that the US Army was using as a helipad. The villagers took matters into their own hands. "Steinstuecken residents promptly chopped holes in the barricade" to enable access across the train tracks, wrote a UPI reporter, "and cleared some more of their land for another landing site."[32]

At the end of 1964, the Berlin Wall finally came to Steinstuecken. GDR workmen erected the same kinds of concrete panels that now divided the main city. Watchtowers appeared. The first ones were wooden; later they were replaced by concrete enclosures on pillars. Guards inside them scanned the exclave and the approaches to it with binoculars and cameras; they also watched their own soldiers on patrol around the fences. The Vopos mounted lights on poles to illuminate the fence line. "They were very bright and lit up the houses inside Steinstuecken," remembers former MP Keith Koziba. "Most of the houses that faced the fence had to have thick blinds on their windows."[33] By the mid-1960s, the GDR barrier was so tight and forbidding that refugee escapes largely ceased.

Heike Behrendt is the daughter of Kurt Behrendt, the photographer who lived in Steinstuecken. She was two-and-a-half when General Clay came, and she watched the Wall grow as she grew up. She remembers an episode from the early days when only a barbed wire fence surrounded the exclave. A young East German girl, five or six years old, had a friend in the hamlet. She would wriggle under the wire to come play with her friend, then wriggle under it again to go home. That stopped when the actual Wall appeared.[34]

Behrendt's parents saw one bright side in the Wall. "When they erected the Wall," and replaced the barbed wire with the concrete panels, "I remember that very well. The adults talked about that. The children stood near them, and we heard" them talk about the strengthened barriers. "The adults said, 'You know, now that they have erected this concrete wall,'" and put "such an amount of material and money" into it—that clarified the situation on the border. The Steinstueckeners saw the Wall as a tacit acceptance by the GDR that the hamlet belonged to West Berlin. The adults "think they are now safer, because the situation is now clear, and they will have the status quo. Yes, they will have to endure the inconvenience of going through border checkpoints" to go to Berlin, "but they will have the border line. They are less afraid of being occupied" by the GDR.[35]

The Vopos built bunkers where the train tracks entered and exited Steinstuecken, "so you couldn't really sneak down those tracks and scamper in" to the exclave, recalled Herbert Judd. Judd remembers tripwires the GDR strung around the fences. They "would be attached to flares and/or noisemakers, to prevent people from trying to sneak across there at night. You could see them if you shone your light on them. They would be at foot or ankle level." If a fleeing East German tripped one of the wires, "it would be just like ringing a bell. It would be like, 'Here I am, come shoot me.'" The Vopos used the same tripwires in Berlin itself, near the Brandenburg Gate—for a while. "They had to get rid of them near the Brandenburg Gate, because there was a big wooded area" near the gate, "and the rabbits would set off the flares."[36]

Charlie Smith, who retired from the Army as a Command Sergeant Major, was a sergeant in the 287th MP Company in the early 1960s. One day, while on patrol in the exclave, he noticed that one of the fenceposts holding up the wire barrier had fallen. The Vopos fixed the fence by standing up the fencepost and tying it with barbed wire to a tree—on the American side of the line.

"I called into G2 and told them what they had done, and told them that it was secured to a tree on our side. They didn't say anything. So, I got some wire cutters and took a patrol out, and I went up and I cut it. When I did, and the tension on that pole went, three or four other poles collapsed, like dominoes. And the Vopos got all upset. They had a bunker there on the corner. And it wasn't long before there was a company of them there. They were all excited. They didn't do nothing, except stand there and look at it, though. Later on they fixed it."[37]

The GDR protested through official channels. "It went all the way up to Willy Brandt," Smith recalls. Berlin Brigade sent a helicopter to Steinstuecken to bring Sergeant Smith back to Andrews Barracks, so he could explain what happened. "I told them, 'I told you about it.' They said 'well, we didn't tell you to cut it.' I said 'you didn't tell me not to. I told you that I was going to cut it, that it was on our side.' They said, 'well, are you sure that it was on the American side?' I said that you could see the border marker there. Then they said that it had gone up to the mayor, Willy Brandt, that I was harassing their troops, and they were young men, and they couldn't be responsible for them."[38] Later on, Smith heard the Steinstuecken mayor had been walking on the *Waldweg* when the commander of the Vopo border guard company appeared. The GDR officer gave him the same warning: The Vopos on guard duty were often young and inexperienced, and they might react rashly if the MPs "provoked" them.[39]

Vopos patrolled the fence lines along the edges of Steinstuecken. So did the MPs. This brought American and East German personnel close enough to shout, or even speak, to each other. The Army discouraged the MPs from trying to engage their counterparts in conversation[40]—and the Vopos certainly did likewise. The language barrier made it hard to talk. Mostly, American and East German guards passed each other in silence. "They'd look at us, as if to say 'Who are you,' and we'd look at them like 'Who are you?'" recalled Ed Hamborski. "They'd be on their side of the fence and we'd be on ours. We'd walk maybe 25, 40 yards together, and then they'd tail off or we'd tail off" in different directions.[41]

Inevitably, though, some greetings did go back and forth across the wire. Mostly it was a simple wave or "*Guten Tag.*" But, sometimes, it was more. "I ran into one [East German], he was by himself, and I tried to talk to him," remembers Herbert Judd. Only a few yards separated them. "I didn't shout at him. He was just right across the fence. He happened to be out patrolling too, just like I was. I asked him, in my crappy German, what he thought, what's going on. I told him that you guys can't even afford butter. He said, yeah that's right, but we think we'll be a powerful nation soon, one of these days. It was kind of sad."[42]

Ed Hamborski was on patrol one day. Near the hole in the fence where the train tracks passed through, he met a Vopo on patrol. "He and I came face to face. He couldn't have been more than nineteen years old; at that time I was 24 or 25. And I thought he was going to come across. We stood there toe to toe. We just looked eyeball to eyeball. And then, he turned around. I thought for sure that he was coming over."[43]

Charlie Smith tried to get a Vopo to defect. "If you could get one of the Vopos by himself—they're always [on patrol] together—but if you could get one by himself, he'd talk to you. I talked to one, I told him 'Come on over here, I'll help you.' He said no. He said that, if he came over, he was concerned about his family, which would still be over there. And I understood that." Smith would set out fresh fruit on the railroad tracks at the exclave's edges. When he returned, the fruit was always gone.[44]

Keith Koziba tells of a fascinating experience in the summer of 1963. One night, the sergeant in charge of the MP detachment called Koziba over to a section of the fence. To his surprise, Koziba found that his sergeant had cut a huge hole in the wires! It went all the way through the GDR fencing. "He cut a hole big enough to walk through, three foot wide, six foot tall." Someone could have walked from Steinstuecken into the Soviet Zone . . . or, walked into the exclave. So, when the GDR guards next came by the area, "they were looking at a door into freedom-land."

Koziba tells what happened next. "We were sitting off out of sight, waiting for some Vopos to come back by there, on their patrol. Eventually two of them did come back," found the holes, "and they got all excited. The senior one stayed there and sent the junior one back to get some help, and eventually he came back with some more Vopos and some workers" to fix the holes in the fence. "In the meantime, [the MP sergeant] is trying to convince him to defect. [The sergeant] spoke pretty good German, and he had [the Vopo] in tears." After the whole episode ended, the sergeant "told me that the guy had wanted to come over, but he had a wife and a child, and if he left, his wife and child would pay the price. So, they stood there together for quite a while, and he couldn't even get him to walk into the hole."

The junior Vopo returned with the repair team, "and they saw us standing there. One of the Vopos lowered his weapon and jacked a round into his AK-47 and pointed it at us, and they were yelling, a lot of different things. Then they got these people working on filling the hole back up, and [the sergeant] and I went back to the mayor's house from there." The next morning, all the holes had been patched.[45]

Ralph Sanchez first came to Steinstuecken in 1965. He remembers a common kind of interaction between MPs and Vopos: barter. "We weren't supposed to [talk with the East Germans]. But, if you wanted an East German hat, or an East German belt buckle, you took a couple of packs of Marlboros, you took a Playboy, and in a discreet fashion, you'd do a tradeoff." Such tradeoffs were common among Western troops who had contact with Soviet and GDR personnel. Sanchez still has a Russian hat he acquired while guarding one of the duty trains.

Tradeoffs were common—but definitely unauthorized. "My guards, the guys that I was with [in Steinstuecken], they'd show me" the souvenirs they acquired in trades, recalled Sanchez. "I'd tell them, don't show that around. Pack it up once you get back to the barracks and send it home. Don't be messing around, because you'd have [Army investigators] knocking on your door."[46]

The East Germans didn't think much of cross-wire barter or chatter, either. From Reuters, in the *Minneapolis Star Tribune* on July 30, 1963:

> *At The Wall: Bum a Smoke, Get A Transfer.*
>
> An escaped East German border guard said here Monday that an East German platoon was withdrawn from border duty after accepting cigarettes from US military police in the West Berlin enclave of Steinstuecken.
>
> The 21-year-old guard told a press conference that soldiers were strictly forbidden to make contact with people on the West Berlin side of the border. 'Even to say "good morning" across the fence,' he explained, 'was a dangerous thing to do.' He said that a week before his escape eight days ago, all portable radios in his regiment were confiscated to stop the soldiers from listening to Western radio stations.

Putting MP "boots on the ground" stabilized the situation in and around Steinstuecken, once and for all. Soviet and East German pressure on the exclave diminished once the Communists saw that the Americans meant business when they said Steinstuecken was West Berlin (and, hence, American) territory—just as Clay had predicted. "You weren't going to make much of an impact" with just three lightly armed MPs, remarked Herbert Judd. "The whole idea was that the United States was there."[47]

The Americans hadn't put the Communists on the spot, either. No tank columns had crashed through the Kohlhasenbrueck checkpoint, and Berlin Brigade hadn't helicoptered in companies of infantry to transform Steinstuecken into a true combat operations base on Soviet Zone territory. Actions like that would have challenged the Soviets and East Germans to respond. As time passed, the Soviets and East Germans saw that the Americans also weren't challenging other more minor Communist restrictions on the exclave. US occupation authorities didn't forcefully resist GDR rules that prevented West Berliners from traveling to Steinstuecken without a GDR pass. Despite Clay's urgings,[48] the American authorities didn't try to assert their rights as occupiers to drive to the hamlet. MPs continued to travel by helicopter, not jeep. The MP detachment preserved but did not expand the West's footprint in the Soviet Zone.

As time passed, and the initial tensions of the Berlin Wall crisis faded, life in Steinstuecken settled into a routine. The residents inside the exclave and the Vopo guards outside it grew accustomed to the sound, every three or four days, of approaching helicopter blades. A Berlin Brigade helicopter would land and drop off a fresh detachment of MPs.

"The children were very fond of the helicopter landings," said Heike Behrendt. "It was an event for them. All of the children who were too young to go to school, when we would hear the helicopters, we knew they were going to land. And we would come running from our houses to the landing zone."

The helicopter pilots greeted them warmly. Usually, the aircrews had some time on the ground, as the incoming MP detachment unloaded its equipment and food and the outgoing detachment loaded its gear. The fliers often let the children climb into the helicopter's cargo bay and sit in the seats. Once, Heike Behrendt remembers, a new MP company commander flew into Steinstuecken for an orientation tour.

Some of the children sang him a song. As a thank you, the pilots fired up the helicopter's engines, got the main rotor blades going, and generated some propwash for the children to enjoy. The children loved feeling the propwash, said Heike. "It was a heavy, heavy wind." The smaller children could lean into it, and the force of the propwash held them upright. It reminded Heike Behrendt of a thrill ride at a carnival.[49]

MPs en route to Steinstuecken got door-to-door service—literally. Their helicopter would pick them up at the MP barracks. A typical tour lasted 3–4 days. However, MP detachments carried a few extra days' worth of food in case bad weather (or Cold War tensions) prevented their relief helicopter from picking them up on schedule.

MP life in Steinstuecken followed a set routine: fence patrol, radio watch, watching the Vopos. Every day, one or two MPs walked the perimeter, looking for any signs of trouble. "We'd go out periodically, every 4 hours, every 6 hours, something like that, and just make a walk around the territory," remembers Herbert Judd. "It was a small village. I don't recall exactly how big it was, but I think you could walk around it in an hour without letting out a breath. It was very small."[50] The MPs patrolled the fence both day and night.

Back at the mayor's house, one MP monitored the radios. "We had two radios in our room, on different frequencies," remembers Jerome Weilmuenster. The MP's duty room wasn't huge: "it seems it was about 12 feet by 12 feet, so there was no problem hearing it if there was a transmission. We did not have to have someone sitting immediately by the radio at all times. But there had to be at least one person in the room at all times. We also had the house phone, but we were in the basement and the phone was on the first floor. 99.9% of communication was by radio. The other end of the radio was in the Provost Marshal's Office, and they received all radio transmissions there."[51] "We'd call in regularly to the Provost Marshal," said Herbert Judd. "And, if we didn't, they'd give us a call in the middle of the night and say 'Hey, c'mon!' That was embarrassing."[52]

The MPs watched the Vopos and reported on their activities. "We had to do spot reports on any types of observations—personnel, vehicles, air transport, whatever it may have been," recalls Ralph Sanchez. "We always had to do a report, to send it back to Berlin Brigade headquarters. From the back yard of the mayor's house, you could look right into a guard tower, and see the changing of the guard, and we'd have to report that. How many guards we saw go up, how many we saw come down, the times, when they brought the food—they'd send the food up on a rope."[53]

Throughout the 1960s, another routine began in Steinstuecken: visits by American and German officials. US military and West Berlin government leaders flew into the exclave regularly to reassure the residents—and remind the GDR—that the Americans remained committed to Steinstuecken's security. West Berlin's mayor, the mayor of the Zehlendorf *Bezirk*, the current USCOBs, and Berlin Brigade commanders were among the dignitaries who visited.

All the important visitors toured the exclave's boundaries, with residents—especially children—in tow. "I remember that when there were visits" by dignitaries, "the adults would all come to the landing zone. It was an event for all the people here," said Heike Behrendt. "The people of Steinstuecken were very fond" of these visits because they knew the visitors were high-ranking officials,[54] and their visits demonstrated that American and West Berlin officials understood Steinstuecken's unique situation.

Steinstuecken duty had its benefits. MPs normally got a three-day pass after a tour in the exclave. That was a nice perk, especially in the early months of the Berlin Wall crisis. Time off was hard to come by then, recalled Herbert Judd. Berlin Brigade "sort of clamped down when the Wall went up. No overnight passes, they were pretty careful about giving out stuff like that. So, it was a good deal if you wanted to volunteer" for Steinstuecken duty. A three-day pass gave you enough time to get away from base. "If you stayed there in the barracks, why, someone was liable to grab you for some screwy work detail."[55]

Another benefit was the duty itself and the location. The peace and quiet of Steinstuecken, the trait that made residents willing to put up with constant hassles (and occasional fears) in order to live there, also made an impression on the MPs. "It was deathly quiet," said Ralph Sanchez. Bernhard Beyer Strasse, the main street in the village, was lined with chestnut trees whose branches had grown together over the road. "It was like a tunnel. [The whole village] was so serene, it was so peaceful—except for the jerks up in the towers."[56]

"Perhaps the 'oddest' thing about Steinstucken," remarked Jerome Weilmuenster, "was that it was really a quiet and normal way of life. Of course, the residents were inconvenienced. But, living in Berlin was an inconvenience. Actually, living in Steinstuecken was one way to leave the hustle

Photo credit: Jerome Weilmuenster

GDR watchtowers around the exclave. Top: 1960s. Bottom: 1970s. Photo credit: Jim Kertz

Photo credit: U.S. Army

Army Signal Corps photographs of a new contingent of MPs arriving in Steinstuecken. The MPs came with enough supplies for several days in the exclave. The village's children usually came to watch the helicopters land, and wave goodbye as they left. The girl in the dark dress with long brown hair is Magrit Wiese, who would later marry MP Ralph Sanchez. Photo credit: U.S. Army

Photo credit: Kurt Behrendt

A lucky MP gets a lift from the helipad courtesy of a Steinstuecken resident with a car. Photo credit: Kurt Behrendt

Above: a view from Steinstuecken, across the death strip, towards Berlin in 1964. Below: a close-up of one of the GDR guard posts. Photo credits: Berlin State Archives, F Rep. 290 No. 0046749. Photographer: Gert Schütz.

Jerome Weilmuenster, an MP in the 287th MP Company, took these pictures on a flight from Berlin to Steinstuecken. Top: the helicopter would land at the MP barracks to pick up the new detachment. The men in white are the mess hall employees bringing rations to the helicopter. Middle & Bottom: views of the death strip. Photo credits: Jerome Weilmuenster

Pictures from a 1967 Stars and Stripes *story on Steinstuecken. Above: many Steinstuecken residents used bicycles to travel daily from the exclave to the entry checkpoint into West Berlin. They would park their bikes at the checkpoint, and then take public transportation to school or work. Below: a West Berlin policeman raises the barrier as a Steinstuecken resident leaves the exclave. Photo credits:* Stars and Stripes

Residents walk and drive into Steinstuecken. Photo credits: Stars and Stripes

East Germans perform maintenance on the fence surrounding the portion of the railway running through Steinstuecken, 1964. Photo credits: Jerome Weilmuenster

The GDR work detail brought a photographer. The Vopos routinely photographed Americans on duty in Steinstuecken. The MP has masking tape over his nametag; this made it more difficult for GDR observers to identify and track Americans who were assigned to the exclave. Photo credits: Jerome Weilmuenster

The West Berlin government paid for this schoolbus, which a Steinstuecken resident drove to take the village's children to and from school in Berlin. Photo credit: Jim Kertz

The helicopter playset Berlin Brigade built for the exclave. Photo credit: Jim Kertz

Photo credit: Kurt Behrendt

A Berlin official uses the playset as a candy launching pad during a party in the exclave. Photo credit: Kurt Behrendt

Photo credit: Kurt Behrendt

American and West Berlin officials paid regular visits to Steinstuecken. Here, West Berlin mayor Willy Brandt and General Albert Watson, the US Commander of Berlin, visit in 1962. Photo credit: Kurt Behrendt

General James Polk, the new US Commander in Berlin (in dress uniform), and General Frederick Hartel, commander of the Berlin Brigade (in field uniform), tour the village in 1963. Photo credits: Kurt Behrendt

The sign outside the house that served as the MP base in Steinstuecken. Photo credit: Wikimedia Commons

"Santa" leaves the exclave, on a Berlin Brigade sled. Photo credit: RBB Media

THE BERLIN OBSERVER

Vol. 24, No. 47 | U.S. ARMY, BERLIN | FRIDAY, November 22, 1968

Steinstuecken Children Will Share Thanksgiving Meal with 287th MPs

The Berlin Brigade will host a Thanksgiving Dinner for all children of Steinstuecken on Thursday, Nov. 28, it was announced this week.

In years past, the Berlin Brigade has sponsored a similar turkey feast for the entire population of Steinstuecken on the Saturday following Thanksgiving Day by transporting the traditional holiday meal and all its trimmings to the exclave of Steinstuecken, which is part of the West Berlin district of Zehlendorf.

This year the program is being expanded. Some 45 children between the ages of 4 and 14, as well as several chaperones, will be transported from the border crossing point at Kohlhasenbrueck to the mess hall of the 287th Military Police Company where they will share with the members of that company the traditional American Thanksgiving Dinner.

In addition, adult members of the Steinstuecken community will have an opportunity to celebrate Thanksgiving with American representatives. As in past years, on the Saturday following Thanksgiving Day the turkey dinner will be flown to the 200 residents of the exclave. Brigadier General Samuel McC. Goodwin, commanding general, Berlin Brigade, and Zehlendorf District Mayor Hans-Joachim Schnitzer will cut the first turkey, signalling the start of the holiday feast on Saturday, Nov. 30.

Two Brigade Tank Crews Earn Distinguished Rating in TCQC

Two tank crews from Company F, 40th Armor, Berlin Brigade scored unusually high and earned Distinguished Crew Ratings in the Tank Crew Qualification Course (TCQC) along with tanks of the 4th Armored Division at their annual qualifica- two platoons were attached to Company B, 4th Battalion, 35th Armor, 4th Armored Division, from Illesheim, West Germany.

Sergeant Wertenberger attributed his success to his smooth-function-

HANS-JOACHIM SCHNITZER, district mayor of Zehlendorf, chats with Corporal Paul Boeher of the 287th Military Police Company during a special Thanksgiving Day Dinner, Nov. 28. The children in the picture are just two of 45 children hosted at the MP mess hall that day. The children came from the tiny Berlin exclave of Steinstuecken which sits to the south of Zehlendorf within East Germany. U. S. Army Photo by Specialist 5 McCormack

Coverage by the Berlin Observer, *the newspaper for the US military community in Berlin. The girls are, l-r, Susanna Weber and Heike Behrendt, daughter of Kurt. Photo credits:* Berlin Observer

OPENING WIDE is one of the 45 children from the tiny Berlin exclave of Steinstuecken who dined at the 287th Military Police mess hall this Thanksgiving. Holding the little tyke is MP Corporal Steve Dragos, a favorite of the Steinstuecken children.

Jorg Behrendt, son of Kurt and brother of Heike, enjoys a piece of wurst. Photo credit: Berlin Observer

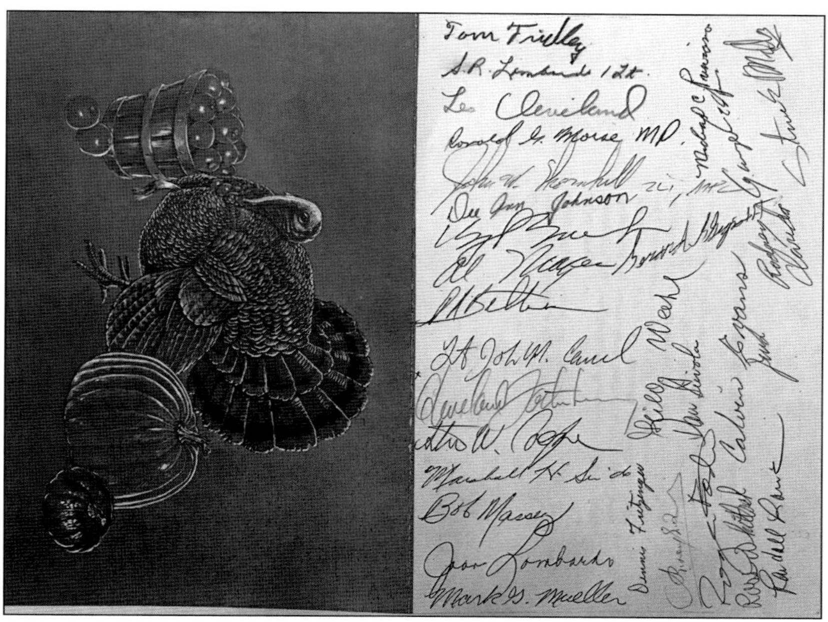

An autographed Thanksgiving menu. Photo credit: Heike Behrendt

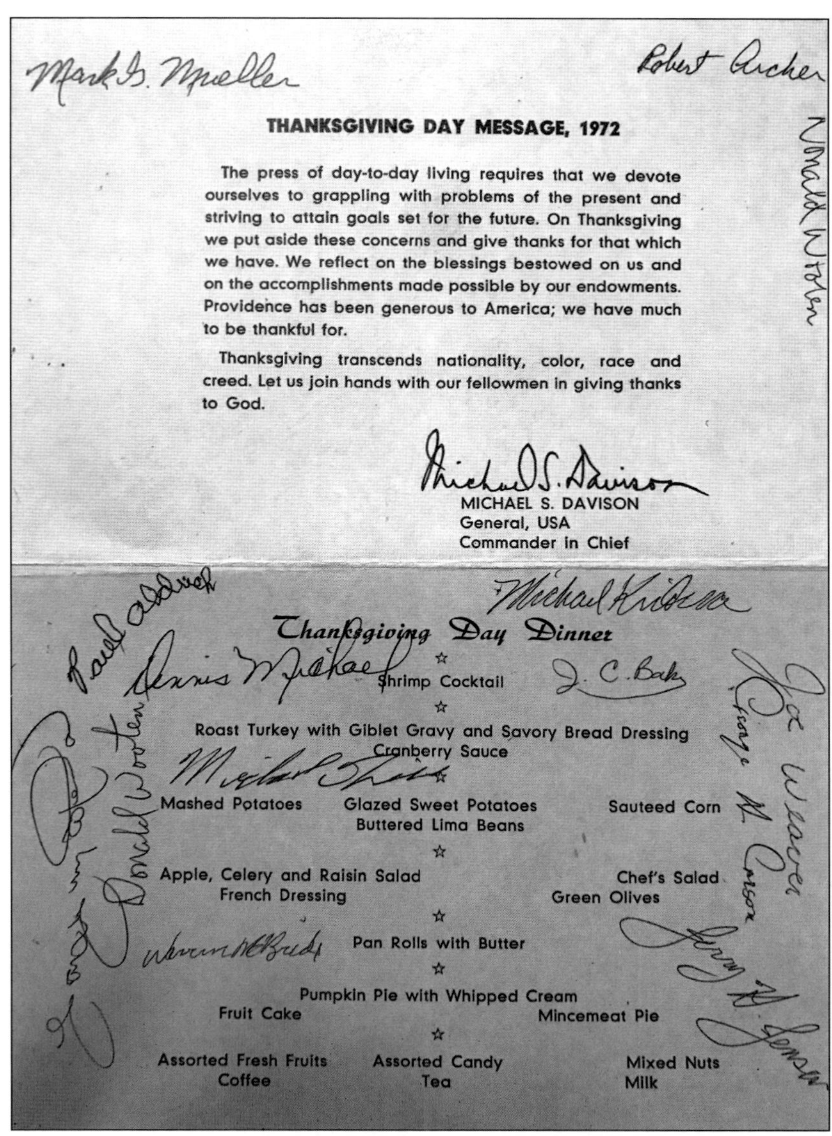

THANKSGIVING DAY MESSAGE, 1972

The press of day-to-day living requires that we devote ourselves to grappling with problems of the present and striving to attain goals set for the future. On Thanksgiving we put aside these concerns and give thanks for that which we have. We reflect on the blessings bestowed on us and on the accomplishments made possible by our endowments. Providence has been generous to America; we have much to be thankful for.

Thanksgiving transcends nationality, color, race and creed. Let us join hands with our fellowmen in giving thanks to God.

MICHAEL S. DAVISON
General, USA
Commander in Chief

Thanksgiving Day Dinner

☆

Shrimp Cocktail

☆

Roast Turkey with Giblet Gravy and Savory Bread Dressing
Cranberry Sauce

☆

Mashed Potatoes — Glazed Sweet Potatoes — Sauteed Corn
Buttered Lima Beans

☆

Apple, Celery and Raisin Salad — Chef's Salad
French Dressing — Green Olives

☆

Pan Rolls with Butter

☆

Pumpkin Pie with Whipped Cream
Fruit Cake — Mincemeat Pie

☆

Assorted Fresh Fruits — Assorted Candy — Mixed Nuts
Coffee — Tea — Milk

An autographed Thanksviving menu from 1972. Photo credit: Heike Behrendt

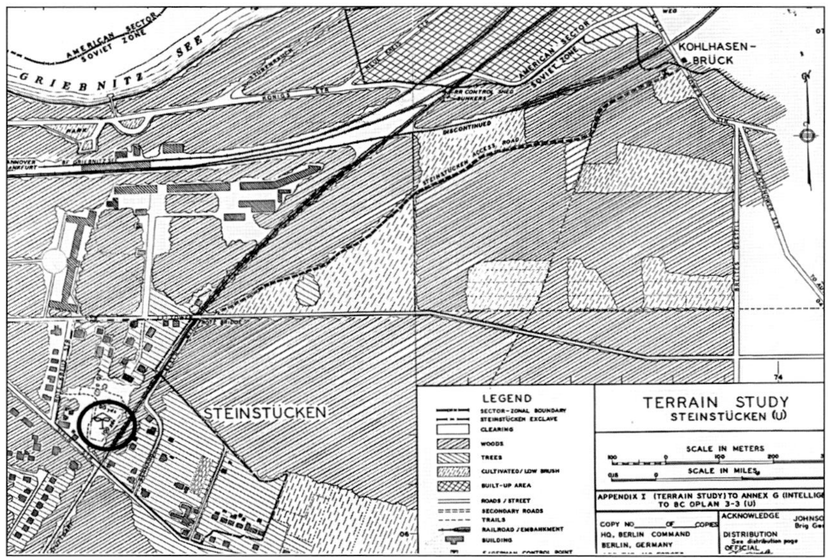

U.S. Army map of Steinstuecken that showed the location of the helipad (circled), the route of the Waldweg (dotted line labeled as "Steinstucken Access Road), and the border between the American Sector and Soviet Zone. This map was part of the Berlin Command's Operations Plan (OPLAN) for the defense of the exclave. Photo credit: National Archives

Vopos (in saucer hats) watch construction of the road to Steinstuecken. Photo credit: Kurt Behrendt

Road construction crews apply the finishing touches to the road. The GDR has already extended the Berlin Wall, so it lines both sides of the new road. Photo credit: Kurt Behrendt

On the day the road opened, hundreds of people walked from Berlin to Steinstuecken. Photo credit: Kurt Behrendt

Berlin Mayor Klaus Schulz (in glasses and spotted tie) USCOB General William Cobb and Mrs. Cobb (in between the two gentlemen) walk on the new road to Steinstuecken. Photo credit: Kurt Behrendt

The finished road, surrounded on both sides by the Berlin Wall. Photo credit: Jim Kertz

U.S. Army units in Berlin often put the names of Berlin neighborhoods on their vehicles. This still shot from an Armed Forces Network video from the 1970s shows a Berlin Brigade Field Artillery M577 command post emblazoned with the exclave's name. Photo credit: Armed Forces Network (AFN)

An aerial photo of Steinstuecken in 1989. Photo credit: U.S. Army

An American UH-1 "Huey" and Soviet MI-8 "HIP" helicopter pass each other as they fly along the border between West Berlin and the Soviet Zone in 1989. British aviators took this photo. Photo credit: Joseph King

Doug Powell, commander of the Berlin Brigade Aviation Detachment from 1988 to 1991, with the detachment's guidon. The Steinstuecken streamer was hand-sewn by exclave residents. Photo credit: Doug Powell

Steinstuecken residents Guenter Rossnagel and Gert Knecht were instrumental in helping the American miltary community reestablish its relationship with the villagers. Here Guenter Rossnagel receives a public service award from Major General Raymond Haddock, US Commander of Berlin. Photo credit: Rossnagel Family

Gert Knecht cleaning the pedestal of the rotor blade memorial. Photo credit: Doug Powell

After riding the length of the Berlin Wall, members and family members of the Berlin Brigade Aviation Detachment prepare to ride down Bernhard-Beyer Strasse to Steinstuecken for the now-enclave's Sommerfest in August 1988. Photo credit: Doug Powell

Youngsters from Steinstuecken explore the helicopter display at Sommerfest in August 1988. Photo credit: Berlin Observer

Festival-goers had the chance to pose for pictures in the helicopters. Detachment personnel then attached the photo to a pre-printed certificate and typed in the person's name, creating a customized memento of the person's time on an American Huey. Photo credit: Doug Powell

....WIRD HIERMIT ZUM EHREN-PILOTEN VON STEINSTUECKEN ERNANNT.
ZUR ERINNERUNG AN DEN ENTSCHLOSSENEN WIDERSTAND VON
STEINSTUECKEN ALS EINE EXKLAVE DER FREIHEIT UND
DIE LUFTBRUECKE DER U. S. ARMY LUFTWAFFE VON 1961-1972,
DIE DEN STOLZEN EINWOHNERN VON STEINSTUECKEN
DIE FREIHEIT BEWAHRT HABEN.

21 AUG 1988

Translated, the caption reads: "____________________" is designated an Honorary Pilot of Steinstuecken, in remembrance of the resolute resistance of Steinstuecken as an exclave of liberty, and the airlift by U.S. Army aviators from 1961 to 1972, which preserved the freedom of the proud residents of Steinstuecken." Photo credit: Doug Powell

Kurt Behrendt shows a collection of his Steinstuecken photographs to Major General Raymond Haddock during the general's visit to the village in 1989. Photo credit: Doug Powell

The last flight by Berlin Brigade helicopters into the "enclave" of Steinstuecken, over the territory of the "German Democratic Republic", on September 29, 1991. Four days later, on October 3rd, Germany officially reunified, and the Allied occupation of Berlin ended. Photo credit: U.S. Air Force

Lester and Jan Feutz in front of the "Spirit of Steinstuecken." Doug Powell received official Army approval to stencil the inscription on one of the detachment's helicopters, to symbolize the close relationship between the people of Steinstuecken and the U.S. military. The helicopter is now on display at the Allied Museum in Berlin, a museum that commemorates the Allied presence in Berlin during the Cold War. Photo credit: Jan Feutz

A patch created to honor both the Lueftbrucke, *the helicopter "air bridge" into Steinstuecken, and the renewed US-German partnership. Photo credit: Doug Powell*

Gail Halvorsen, the "Berlin Candy Bomber," describes to two children how he and other American pilots dropped candy to Berlin children. Photo credit: Gail Halvorsen

Halvorsen as commander of Templeof Airbase, holding one of the candy parachutes. Photo credit: Gail Halvorsen

Russian Air Force Major Yuri Gidzenko and U.S. Army Lieutenant Colonel William S. McArthur holding Gert Knecht's candy parachute during their space flight. Photo credit: Doug Powell

Gail Halvorsen visits Steinstuecken in 2005. With him is Mercedes Wild and her husband, Peter. Mercedes wrote to Halvorsen during the Berlin Airlift, asking him to try and drop a candy parchute on her Berlin home. Halvorsen mailed her some candy and later paid her a visit. When he commanded Templehof Airbase, Colonel Halvorsen visited the Wild family and began a lasting friendship. Photo credit: Gail Halvorsen

One of the most widely-reported episodes of the Berlin Wall crisis: a boy who lived in an exclave in the British Sector received an armored car escort to and from school, to deter the Vopos from harassing him. An interpretive sign along the modern-day Berlin Wall trail commemorates the event. (UK National Army Museum). Photo credit: UK National Army Museum

Colonel Christopher Waters and Command Sergeant Major Osvaldo Martell, the commander and senior non-commissioned officer (NCO) of the Army's 16th Combat Aviation Brigade present the St. Michael Award to Lorenz Knecht (son of Gert) and Gitte Rossnagel (wife of Guenter) in 2017. Photo credit: U.S. Army

Elke Hammer (center) poses with former Berlin Brigade pilot Wilbur Wolf and his wife, Amy, in front of the rotor blade memorial in 2017. The helicopter playset, newly-refurbished and still in use, is visible in the background. Photo credit: Wilbur Wolf

Mementos to the American presence that are still in the Steinstuecken community clubhouse. Photo credit: Elke Hammer

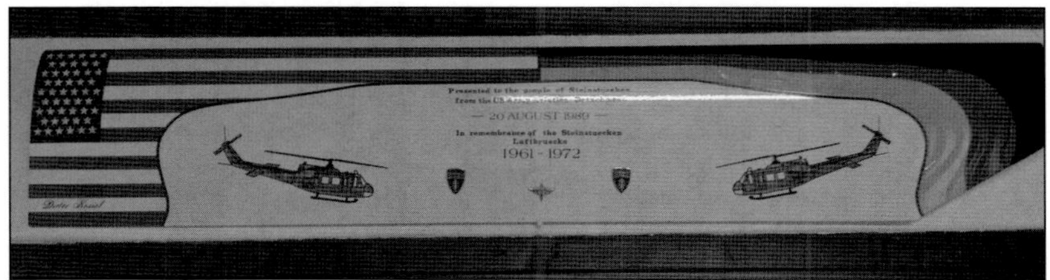

Photo credit: Wilbur Wolf

The helicopter playset in 2019, newly refurbished by Steinsteucken residents. Photo credit: Elke Hammer

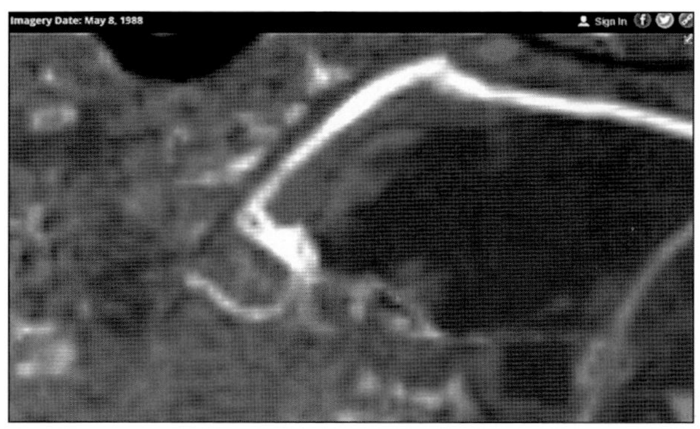

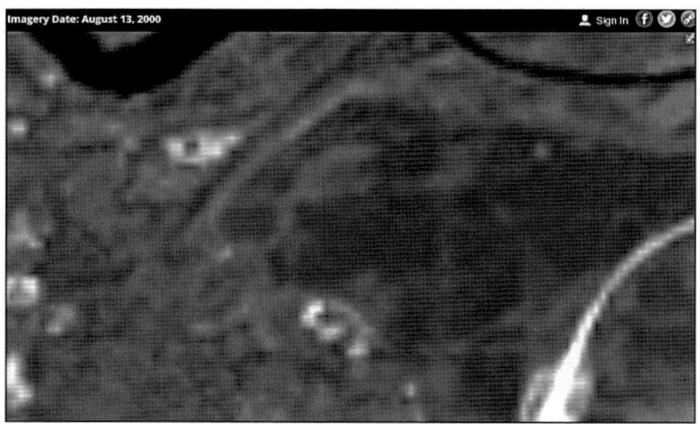

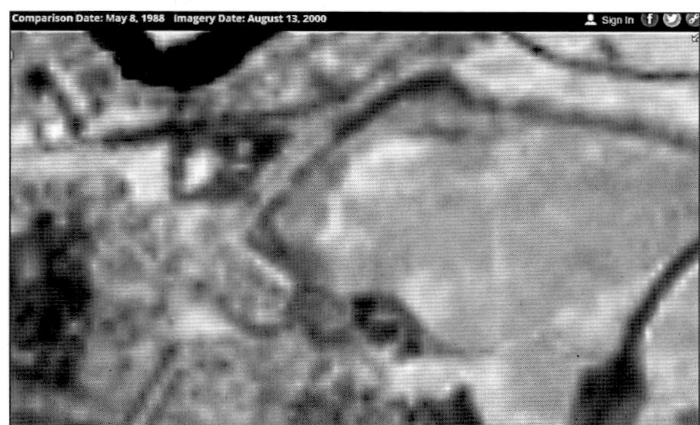

These image products were created from LANDSAT, a satellite imagery system used to measure vegetation health. They show how the areas around Steinstuecken changed in the years after the Cold War.

In the first image, taken in 1988, the cleared areas of the death strip, colored light grey, are clearly visible around the edges of the exclave.

In the second image, taken in 2000, new vegetation and construction have covered the strip.

The third image is a "change detection" product, which highlights changes on the ground in between the first and second images. "Changed" areas show up in dark shades—like the dark line that shows the trace of the former death strip.

Photo credits: ESRI

and bustle of the big city, live in a quiet area, yet still have the amenities of the city—restaurants, hotels, a large international airport, the University of Berlin, etc...—close by. If you could just put up with the checkpoints."[57]

Life in Steinstuecken wasn't all peace and quiet. Some flareups occurred. While the Soviets had forced the East Germans to grudgingly accept a parcel of West Berlin guarded by Americans on "sovereign" GDR territory, the Vopos didn't back off completely. Periodically throughout the 1960s, US authorities had to deal with various GDR harassments. In April 1962 the Vopos prevented West Berlin firemen from going to Steinstuecken to trim trees. A year later, the GDR put new barriers on the *Waldweg*. They erected low concrete walls and a fence of iron rails. This created a narrow zigzag path for vehicle traffic.[58] West Berlin officials feared their fire trucks couldn't get through.

The Americans had to step in. "US Pledges Aid to Protect Road" was the headline for a May 26 UPI report in the *Cincinnati Enquirer* on the latest Steinstuecken "crisis":

> The United States pledged Saturday it would keep open the route through East Germany to a tiny American sector enclave surrounded by Communist territory. US officials assured West Berlin officials that new barriers built by Communist police on a mile-long narrow country road to the hamlet of Steinstuecken would not be allowed to cut off the tiny community. The pledge was given at a meeting of American and West Berlin officials which was requested by the city government to map measures to meet new Communist harassment of Steinstuecken.
>
> A communique on the meeting said 'All necessary measures will be taken to safeguard access to Steinstuecken.' It said new meetings would be held if necessary.
>
> It was felt that Steinstuecken faced no immediate threat and that apparently the Communists only were tightening their controls around the hamlet, rather than taking action against it.

Whatever the Americans did worked. Four days later, this headline appeared over a UPI report in the *Pittsburgh Press*: "Reds Back Down on German Road." "The East German Communists backed down in the face of American determination and opened the road to Steinstuecken, a tiny US enclave a mile inside East Germany. East German police worked through the night to remove barriers on the road linking the village to West Berlin so fire engines and other utility vehicles could reach" the village. AP relayed a report from the West Berlin police "that the Vopos uprooted the rails with a mobile crane and replanted them farther apart."[59] "After the last barrier was removed," wrote UPI, "a West Berlin fire truck made a dry run test past the iron barriers and concrete blocks to Steinstuecken and back."[60]

Not all the flareups were so mild. Bill Bacon flew helicopters for the Berlin Brigade in the early 1960s. He was one of the first pilots to fly missions in and out of Steinstuecken. He remembers one dramatic evening. "I nearly had three heart attacks that night." Berlin Brigade had an emergency evacuation plan for the MPs. If necessary, a helicopter would fly into the exclave and rescue them.

> There was a codeword, and if you got that codeword, by the time you got your flight suit on and got to the parking lot there'd be a vehicle to pick you up and take you immediately to the airfield. The aircraft would be running, and you'd go into Steinstuecken to extract the MPs. And that happened one time with me. In fact, I don't think it ever happened but one time.
>
> By the time I got down to the parking lot there was someone waiting on me. Lights and sirens all the way to the airfield, and the aircraft was running when I got there and away we went.
>
> Berlin, especially out in those parts [i.e., the edges of the city], was just black, it was so dark. We'd flown that route so many times, we could fly it in the dark, almost with your eyes closed. So we flew into Steinstuecken....and we made a few calls over the FM radio to the MPs and never got a reply. So we didn't know what was happening, we didn't know why we were going to begin with. It was supposed to be an extraction, and we didn't know if anyone was alive or what had happened. And we sat out there and circled for about 15 minutes. [My copilot and I], we weren't arguing, we were looking at each other as if to say 'What do we do now?' There wasn't anybody to get any instructions from, so we decided to just go in there and land.
>
> [The helicopter they were flying, the Sikorsky H34, had enough power that] you can land with the tail wheel on the ground and the front wheels off the ground. And that's how we sat, for what

seemed to me like 30 or 40 minutes, before some GI came out there all blurry-eyed and wanted to know what we were doing. When we found out what had happened, we took off and went back to Templehof and tried to get some sleep.[61]

Later on, Bacon heard that an official in the Provost Marshal's office, newly assigned to Berlin and inexperienced, had mistakenly issued the codeword. "Silly things happen when you're in those types of situations," said Bacon, with a slight chuckle.[62]

Another flareup happened on the morning of March 19, 1966. This one was lethal. An AP reporter called it "one of the most violent escape attempts by Easterners trying to come West."[63] An East German border guard, Willi Marzahn, tried to flee. Marzahn and another fleeing border guard passed by Steinstuecken undetected, but Vopos caught them as they tried to cross into West Berlin near Kohlhasenbrueck. Both refugees were armed, and a brief gun battle ensued. Marzahn's colleague made it into West Berlin, but Marzahn died of gunshot wounds.[64] A memorial to him exists to this day in Zehlendorf.[65]

"I was in the bathtub," recalled Ralph Sanchez. The mayor's house had no shower, so MPs used the family bathtub. "I'd just got in the thing, and lathered up, when a machine gun went off. By the time I got my fatigues on, my flak vest, my helmet and got my M3 grease gun cocked and loaded . . . we couldn't see nothing. It was over the wall." Berlin Brigade radioed the MPs, "and we told them we had a negative report. We didn't see anything. We heard, but we didn't see anything. The next day, we learned that an East German guard had been killed out there."[66]

As former members of the 287th MP Company shared their memories of Steinstuecken for this book, one event in particular stood out. Every interviewee had heard about it. It made headlines in the summer and fall of 1963. From *Stars and Stripes*, September 26:

Gun Firing Costs MP Sergeant

A 28-year old U.S. Army sergeant accused of shooting out light bulbs strung by East German border guards has been convicted of disobeying a superior officer and of being disorderly in a public place.[67]

Long story short: One night, a 287th MP company sergeant who was the detachment NCOIC (Non Commissioned Officer in Charge) in Steinstuecken might have had too much to drink, walked out to the border fence, and shot out several of the GDR border lights.

Keith Koziba was there; he remembers the event vividly. But first a side note: This book will not identify the sergeant by name. What happened in Steinstuecken that night was extraordinary. The sergeant suffered for his actions. This whole affair was undoubtedly a very uncomfortable experience for him—and one he might wish to forget. Moreover, the author has been unable to contact the former sergeant and get his side of the story. This account you are about to read relies on newspaper articles and recollections of other MPs.

Here is how Keith Koziba remembers what happened. It was the night of July 3, 1963. Koziba was patrolling the fence line with the sergeant.

> It was probably 1 or 2 in the morning. We were just walking out there, and those lights were on, and they really lit up Steinstuecken, pretty powerful lights. And he stopped, and we were standing under one light, it was probably about 40 yards away, and 'I'm going to shoot those lights out.' I either said 'OK' or 'go ahead,' I didn't really think that he was going to do anything. And we'd been drinking some beer and he'd had quite a bit of cognac, I didn't realize he was that far gone.
>
> So he pulls out his pistol and he fires seven rounds. I think he hit the reflector once but he didn't knock a light out. And that just made him more upset. And about that time I went down on the ground under a bush, and I could hear what sounded like a machine-gun bolt in the tower, which wasn't that far, about a hundred yards, and I'm thinking "Oh boy, they're going to start shooting."
>
> So we had the grease guns for patrolling there … we were both carrying grease guns. And he opened up with that, and he fired seven or eight rounds, he blew that light out, and from that point he aimed at the next one, which was quite a ways, and he shot that one out, and then he emptied it out on the third light. He shot out all three. And then he decided 'Well, we'd better get back.' So we went back.
>
> A lot of lights went on and off, in a few houses around there, and apparently some of the civilians called Berlin, I don't know if

they talked to the police or the military. And it was about a half-hour later that we got a helicopter out there.[68]

The helicopter carried a relief MP detachment, and several agents from the Army's Criminal Investigation Division (CID). The agents handcuffed the sergeant, Koziba, and the other member of their three-man detachment (who had been back in the mayor's house when the event occurred). They flew all three back to West Berlin. The sergeant confessed immediately, assumed full responsibility, and absolved Koziba and the third MP of any wrongdoing.[69]

The Army suddenly had a public relations stink on its hands. "It was an international incident," said Keith Koziba. The East German Defense Ministry complained formally. It claimed that the sergeant "damaged border installations and threw tear gas grenades into Communist territory."[70] The incident thrust Steinstuecken back into the American newspapers. This UPI wire story ran in the *Fresno Bee* (Fresno, California) on July 8.

East German Reds Charge Attack by US

The East German Communists tonight accused US troops of firing machine gun bullets and tear gas grenades at East German border guards and destroying border fortifications at the US sector enclave of Steinstuecken. The charges apparently are the Communist version of an incident last Wednesday, when a US soldier shot out four of the East German searchlights that ring the isolated hamlet, informed sources said.

A US Army spokesman said 'An incident occurred at Steinstuecken early on the morning of July 3rd. A US military police noncommissioned officer is in custody. We are investigating.' The Communist charge, published by the East German news agency ADN, said the incident took place last Tuesday.... 'Thanks to the restrained attitude of the border troops of the East German national people's army, this attack did not lead to serious consequences,' the Communist statement said.

Another UPI report comes off a bit tongue-in-cheek. "American officials granted that the sergeant had proved himself a good marksman.... The sergeant, apparently bored by his weeklong assignment in an isolated community of only 159 persons, allegedly had a few drinks last Wednesday.... US officials said of the charges against the soldier that it was a serious matter for a military policeman to drink and shoot his gun for the fun of it."[71]

The sergeant was court-martialed in September. He pled guilty. He was reduced in rank to private and fined $50 for three months.[72] (And he never went back to Steinstuecken again.) Neither Koziba nor the other MP were punished.[73]

Public reaction was mixed. "The West Berliners considered [the sergeant] to be a hero," said Koziba. But some of the Steinstueckeners weren't happy at all. "The events along the border like cutting wires or shooting out the lights by MPs were not at all seen as heroic actions," said Elke Hammer. "The exclave's inhabitants feared that such actions, especially by bored or maybe even alcoholized policemen, could lead to unnecessary confrontations" with the Vopos.[74] Steinstueckeners realized what the MPs openly admitted: Three men with grease guns couldn't repel a determined GDR encroachment. Even if the Vopos stopped short of a full invasion but simply harassed the hamlet instead, the peace and quiet that made Steinstuecken special could vanish.

The resident's fears were validated in the same month the sergeant was court-martialed when trouble flared up around Steinstuecken again. From *Stars and Stripes*, September 5, 1963.

> *Red Guards Stone GI Patrol in West Berlin Exclave*
>
> BERLIN (*Stars & Stripes*)—An East German officer exploded two smoke grenades near an American foot patrol Tuesday evening and, a short time later, a group of Communist guards threw stones at the soldiers, hitting one of them in the shoulder, the Army announced.
>
> The two-man patrol, consisting of PFC John A. Craig of Modesto CA and SP4 Francis Reick of Philadelphia, were walking along the border of Steinstuecken, an exclave of West Berlin, when the incidents occurred.
>
> The smoke grenades were thrown at 7:25 PM. They landed about six feet from the patrol and just inside East German territory.
>
> The stone-throwing took place at 8:30. Craig was struck but not injured. Both of the Americans, members of the 287th MP Company, insisted they did nothing to provoke the attack.[75]

In early October the Vopos threw rocks at the MPs and fired smoke grenades again. This is a portion of a UPI wire report on October 3, as it appeared in the *Pasadena Independent* (Pasadena, California).

> An Army spokesman said yesterday that American troops fired tear gas grenades at Communist border guards Monday to protect themselves after the East Germans hurled stones at US military police. The US MPs in the isolated American sector enclave of Steinstuecken 'were following orders,' the spokesman said, when they replied to the Communist stoning with two tear gas grenades and two smoke grenades.
>
> The spokesman made his statement after the East German news agency ADN complained Monday night that US troops had attacked the Communist guards and that the tear gas grenades had landed on the main rail line near the enclave, endangering train traffic. The spokesman described the Communist stone-throwing as 'unprovoked.' He said military police had been authorized, in the face of such provocative action, to take necessary countersteps to protect themselves and West Berlin property.

This time, Berlin Brigade took some of those countersteps. It flew twenty infantrymen into the exclave to reinforce the MP detachment.[76] "The US Army flew combat-equipped infantry to a troublesome sector of the Berlin border Thursday to counter harassment of US patrols by stone-throwing East German border guards," wrote the AP. "MG James H. Polk, the US commandant in Berlin, sent part of an infantry platoon into Steinstuecken by helicopters with orders to stay there as long as there was trouble with the East Germans."[77] The infantry pitched tents in a meadow, then waited to see if the Vopo provocations would cease. They did, and a week later, the Army withdrew the infantrymen.

The light-shooting and stone-throwing incidents were exceptions to the rule. Life in Steinstuecken was mostly quiet after the 287th MP Company arrived. Before then, exclave residents "had felt captured," said Magrit Wiese. They knew their exposed position left them vulnerable. The MP's arrival essentially removed that threat. Steinstuecken could finally relax and enjoy its unique serenity less than a kilometer from the hustle and bustle of West Berlin. A 1967 *Stars and Stripes* article reported that the West Berlin real estate market had noticed. "Last year, German newspapers reported, there were even buyers from West Berlin and West Germany for houses in the exclave."[78]

That same *Stars and Stripes* article made it clear that Steinstuecken was still not a typical West Berlin neighborhood. "At night, the area is lit up like a Christmas display and residents frequently complain of gunfire and flares."[79] But the MPs, now a regular fixture in Steinstuecken, saw no signs of panic. "Nobody was busting their hump to leave," said Ed Hamborski. He sensed no overbearing feeling of fear and dread amongst the residents. "It [i.e., the hamlet of Steinstuecken] looked normal to me. Everybody was casual. The burgermeister's wife was friendly, the fireman's wife would come over and we'd talk. And as we made our rounds the kids would come, and some of them would follow us. People would wave or smile, and just keep going about their business. I never had anybody run up to me and say 'Hey, where are the Vopos today?' It looked and felt like a normal village to me." Hamborski said that Steinstuecken reminded him of his own hometown in western Pennsylvania[80] instead of a Western outpost in the Cold War.

Lucius Clay's determination in September 1961 had paid off. When the 287th MP Company put boots on the ground in Steinstuecken, that finally put the exclave on the path to achieving the same levels of security and peace of mind that other neighborhoods in West Berlin enjoyed. As the 1960s progressed into the 1970s, the Soviets (and their GDR allies) continued to respect the occupation rights of the Western Allies. As of September 23, 1961, those rights included safeguarding Steinstuecken. The Americans didn't press their luck. MPs continued to rotate in and out of the hamlet by helicopter, not truck or Jeep. The US did not push the Communists, and they didn't push back. Life in and around Steinstuecken settled into a cautious but accepted routine. The MP presence made that routine possible. And as the years passed, the MP's friendship and personal relationship with the people of Steinstuecken grew, as the next chapter will show.

CHAPTER NINE

"We know almost everyone in there by name and they know us."
—A West Berlin policeman who manned
the checkpoint on the *Waldweg*, 1967.

The one-man checkpoint on the southwestern fringe of West Berlin has no catchy name, and few camera-toting sightseers manage to find their way there.

There isn't much to it, anyway. A lone cop, a road block that can be raised, a bicycle stand with a few two-wheelers. And the inevitable four-language billboards of the divided city: 'You are leaving the American Sector.'

Beyond that, a dirt road runs through swampy meadows and sparse pines and the 'death strip' to another checkpoint, this one manned by the East Germans.

At the other end of the road—blocked in by coiled barbed wire, concrete obstacles and a wall—lies Steinstuecken, a tiny chunk of West Berlin surrounded by East Germany.

Peter Kuhrt, a *Stars and Stripes* writer, wrote an article about the exclave, "Berlin's Own Little Island," for the military newspaper's May 4, 1967, edition. The opening lines of this chapter, plus the quote at the top of the page, come from that article.

Nearly six years after the Berlin Wall crisis, the Wall had become a tourist attraction. People came to the Brandenburg Gate to see the drab, forbidding barrier that now sealed off the gate, one of Berlin's iconic symbols, from West Berlin. They visited Checkpoint Charlie, the crossing point with the catchy name known around the world, now the only place where Allied personnel could enter East Berlin. Elevated platforms allowed tourists to look into East Berlin. The West German and American governments urged people to come see the Wall for themselves. There was no better place on Earth to compare the Communist and Free Worlds. Pictures of dignitaries like John F. Kennedy, Ronald Reagan, and Martin Luther King Jr. visiting the Wall or giving speeches in front of it appeared often in the Western press.

The checkpoint controlling access from Zehlendorf to Steinstuecken was a much more modest affair than Checkpoint Charlie and in a much calmer corner of Berlin. Peter Kuhrt's description of the activity at the end of a typical workday conveys a sense of quiet routine. "It is 5:30 p.m., about the time when many residents of the 30-acre exclave return from their jobs in the city. Many drive their own cars, but some use the city bus and then mount the bikes they have left in the trusted care of the police guard to pedal to their homes less than a mile across the border. The [West Berlin] policemen posted here usually raise the bar well in advance of approaching cars and are thanked by a brief wave." When the guards knew everyone who's passing through, there was no need to check identity cards. Once the Steinstueckeners cleared the West Berlin police checkpoint, they then went through two GDR checkpoints on the *Waldweg* on their way home.

As a child, Heike Behrendt would go to the GDR checkpoint at the edge of Steinstuecken and wait for her father to come home from his job in Berlin. Normally the Vopos "would keep their distance" from Steinstueckeners, said Behrendt, "because they had been told by their government not to be our friends." But sometimes the children found guards who "were not so strong in their government line. You could have a little conversation with them." Behrendt remembers some of the nicer guards letting her play around the barrier and even sit on the crossbar barrier as she waited for her father.[1]

By mid-1967, life in Steinstuecken was calm and secure. In fact, West Berlin was pretty much calm and secure. The Berlin Wall, that perverse monstrosity that slashed a great city in two, had brought calm. The Wall had kept East Germany from bleeding to death. GDR citizens could no longer use West Berlin as an escape chute to the West.

The Wall was also a shield. It made it much easier for the Communists to shield the GDR's citizens and Eastern Europeans from the West and its corrosive ideas. Free speech, free elections, free enterprise, and other such concepts made it harder for the Communists to indoctrinate—sorry, groom their young people. The Berlin Wall made it much easier to keep those contaminants out of the Soviet bloc. It kept the West out and the Easterners in.

For the Germans, both East and West, the Wall symbolized finality: A door slammed shut and then locked loudly. Before the Wall went up, it was easier for Germans to imagine an end (perhaps soon?) to their country's division. Sure, most Germans understood that was wishful thinking. The Cold War's battle lines were clearly drawn. The incompatibility of communism and the West was unmistakable. No rational German expected a meeting of hearts and minds between Moscow and Washington anytime soon, if ever. But as long as people could move somewhat freely between East and West Berlin, there was always hope.

The Wall dashed those hopes. Once it appeared, and then grew stronger and more forbidding, Germans on both sides of it finally started to drop any hopes that their homeland would reunify anytime soon. They began to sadly think of, and move on with, life in a divided country.

The ugly Wall brought some stability to Berlin. Both sides in the Cold War accepted it. The tensions caused by thoughts (or hopes) of reunification began to lessen. Both sides settled into a sort of normalcy. The American occupiers welcomed this normalcy, especially around Steinstuecken. "We were not going to abandon our position in and around Steinstuecken," recalled W. R Smyser, "but we were not looking to expand it, either."[2] The Americans wanted the Communists to leave Steinstuecken alone, undisturbed. Accordingly, the US avoided making a public issue of this little pocket of the West on Soviet Zone territory. The Americans reasoned that, as long as the exclave wasn't an irritant or embarrassment, the Soviets and East Germans would leave it and its residents in peace.

Life in Steinstuecken was more secure, but it still had many inconveniences. There was still no bus or taxi service. No school buses came from Zehlendorf for the children. If a resident ordered a sofa or refrigerator from a department store in West Berlin, it was very difficult (and often impossible) for the vendor to deliver it. Access rosters still controlled travel into and out of Steinstuecken. The exclave's "mayor" gave the Vopos a list of people who lived in the exclave or had regular business there (e.g., the priest, the postman, the doctor). Anyone not on the list had to request permission. Steinstueckener Annemarie Knecht shared memories of (and frustration with) the permission process with Cold War author Leland McCaslin. "You waited three days for an answer, and in half of the cases that answer was 'NO.'"[3]

As a result, people in West Berlin didn't just "pop in" on their friends or family in Steinstuecken. Annemarie Knecht told Leland McCaslin of one time when her husband Gert decided to skip the whole process. "My father-in-law just wanted to visit us for a cup of coffee. So, my husband took a big risk and smuggled him into the exclave! Gert ran a shop for electric devices, and he was known to handle huge packages in his transporter. He was hardly ever inspected while passing through the checkpoints. So he offered his father a big box to climb into. The border guards thought he was delivering a refrigerator and waved him through. We spent a nice family afternoon."[4] Some people went to the trouble of officially establishing a second residence, or address, in Steinstuecken. This was possible when someone had friends or family in the village or when an exclave resident agreed to sponsor them. People with second "residences" in Steinstuecken could get on the access roster.

The separation from West Berlin was especially difficult on the exclave's children, who had friends in Zehlendorf. "For any kids coming from the Zehlendorf area," said Ralph Sanchez, the distance they'd have to travel "wasn't just a walk across the block. People would be somewhat apprehensive because that roadway [the *Waldweg*] from the West Berlin barrier to the East Berlin barrier was one kilometer, and it was all in the forest." Parents could escort the children—if they were on the access roster.

"My birthdays were so boring because I couldn't invite my classmates and friends," exclave resident Gudrun Neumann told Leland McCaslin. "They would have to go through permission paperwork and were usually denied. Or, their parents were too anxious to let the kids go to the exclave. So we celebrated with our neighbors and two boys who were much older than me. I still get tears in my eyes when I remember my biggest birthday party, with twelve classmates and wonderful outdoor games, held in Wannsee—organized by one of my closest friends as a surprise for me!"[5] Heike Behrendt said that she had two sets of friends—those in school and those in the exclave.[6]

Steinstuecken's isolation had some upsides for its children. Because there was little to no car or truck traffic, the streets were usually empty. Ralph Sanchez said that, whenever he wanted to throw the football with an MP colleague or some of the children, there was always an open street to play on.

Another benefit to living in a neighborhood that was walled in and heavily guarded: no crime. "We kids were super safe because no stranger could get in," said Heike Behrendt. "Our parents let us go free in the evenings to play." The parents would even go to the Vopos at the checkpoint and tell them which children were too young to leave the hamlet. If these children tried to walk or ride up the *Waldweg*, the Vopos would refuse to lift the barrier.[7]

The Wall relieved (or at least lessened) one ongoing fear: being snatched by Vopos. Before the Berlin Wall crisis, Vopos could simply walk across the street and enter the village. Johannes Niemeyer wrote of an eerie encounter he had with some GDR guards and workmen who'd trespassed into Steinstuecken. When Niemeyer told them to leave, one of the Vopos warned that, if he wasn't careful, he might disappear someday.[8] The permanent barbed-wire barriers, followed by the concrete Wall, made it difficult for Vopos to enter Steinstuecken.

Some residents who lived next to the border found it difficult—if not impossible—to use the front doors of their own houses. Christine Clark and her husband Tom, one of the helicopter pilots who flew Clay into Steinstuecken on his historic visit, became friends with Kurt Behrendt and his wife Helga. In her book *Letters from Berlin*, Clark remarks that the Behrendt's home "during the Cold War could only be entered through the back door, as the front yard was fenced in and not accessible because it fronted the East German border."[9] Dieter Giertz recalled that "the borderline divided the Steinstrasse (one of the boundary streets) in the middle, and the no man's land included the sidewalk and parts of peoples' gardens." Residents had to build alternate paths to enter their houses.[10]

Another upside to living in an isolated place: It made the exclave (and its residents) somewhat mysterious. Imagine if you had been a West Berliner during the Cold War. There would have been one neighborhood in your city that you often read about in the newspapers—but you could not visit it, drive through it, or even look at it from a distance. (You couldn't see Steinstuecken from Zehlendorf because of the woods.) That made some people curious. Checkpoint Kohlhasenbrueck wasn't nearly as famous as its Charlie counterpart, but it still drew visitors. When Steinstueckeners passed by, the tourists would occasionally ask questions about the exclave.

The children gladly answered. "People would be standing at the first checkpoint in Kohlhasenbrueck, and asking 'What is it like in there,'" recalled Magrit Wiese. "They would ask, 'Do you have cows?' They had no idea."[11] Some youngsters proved to be *bona fide* entrepreneurs. "We children went to Kohlhasenbrück on Sundays to explain to 'Wall-Watchers' the situation in Steinstücken," remembered Heike Behrendt. "Often they rewarded us with 10 pfennings, and we spent that money to get ice cream."[12]

Even after the Berlin Wall went up, the hamlet still needed an official representative to deal directly with the Vopos and the GDR authorities. West Berliners and the Americans could avoid contact with the East Germans, but the Steinstueckeners couldn't. The duty fell to the Zehlendorf administrative representative.

Often referred to as the "mayor" of Steinstuecken, the administrative representative was a hamlet resident who worked for the Zehlendorf *Bezirk* government. He/she was a liaison between the Brandenburg authorities and Zehlendorf. Vopos and other GDR officials came to the administrative representative to complain about West Berlin or American personnel or policies. Steinstuecken residents came to her/him when they had problems with the American MP detachment. When the hamlet needed to talk to the East Germans about matters like road maintenance on the *Waldweg* or trash removal, the administrative representative would contact the Vopos. Zehlendorf keeps copies of the reports the administrative representative sent during the Cold War years. They offer a good (and often entertaining) insight into some of the problems caused by the hamlet's isolation.

On January 5, 1962, the Vopos requested a meeting with the mayor, Herr Reichow. In his report, Reichow said that a Vopo lieutenant told him that several Steinstueckeners had complained to the GDR border guards. Their concern? Some "Steinstuecken motorists weren't complying with the speed limit on the *Waldweg*." The complainers claimed the reckless driving put them "constantly in mortal danger."

The Vopos didn't care. The lieutenant said they "have no interest in issuing tickets for an infringement that, in West Berlin, would cost 5 DM. But, if the Vopos keep getting complaints, measures would be taken." Any speeding Steinstueckeners would "have to travel by foot" from the hamlet to Zehlendorf.

Reichow replied that he, as a Zehlendorf *Bezirk* employee, had no authority to punish drivers for anything they did on the *Waldweg*. The *Waldweg* ran through Brandenburg. All he could do was "remind the people who use the road." Reichow then countered with a complaint of his own. "A greater danger on the road, according to the residents, is that in the case of black ice and snow the *Waldweg* is not cleared. We have been forced to hire a private company to clear the *Waldweg* and carry out the trash, after the [West Berlin] city street cleaners and garbage services were denied access to our neighborhood. The Vopos also deny access to East German electricity, gas and waterworks personnel, even though we have paid our fees and the GDR must have an interest in keeping these services regulated and maintained."[13] Steinstuecken homeowners used Potsdam utilities and paid for those services. A Vopo officer responded that "the obligation to remove trash, remove snow and ice from the Waldweg and the entrances to the city are our [i.e., the exclave's] responsibility."[14]

Utilities and public services were a constant irritant. The road surface on the *Waldweg* was often bad. For tires, it could be fatal. A report from the Zehlendorf administrative office, dated November 1, 1968, stated the following: "Today, Herr Blischke informed the office that he had an accident" on the *Waldweg*. "His vehicle struck one of the potholes and it burst his right front tire."[15] When exclave residents asked *Land* Brandenburg to provide public services, the GDR often claimed that it was West Berlin's responsibility.

The Vopos made it difficult for West Berlin city maintenance to support the exclave. The GDR's guidelines on which city employees could visit the hamlet, how much advance notice they had to give, or what kind of pass they had to obtain changed constantly. The administrative representative was forever chasing down the latest GDR position on who could visit when and under what conditions. For instance, Reichow received this guidance from the Vopos on April 7, 1962: "In the matter of the fire department: In case of an emergency, the fire department can come to Steinstuecken without permission. For special work that the fire department needs to carry out, it must request permission in writing from the Vopos. Then the work can occur."[16]

The Vopos hindered commercial traffic, too. On January 5, 1962, when the Vopos met with Herr Reichow about speeding on the *Waldweg*, they also discussed freight deliveries. "A border patrol lieutenant said that, in the future, when individual companies want to make a delivery to Steinstuecken, they have to clear it with the border post. It doesn't matter who is getting the delivery" or what the cargo was. Reichow replied that West Berlin companies would "be informed of the new provisions and that the administrative office" would notify the Vopos in advance of future deliveries.[17] Throughout the 1960s—just as they had in the 1950s—the GDR tightened restrictions on deliverymen, then relaxed them, then tightened them again.

When the Vopos felt that hamlet residents or American MPs were misbehaving, they'd demand to meet with the administrative representative. "Residents of Steinstuecken curse at and harass our sentries, when they are in the presence of the Americans," the Vopos told Reichow at their April 7, 1962 encounter. "We know these people. We will take measures here, if necessary. These residents will in the future not be allowed to leave or enter Steinstuecken. Please warn them."[18] (Apparently nothing came of this threat. There is no known instance of the Vopos ever forbidding a resident from leaving the exclave in the 1960s).

Six months later the Vopos were back, this time to complain about the MPs. "The MPs have damaged the border fence, which belongs to the GDR, and which the MPs may not search, in 11 places by cutting through it. The MP guards were drunk and scolded our soldiers, even loaded their submachine guns and threatened to shoot. We will not allow this any longer. We are concerned, because we also have some very young soldiers on duty, who might, in a very tense session, be provoked into shooting. It is therefore certainly possible that there could be an innocent shooting incident."[19]

If this sounds familiar—it is. In the previous chapter, Charlie Smith, a former MP, said he had cut down a section of border fence that the Vopos had fastened to a tree inside Steinstuecken. Smith later heard the Vopos had approached the Zehlendorf administrative representative with a warning: Some of our border guards are young and inexperienced and might react violently if the MPs continue to provoke them.

The Vopos and the MPs never traded gunfire, ever, as far as the author can tell. Steinstuecken residents interviewed for this book remember the MPs warmly. The author's impression—-a very strong impression—is that the people of Steinstuecken in general felt that the 287th MP Company's duty performance in the exclave and the behavior of its personnel was professional and often exemplary.

But no one is perfect. From time to time the Zehlendorf administrative representative received complaints from villagers about MP behavior.

> May 26th, 1962: At night, a family discovered 3 drunk MPs violently kicking and pounding the door of the closed restaurant. When someone opened a window and asked them what they were doing, they demanded that the restaurant be opened immediately, so they could watch television.
>
> April 6th, 1966: Herr Grutzmacher shared this today: An American sergeant complained that the Steinstuecken resident hired to cook for the Americans often didn't prepare food for them. The residents observed that, at mealtimes/gatherings the sergeant consumed beer and spirits from a flask. The group of soldiers he was part of also had beer in their quarters. This irritated some of the exclave residents. The office of Major Baker {presumably a US Army officer] was telephoned, and informed about the matter. The office asked that the Burgermeister's office not be immediately informed of this matter, but instead allow the matter to be handled unofficially.

The 287th MP Company's leaders knew their men in Steinstuecken were on display. They were keen to avoid problems and quickly squelch any that did arise. One month later the MP sergeant caused more trouble. In early May 1966 the administrative representative complained to the Americans again. The sergeant had reportedly brought more beer to the exclave. He was openly unhappy with the meals his host fed the MPs. He got into an argument with a Steinstuecken resident in which he supposedly used "a harsh and unruly tone."

This prompted a visit from a US Army captain named Schneeweis. Presumably, he was the 287th MP company commander. He expressed his regrets and affirmed that MPs were not allowed to use alcohol while in Steinstuecken. The captain asked the administrative representative to call him if similar problems reoccurred. He gave a phone number where he could always be reached, and he promised to intervene immediately. Captain Schneeweis said that his soldiers liked duty in Steinstuecken, and he only wanted to send good soldiers there. The administrative representative replied that, except for this one sergeant, all the other MPs had behaved impeccably.[20] "During my time in Steinstuecken, I had one guy that got pretty 'tipsy' once," recalls Jerome Weilmuenster. "I had a conversation with the first sergeant, and he was not assigned to Steinstuecken again."

Magrit Wiese, the girl whose parents smuggled a refugee to West Berlin, was featured in several reports from early May 1962.

> "May 8 1962: Frau Wiese brings Magrit to the *Nebenstelle* [the Zehlendorf government office in Steinstuecken]. Magrit reports that, earlier in the day, at 11:30, she was coming home from school. On the Waldweg, she was summoned to see a GDR officer in their watchroom. The officer showed her a magazine photo, in which she was visible." He wanted to know who took the picture. "He asked: 'You really don't know who took this picture? You are looking into the camera.'" [Apparently the Vopos had already questioned Magrit about this photograph.]
>
> Magrit answered: 'No, I really don't know who took the picture, there were many people in Steinstuecken who took pictures that day.'
>
> 11 May. This morning her daughter Magrit was again questioned by a Vopo officer. 'Do you know now who took the picture?' 'No.'
>
> Herr Wiese had complained the previous day to the Grenzpost [border police checkpoint] and said that they should leave the children alone. The post replied: We know nothing about this!
>
> The Warlich parents are saying that their child, after the US helicopter came, was questioned by a GDR officer at the railroad crossing at Steinstrasse: 'Who came in on the helicopter today?' The parents mentioned this to the US sergeant on duty.

Some reports tell of refugees escaping into the exclave. On August 9, 1962, Reichow wrote that a Vopo escaped into Steinstuecken by hitching a ride on a freight train passing through the hamlet. He appeared at the *Nebenstelle* with all his equipment. Immediately afterwards, the Vopos asked to meet with Reichow. This prompted a visit the next morning from Lt. Vern Pike of the 287th MP Company. Pike thought the Vopos might retaliate against Reichow. "Our concern was that Herr Reichow not put himself in a delicate situation with the Vopos, that may require we Americans to bail him out," Pike told the author in an e-mail. Reichow told Pike that he was careful to limit his activities to administrative matters only.[21] One month later, Reichow had more visitors. Four refugees contacted MPs near the *Nebenstelle* and asked for asylum. A fifth refugee had a mental breakdown as he tried to breach the barbed wire fence, and the Vopos caught him.[22]

Some of the reports are quite funny. "Feb 19th 1962: Report from Herr Reichow. [A resident] comes to the office. He says that the three Americans in Steinsuecken have plenty of free time on their hands. He would like to ask that this office arrange for the MPs to be tasked to clear away some cut-down trees that are lying on exclave property. He will donate a bottle of schnapps as payment. The representative [Herr Reichow] explained that his office cannot issue instructions to the MPs. They are here to protect the inhabitants."

Later that year, the GDR border guards apparently decided to have some fun at Herr Reichow's expense. On October 17 Reichow summoned a Vopo officer to complain. One morning, he drove through the Kohlhasenbrueck checkpoint and headed into West Berlin. Once in the city, several people came up to him and asked if he now supported the GDR. They pointed to his car bumper—which sported a GDR banner. Reichow was sure the Vopos had put it there. "I consider this matter an episode of gross mischief," he told the Vopo officer. "The GDR officer clarified the date and time of the event, and said this was a dumb, juvenile prank. They will try to determine who did it. The consultation was conducted in a friendly tone. The officer said goodbye with a handshake."[23] Many of the Zehlendorf administrative representative's meetings with Vopo officials were cordial and professional. It seems that everyone—the Americans, the Steinstueckeners, and the local GDR authorities—recognized the value in getting along with each other as much as possible.

The adults in Steinstuecken did their best to mitigate all the inconveniences of exclave life. They organized and improvised to provide the services that would be an afterthought in any other Berlin neighborhood. "During the 60s our community grew very close together," said Wilfried Hammer. "Everybody watched out for each other and many of us took over social duties. Herr Tauchert collected trashcans, and Frau Behrendt drove the kids to school."[24] The West Berlin government subsidized a small bus, and an exclave resident drove it.

Frau Behrendt's mother once tried to sneak her nephew, who lived in Berlin, into Steinstuecken for a quick visit. He was twenty, so she hoped the Vopos at the checkpoint would think he was one of the exclave's high-school age residents. She loaded her nephew into the bus with the other high school children and drove up to the GDR checkpoint. The Vopos weren't fooled. But these particular guards were, as Heike put it, not so strong in the GDR government line. They let Frau Behrendt and her nephew pass—but they warned her to have the boy out of the exclave before the next shift change at the checkpoint. Who knew how "strong in the government line" the next guards would be?[25]

Herr Steinweg continued to operate his grocery store. This gave Steinstueckeners a local source for basic food and household items. Fresh rolls and bread are a passion for Germans at breakfast. "Every Berliner—and every Steinstückener, too—loves freshly baked 'Schrippen' [small rolls with a hard crust] in the morning," said Wilfried Hammer.[26] *Stars and Stripes* reporter Peter Kuhrt wrote that the store's operators took "special pride in providing milk and fresh rolls by their 8AM opening time."[27] However, the Steinwegs' store didn't have its own bakery. Fresh bread had to come from Zehlendorf. So, someone from the store made the trip up the *Waldweg* and back, several times a week, *very* early in the morning, to fetch it.

Wilfried Hammer helped. Even though he worked a full-time job in West Berlin, he made time to fetch groceries. Wilfried drove an Isetta, a tiny three-wheeled microcar with only one door, on the front of the car. Some days he had to go by bicycle instead, pulling a cart big enough to carry all the supplies.[28] "On sunny summer days it was fun, but sometimes, when there was wind and snow, I regretted having taken the job," Wilfried Hammer told Leland McCaslin. "Mostly I did my job well and on time—but I was a young man then. I spent some evenings with friends, going to the movies, and came home very late. Every once in a while the Steinstückeners had to wait a little longer for their breakfast." After he delivered the groceries, Wilfried "had to make the 25km to my office racing the poor Isetta. My boss frowned at me for being late on the job, but he never threatened me with any penalties since he knew about the special situation of our exclave."[29]

As for the MPs, the nature of their duties complicated efforts to make friends with the exclave residents. The people in Steinstuecken were very friendly. However, with only three or four soldiers in the exclave at any one time, the MPs didn't have lots of free time to spend visiting the neighbors. They were generally on patrol, on radio watch, or sleeping. "We didn't go socialize," remembers Herbert Judd. "We didn't go next door and say, oh 'How are you doing?' We just made our patrols."[30]

The MPs interviewed for this book shared some stories of the time they spent with Steinstueckeners. The MPs often ate dinner with their German hosts. Jerome Weilmuenster remembers the conversations at those meals. "One of the guys in my squad could eat a dozen scrambled eggs in about 15 seconds. Our host lost a 5 DM bet on that one." Weilmunster also remembered "the deep, absolute hatred our host had for Communists. After he had had a couple of drinks, the only thing he would talk about was the number of Communists he had killed in the war."[31]

Heike Behrendt's parents talked the MPs into helping them around the house. They needed to go into Berlin one day, and they couldn't take Heike and her baby brother Jorg. So....

> I remember one time the Americans came to babysit, when my brother was a half-year old. They came in from patrol, and they were in uniform with all their weapons. And they put their weapons on the cupboard, to make sure the children could not reach them, for safety. My mother showed them in the kitchen where to warm up the milk for the baby. And then my parents left, and the MPs were babysitting there, in their uniforms and helmets. If you would tell that to somebody outside of Steinstuecken, in Berlin or in West Germany, it was very strange for them to imagine that people in uniform can be used for babysitting.[32]

"In our life" in Steinstuecken, said Behrendt, "we came in contact with people with weapons and with uniforms every day. We found them to be nice and friendly, and we knew what they were doing there. We knew that they were there to help us for our security, and so it was not a strange feeling for us. It was very common."

Dieter Giertz told McCaslin of another, much-less-happy occasion when the MPs came to visit—the assassination of President Kennedy. Here is Dieter's diary entry from that day:

> 22 November 1963: John F. Kennedy was shot dead! The three American MPs who were on guard asked my parents if they could watch TV for that matter. At that time there were just two TV sets in Steinstücken: the official one at Steinweg's restaurant and ours. Since the MPs were stationed in the basement of Herr Amtsvorsteher Reichow's house, and my parents often invited Mr. and Mrs. Reichow to watch TV with them, it was not too strange to see the soldiers come with them. But they came in full arms! So they put their weapons, helmet etc., on my parents' bed before getting settled in the living room.[33]

The Army did more for Steinstuecken than just send helicopters loaded with soldiers and VIPs. The Berlin Brigade performed several public service projects for the exclave. These projects demonstrated the Americans' commitment to the hamlet and also brightened life there. (They also made for great public relations).

Berlin Brigade built a playset for the children. It was shaped like a helicopter. "They brought that in by helicopter," recalls Ralph Sanchez. "They made a gigantic sandbox, and that's where the kids from Steinstucken used to congregate and play."[34]

The 287th MP Company included Steinstuecken in one of the Army's finest traditions: Thanksgiving and Christmas dinners. Army posts worldwide bend over backwards to stage lavish holiday meals. The mess halls cook a wide variety of side dishes and desserts to complement the hams and turkeys that are the stars of the show. The cooks and servers wear their best outfits. Commanders and senior NCOs wear their dress uniforms and medals and often carve the hams and turkeys. Soldiers bring their families, and everyone feasts. For Army units deployed overseas, the Thanksgiving and Christmas dinners are a welcome reminder of home. Weeks in advance, commanders track the planning of the holiday meals to ensure plenty of food will be on hand.

Starting in 1961, the 287th MP Company invited the people of Steinstuecken to join in the company's holiday dinners. For the first few years, the MPs brought dinner to the exclave. John Mentor, a lieutenant in the company during the Berlin Wall Crisis, remembered the very first dinner. "I don't know why, but someone had that idea" to take Thanksgiving dinner out to Steinstuecken.. "I happened to be the duty officer" on Thanksgiving Day," so I flew out with the other MPs, on the helicopter, and we took Thanksgiving dinner out to the people of Steinstuecken. We brought out the turkey and the mashed potatoes and the pumpkin pie—it was a typical American Thanksgiving dinner."

It was a smashing success. "The people were really happy about it, and it was a wonderful community relations gesture on our part," says Mentor. "We took the marmite cans with the food out there, and all the people gathered and came into what seemed to be a large community room. I think they knew we were coming, because they all gathered at a certain time, and they seemed to have a good appetite."[35]

Dieter Giertz recalled the event in his diary:

> 23 November 1961: I was invited along with all kids of Steinstücken to participate at an American Thanksgiving dinner at our local restaurant Steinweg. All supplies came by helicopter, even the cook! I didn't know turkey could taste that good. All in all life isn't quite bad here.[36]

"We learned about a lot of new American foods, things we Germans did not know before," said Heike Behrendt. "Sweet potatoes, nobody knew about them," and also cranberry sauce and pumpkin pie.[37]

At Christmas time, the Army brought another visitor to the exclave—Santa Claus. From the December 21, 1962, issue of *Stars and Stripes:*

> *Copters Fly Toys to Steinstuecken*
>
> A fleet of four helicopters substituted for Santa Claus' reindeer to fly toys to the children of isolated Steinstucken, a small exclave of West Berlin. Members of the 287th MP Company took toys to the 46 children of the agricultural community which lies southeast of West Berlin. The area is completely surrounded by the Soviet Zone. PFC Winfred Radoch, a German-speaking soldier, took the role of Santa Claus at a party Wednesday afternoon.

In 1969, West German television showed elderly retirees receiving television sets and other Christmas goods. "Santa Claus is not only on a sledge this year," the narrator said. "Presents destined for the exclave of Steinstuecken, a little West Berlin island in GDR territory, are being flown in by helicopter." The telecast showed Santa Claus waving as he left the exclave ... in a Berlin Brigade Huey.[38]

A few years later, the MPs added something more to the holiday festivities. They invited the exclave's children to join them at the company mess hall for Thanksgiving and Christmas. A new tradition started. Steinstuecken children (and a few chaperones), dressed for a holiday party, traveled up the *Waldweg*, through the Vopo checkpoints, to Army buses waiting at Kohlhasenbrueck to ferry them to the MP mess hall at Andrews Barracks.

The *Berlin Observer*, the newspaper for the American military community in Berlin, covered several of these parties. The *Observer* ran this article on December 6, 1968.

> *MPs, Exclave Kids Share Thanksgiving*
>
> The 287th Military Police mess hall bore more than a little resemblance of the Peanut Gallery of the old 'Howdy Doody Show' this past Thanksgiving Day as 45 children from the tiny Berlin exclave of Steinstuecken were hosted to the traditional turkey-with-trimmings meal.
>
> The children were met at the East German barrier and bussed to the company in mid-afternoon. Accompanying them to the company were members of the Military Police.
>
> This year marked the seventh time that the Divided City MPs, in keeping with the American tradition of sharing, invited Steinstuecken residents to take part in a Thanksgiving dinner.
>
> However, this year a departure from the ordinary was made in hosting the children to a special meal at the MP company.
>
> Two days later, November 30, Thanksgiving was taken to the adult population of the isolated village cut off from the rest of West Berlin by the East German Border.
>
> A heavy fog made carrying the dinner and personnel to the village via helicopter inadvisable. The entire meal was transported to the border by Berlin Brigade trucks where it was then transported to the community by volunteer Steinstuecken residents.

Heike Behrendt and her friends would collect autographs from their American hosts. The soldiers gladly obliged, and sometimes drew cartoons on the menus. One year, the MP company commander heard how the children liked to gather autographs. He escorted the children and their chaperones to the MP barracks. There they saw "a big line of soldiers, and they all had a pencil or pen," recalls Behrendt. "They were standing straight in one line, like a parade."[39]

For one MP and one Steinstuecken lady, the Cold War led to something positive and permanent: marriage. Ralph Sanchez, the MP who leapt out of his bath when Willi Marzahn's escape attempt led to gunfire, met and fell in love with Magrit Wiese. *Stars and Stripes* wrote about their romance in its January 28, 1986 issue. The article was titled "Courting in Steinstuecken."

> Magrit Sanchez said she first met the young MP who would become her husband one day when the Americans were playing with some local children and one boy was injured. Ralph Sanchez picked up the child and took him home to explain what had happened. Magrit went along and the two hit it off.
>
> A Cold War romance was not without its problems, the couple said. One big problem was the hot war going on thousands of miles away in Vietnam that claimed Ralph Sanchez as a participant. He returned to Berlin in 1968, nourished by the German delicacies shipped to him in Vietnam by the Wiese family.
>
> Sanchez, by then a sergeant, had to wangle helicopter rides into the Steinstuecken exclave. 'Instead of going home I elected to take my leave in Steinstuecken,' he said.... When Ralph was unable to drop in, Magrit would meet him at the Kohlhasenbrueck border checkpoint in a forested section of West Berlin.
>
> The flowering romance between a young German girl and an American GI did not go unnoticed by the East Germans, who studied Magrit's identification card each time she made the trip to West Berlin. At times, the future Mrs. Sanchez was subjected to minor harassment, she said.
>
> 'They knew everything. Even from the towers they watch you with binoculars,' said Sanchez. 'It was uncomfortable.'

Ralph Sanchez remembers a time when he made the Vopos uncomfortable. One Christmas, Ralph got permission to fly into Steinstuecken with the next relief MP detachment, so he could spend the holiday with Magrit and her family. When the helicopter landed and the MPs offloaded, the watching Vopos got a surprise. They saw a typical MP detachment get off the helicopter—three soldiers in fatigues. But they also saw a fourth MP get off, wearing the more formal Class A uniform, normally worn only at official functions. Soldiers also wear the Class A uniform when traveling on leave, as Ralph was. But the Vopos didn't know that. They didn't know what to make of this extra MP in formal attire. To this day Ralph Sanchez chuckles as he recalls the Vopos in the nearby watchtower grabbing binoculars to watch him and radioing their superiors.[40]

Ralph and Magrit Sanchez married on June 6, 1969, in a small church on the West Berlin border.[41] Magrit eventually left the exclave to start a family and travel with Ralph throughout his Army career. Ralph retired from the Army after twenty-three years of service. He, Magrit, and their children then lived in West Germany while Ralph taught law enforcement classes for an American college that served military personnel.[42] When American forces in Germany downsized after the Berlin Wall fell, Ralph and Magrit moved to El Paso, where they live today.

By the 1970s, life in Steinstuecken had settled into a quiet routine. Its people felt secure. "We were a very tiny community," said Heike Behrendt. "Everyone knew that we did not do very bad things, to each other or to the East German soldiers or the Americans. We were quite harmless."[43]

Yet there was always some uncertainty in the air. The watchtowers, the searchlights, the Wall, the barbed wire fences surrounding the *Waldweg*—they constantly reminded exclave residents that, if the Cold War went sour, their lives could quickly go sour too. But in the meantime, as long as the war stayed cold, the people of Steinstuecken could live a relatively normal life. The villagers, the West Berlin government, and the American and Soviet occupation authorities all wanted Steinstuecken to stay an unnoticed place that didn't spark controversy. So, it did. (The East Germans were unhappy, but the Soviets kept them in line).

In 1972, as détente lessened tensions between the US and USSR, a breakthrough occurred that changed life in Steinstuecken forever. The Soviets and East Germans finally agreed to give West Berlin its very own road to the exclave.

CHAPTER TEN

"...from now on, we know we really belong" [to West Berlin]
—Steinstuecken resident Gertrude Vogel, on the meaning of the new road from Steinstuecken to Zehlendorf. (From an Associated Press article in *Stars and Stripes*, December 25, 1971).

The Berlin Wall crisis didn't just make the people of West Berlin fearful and uncertain. It made them angry, too. Angry at the Communists, of course—the people who'd strung the wire and tore up the streets. But many West Berliners were also angry at the Western Allies, especially the Americans. Many had assumed that the Western Allies would use force to keep access to East Berlin open. When they didn't, outrage erupted in the Western sectors. A headline in the German newspaper *Bild* shrieked, "The East acts—and what does the West do? The West does NOTHING!"[1]

Lucian Hechler, a State Department political officer in Berlin, felt some of that outrage firsthand. Hechler had the thankless duty of giving West Berlin Mayor Willy Brandt a copy of the Western Allies' formal protest note to the Soviets over the border closure. How did Brandt react when he read it?

"Oh, he boiled over," Hechler said. "The whole wrath of this man—and he really could get pretty angry—descended upon my innocent, junior shoulders. I was given a history lesson unlike any other I have ever received, because he started to lecture me. ... For some surprising reason Brandt had believed—rather naively—that the 'Protective Powers,' as he called the three Western Occupying Powers, would move with courage and dispatch to stop this latest Eastern outrage."[2]

Willy Brandt wasn't the only German leader to remark on the Western Allies' lack of action. On September 15th, Walter Ulbricht, the GDR's leader, wrote Khruschev on the results of the border closure.

"The tactic of gradually carrying out the measures made it more difficult for the adversary to orient himself with regard to the extent of our measures," he said. "I must say that the adversary undertook fewer countermeasures than was expected."[3]

"The building of the Wall had a very important effect on German policy on the part of Willy Brandt in particular," recalled Arthur Day, chief of the State Department's political section in Berlin from 1962 to 1966. "He read the American response to the building of the Wall quite correctly as being an abandonment really of the concept of reunification, at least for the foreseeable future, and a willingness to abide by a *de facto* division of Germany which would be maintained by the Soviets on one side and the Allies on the other peacefully and not challenged by either side."[4] "Reunification of Germany seemed a fading prospect, and was mentioned less frequently in the West," said Brandon Grove, a US liaison officer in Berlin from 1965 to 1969. "The division seemed nearly complete."[5]

That didn't sit well with Willy Brandt. By August 1961, Germany had been shorn in two for sixteen years. The eastern and western halves of Germany had begun to morph into different entities—a capitalist West Germany and a communist East Germany. As children were born and grew up, they adopted the beliefs and attitudes of their surroundings. By August 1961, a child growing up in Dresden (an East Germany city) lived in a different society and economy than a child growing up in Dusseldorf (a West German city). Nine years later, in 1970, Brandt warned that two different and opposing "state and social systems" had taken root on German soil. These two systems "manifest entirely different and incompatible views on what constitutes German unity, and what a common future looks like and how it is to be achieved."[6]

Brandt passionately wanted to reunite Germany. He saw Germany as still one nation, just temporarily divided. "The word 'nation' encompasses and means more than common language and culture, more than state and social system," Brandt told the *Bundestag* in January 1970. "The word 'nation' is based on the continuous feeling of belonging together, held by the people of a nation."[7]

Brandt feared that Germans on either side of the East-West border were gradually losing any "feeling of belonging together." The Western Allies' muted response to the Berlin Wall led him to conclude that West Berlin's "Protecting Powers" had pretty much given up on German reunification. Willy Brandt couldn't accept that. "We must prevent a further drifting apart of the German nation," Brandt told the *Bundestag* in October 1969.[8]

Many Germans felt the Cold War separation personally; they had family on both sides of the border. The GDR was stingy with border crossing passes. It was difficult (if not impossible) for people in the West to visit the East. Many West Germans hadn't seen friends and family there for years. Gail Halvorsen was an Air Force pilot who flew supplies into Berlin during the airlift. He returned to West Berlin in 1970 as the commander of Templehof Airbase. Halvorsen remembered a sad—but, sadly, not uncommon—sight: People on opposite sides of the Wall waving to each other. Halvorsen said that families divided by the border would send letters to one another and schedule a time and place to meet along the Wall.[9]

West Berlin itself was still in Cold War limbo. There was no formal diplomatic agreement between the two sides for a lasting coexistence. The GDR didn't accept West Berlin as a freestanding political entity. It claimed that *all* of Berlin sat on the territory of—and belonged to—the GDR. The Soviets supported the GDR's legal position. The Soviets did prevent the GDR from permanently blocking traffic between West Germany and West Berlin. They did restrain the GDR from threatening West Berlin's internal peace and security. But they hadn't given any written assurances they'd restrain the GDR forever.

That left West Berlin in a tough spot. The GDR had shown time and time again that, if they wished, they would harass commerce between the Western sectors and West Germany. Here is an excerpt of a State Department report on one example: "All German surface traffic was stopped by the GDR for one day in October 1957 to facilitate the East German currency conversion. At the same time the East Germans detained, examined, and in some cases confiscated, West German parcel post shipments."[10] They also raised tolls arbitrarily.

The West German government mitigated the impact of those toll increases, by helping pay the costs. The legal issues, however, remained murky. When Khrushchev threatened to sign a separate peace treaty with the GDR in 1958, the Eisenhower and Adenauer administrations looked for existing legal precedents that supported uninterrupted access to West Berlin. They "found that the access rights of the Allied garrisons were clear but that the legal basis of civilian access was muddy because the 1949 agreements had merely confirmed a situation which had not been clear before."[11]

The New York Agreement of May 4 and the Paris Four Power Communique of June 20, 1949 were the only formal agreements between the Soviets and the Western Allies since the Berlin Blockade ended that touched on civilian traffic. The New York Agreement said only that the Soviet Union and the Western Powers would drop the traffic restrictions levied during the blockade and then would meet later for further discussions that would "consider questions relating to Germany and problems arising out of the situation in Berlin."[12] The Paris Four-Power communique was more detailed. But it contained no explicit Soviet assurances that civilian traffic between West Germany and West Berlin could move freely.

In other words, neither of the two primary diplomatic agreements controlling civilian travel between West Germany and West Berlin specifically and unambiguously guaranteed that commercial and personal traffic could continue by rail, road, or waterway forever. (Air travel was covered by separate Four-Power agreements). The Eisenhower and Adenauer administrations "feared that the Soviets might concentrate on the attrition of civilian communications rather than Allied access,"[13] as a way to smother West Berlin. West German Foreign Minister Heinrich Brentano said that "the situation would be dangerous if the Soviets should accept Allied rights of access but contest the right of civilian."[14] Khrushchev said again and again that, once the USSR signed a peace treaty with the GDR, it would let the GDR control any civilian traffic through "its" territory. Once the Wall went up, the USSR ensured the GDR respected the travel rights of the Western Powers. But it did let the East Germans impose restrictions on German civilian traffic.

In the early 1970s, West Berlin was in good shape. The city's people and economy were doing well. But West Berlin was still in limbo. And you really can't plan for (or count on) the future if you're in limbo. Konrad Adenauer had voiced that concern years earlier, in discussions on possible solutions to Berlin's problems in March 1960. Adenauer felt that a "temporary agreement" with the Russians on West Berlin would be "dangerous." "To conclude a contractual arrangement for one, two, or three years would mean constant blackmail thereafter. A contractual arrangement would bring insecurity and uncertainty; there would be a bad effect on the Berlin population, and large numbers would leave the city."[15] West Berlin needed an explicit, lasting agreement with the USSR in order to have a bright future.

By the mid-1960s, Willy Brandt had doubts about the Western Allies' ability, and especially their desire, to solve all these problems. Lucian Hechler recalled that, when the Western Powers didn't tear down the GDR's hasty barbed wire barricades in the early days of the Berlin Wall crisis, Brandt "suddenly lost his faith in the Allies; his confidence in the West collapsed all of a sudden."[16] State Department official William Bodde said that Brandt was "disenchanted with the lack of action on the part of the U.S. when the East Germans erected the Wall." So disenchanted, in fact, that he looked for a new approach for dealing with the East. Bodde said Brandt apparently "decided it was up to the Germans themselves to find a solution to the division of their country."[17]

"Brandt felt," recalled Arthur Day, "that if this was the way the Allies were going to play the game, it was time to stop entertaining hopes for reunification and to begin to think about improving the lives of people of the two sides of the Wall, but especially on the East side, in what was likely to be a long reality of separation."[18] Brandt "developed the concept that something had to be done to change what he called this 'frozen landscape' between East and West," said Lucian Hechler.[19]

"The job of practical politics in the years lying ahead of us is to maintain the unity of the nation by easing the current tensions in the relationship between the two parts of Germany," Brandt told the *Bundestag* in October 1969. "We are not abandoning ourselves here to any deceptive hopes: interests, power relations, and societal differences can neither be dialectically dissolved, nor hidden beneath a cloud of smoke.... We are free from illusions that the work of reconciliation will be easy or quickly accomplished. We are dealing with a process, but it is time to move this process forward."[20]

Under Konrad Adenauer, West Germany kept the GDR at arm's length. The FRG only dealt directly with GDR officials on a limited range of subjects, like trade. Adenauer resisted treating the GDR as an equal, a government of a separate and sovereign nation. One tenet of West German foreign policy was the "Hallstein Doctrine." It punished countries that officially accepted the GDR as a sovereign country. Named for West German diplomat Walter Hallstein, it held that West Germany could cut off diplomatic relations with countries that gave the GDR diplomatic recognition.

Brandt "felt that Adenauer's policy of simply standing firmly with the West was a dead end," said Lucian Hechler.[21] The Berlin Wall reinforced that feeling. Brandt and others in his political party, the SPD, began looking for a different approach to the "German question."

A landmark event in that search occurred on July 15, 1963. Egon Bahr, a West Berlin official and a leading figure in the SPD, gave a speech titled "Coming Closer Together through Rapprochement." It came to be known as the "Change Through Rapprochement" speech. The "previous policy of pressure and counter-pressure" against the GDR had failed, argued Bahr. The Hallstein Doctrine had projected that a Western policy of pressure and isolation would bring the East German state to collapse. Instead, it "led only to a solidification of the status quo." Now it was time to try a different policy.

It was time to "renounce previous notions about liberation" of East Germany as the West's immediate goal. The "policy of all-or-nothing must be ruled out. Either free elections or nothing, either all-German freedom of choice or an obstinate 'no,' either elections as the first step or rejection—all this is not only hopelessly antiquated and unreal, but in a strategy of peace it is also meaningless. Today it is clear that reunification is not a one-time act that will be put into effect by a historic decision on an historic day at an historic conference, but rather a process involving many steps and many stations."[22]

The word "rapprochement" means "an establishment of harmonious relations." It's used often in foreign relations.[23] Bahr was calling for a major change in West Germany's approach to the East Germans. Bahr urged West Germany to reach out to and work with the GDR, not push it away. "If it is correct, and I believe it is correct, that the [Soviet Zone of occupation in Germany] cannot be snatched away from the Soviet sphere of influence, then the logical consequence is that every policy aimed directly at toppling the regime over there is hopeless. This conclusion is excruciatingly uncomfortable and runs counter to our feelings, but it is logical. It means that changes and alterations coming from the current regime are the only ones that are attainable."[24] If the FRG couldn't get rid of the GDR, then it only made sense to try to work with it.

The new approach became known as *Ostpolitik*. *Ost* is German for "East." "The goal was to put aside the ideological refusals to have any dealings with the East and to begin talking with East Berlin and East Germany to the effect and hope that this would improve the lot of the people behind the Curtain and enable the people on the West and on the East to move back and forth to some extent," said Arthur Day.[25] *Ostpolitik's* goal, said Brandon Grove, "was to achieve a more healthy and human relationship among Germans."[26]

Ostpolitik, said Brandt in October 1969, would pursue actions intent on "improving political, economic, and cultural relations between the two halves of Germany."[27] "The job of practical politics in the years lying ahead of us is to maintain the unity of the nation by easing the current tensions in the relationship between the two parts of Germany."[28] The FRG would now "actively promote objectively possible historical developments in the relations between" it and the GDR, Brandt said in a January 1970 speech. "Patriotism calls for realizing the facts and trying over and over again to seek new possibilities. It demands the courage to recognize reality."[29] Those possibilities, said Lucian Heichler might be "only small technical steps, that could gradually evolve into larger political steps."[30]

Adenauer and the Christian Democrats had refused to grant the GDR any public legitimacy. They (and the Western powers) referred to it derisively as the "so-called GDR." Adenauer-led governments insisted that only the FRG could speak for Germans, east or west, because only the FRG had a leader legitimately chosen by its people, through free elections. Brandt rejected that approach. He proposed a new way to think of Germany's current situation: two German states in one German nation. Brandt and the Social Democrats were willing to deal with the GDR on the diplomatic level as equal partners in order to improve the lives of Berliners and Germans.

Brandt and the Social Democrats were not willing, however, to accept that Germany had split in two forever. "Germans are not only linked by their language and their history—with all its glory and its misery; Germany is home to all of us," said Brandt in October 1969.[31] He expanded on that theme in a speech the following January. "Nobody can deny the fact that in this sense there is and will be one German nation, as far as we can think ahead. As long as the Germans muster the political will not to abandon this demand the hope remains that later generations will live in one Germany in whose political system the Germans in their entirety can cooperate."[32]

Brandt and the Social Democrats did adopt one of Adenauer's long-standing preconditions for German reunification: The political system that the future "one Germany" adopted must be based on German popular will. "Nobody can tell us that the Germans do not have the same right to self-determination as all other peoples," said Brandt. "What remains unchanged is this: the FRG and GDR are not foreign countries to each other. And what also remains is this: recognition of the GDR under international law is out of the question for us."[33] *Ostpolitik* was a temporary approach, pending the future reunion of the German nation into one state.

Brandt got the chance to put *Ostpolitik* into practice in the fall of 1969. In national elections, West German voters put the Social Democrats in power. Willy Brandt became the new West German chancellor. Under the leadership of more moderate politicians like Brandt and Bahr, the SPD had softened its image as a Marxist-leaning party and accepted free-market economics.

It also committed to keep West Germany in the greater Western alliance. Many in Washington had feared that if the SPD won power, it might pursue policies that would lead to German neutrality in the Cold War. Brandt calmed those fears by making clear that the SPD would not break with NATO or the West. "The North Atlantic Alliance, which, in its twenty-year existence, has stood the test of time, will also guarantee our security in the future. Its tight cohesion is the precondition for the common effort toward détente in Europe," said Brandt in October 1969. The SPD viewed "our state's external security as a function of the alliance to which we belong, and as part of which we will contribute to the equilibrium of forces between West and East. Our national interest does not permit us to stand between the West and the East.... Our country needs cooperation and coordination with the West and understanding with the East."[34] Reassurances like that helped convince West German voters to put the SPD in power and oust the Christian Democrats, who had run West Germany since the FRG was first created in 1949.

Late 1969 was a time of cooperation and a lessening of tensions in the Cold War. The major "combatants" actively sought ways to coexist peacefully. They'd all taken the same lesson from the Berlin Wall that Willy Brandt had—the division between communism and capitalism seemed sure to last for a long time. This change in the diplomatic winds acquired its own nickname: *détente*, a French word that means "the easing of hostility or strained relations, especially between countries."[35]

Richard Nixon, the new American president, called for greater East-West cooperation. In February 1969 he addressed the *Bundestag*. Nixon said the West was entering "what I have described as a period of negotiations with those who have been our opponents."[36] That same month, as he toured a West Berlin factory, Nixon said this: "The men of the past thought in terms of blockades and walls: the men of the future will think in terms of open channels."[37] The final communique from the NATO Ministers' Meeting in December 1969 said that, "in an era of negotiation, it should be possible, by means of discussion of specific and well-defined subjects, progressively to reduce tensions. This would in itself facilitate discussion of the more fundamental questions."[38]

One of the Cold War's most "fundamental questions" was Berlin. In April 1969, the NATO ministers said that "a peaceful European settlement presupposes, among other things, progress toward eliminating existing sources of tension in the center of Europe." Achieving "concrete measures aimed at improving the situation in Berlin, safeguarding free access to the city and removing restrictions which affect traffic and communications between the two parts of Germany would be a substantial contribution toward this objective."[39] They expanded on that sentiment later that year. "The elimination of difficulties created in the past with respect to Berlin, especially with regards to access, would increase the prospects for serious discussion on the other concrete issues which continue to divide East and West. Furthermore, Berlin could play a constructive role in the expansion of East-West economic relations if the city's trade with the East could be facilitated."[40]

In 1969, American, British, and French diplomats reached out to the Soviet Union to explore ways to improve the situation in and around Berlin. The Russians were receptive. They wanted détente to work, too. In specific, the Soviets were pushing for a European security conference. The Western Powers said a Berlin deal had to come first.[41] In late March 1970, ambassadors from the four WWII Allied countries convened in Berlin to start formal negotiations on what the State Department called "the Berlin questions."[42]

In a speech to the Berlin Chamber of Commerce, US Ambassador to West Germany Kenneth Rush described the early phases of the talks. The initial Soviet draft for a proposed agreement did not seem promising. It "did not contain provision for unimpeded access, for specific measures to secure such access, or for Soviet responsibility with access or travel by West Berliners to East Berlin and the GDR. It did contain provisions which might have weakened the ties between the Western sectors and the FRG and resulted in the removal of many FRG agencies and institutions from the Western Sectors...Some on the Western side felt the Soviet draft evidenced the impossibility of reaching some compromise. Nevertheless the Allies negotiators plugged on step by step... We tried to identify common concepts and language,"[43] hoping for a breakthrough. The talks trudged on into 1971.

In March, a breakthrough came. There was, as Ambassador Rush put it, "finally a move on the Soviet side to undertake a Soviet commitment that access to and from the Western sectors would be unimpeded."[44] This was monumental. West Berlin could not be a viable place to live or do business without guaranteed access to the West. The threat that the USSR might let the East Germans harass (or totally block) road, rail, and waterway transit to the West had always hung over the Western sectors. Now, for the first time since the Allies occupied Berlin, the Soviets seemed willing to guarantee, in writing, that the lifelines to the West would stay open.

The pace of negotiations picked up. In August the ambassadors themselves "initiated a series of marathon sessions," in Ambassador Rush's words, to work out the final details. One session lasted fourteen hours and ended well after midnight.[45] After "some further dramatic moments,"[46] the final agreement was signed on September 3, 1971.

The deal came to be known as the "Quadripartite Agreement," or the "Four-Power Agreement." It was a major world event. The leading powers in the Cold War had just agreed to normalize relations and reduce tensions in Berlin, the most sensitive of all the Cold War hotspots in Europe.

The pact basically confirmed the status quo in and around Berlin. Neither side had to make any major changes in their critical policy and legal positions. The GDR didn't have to tear down the Berlin Wall; the Western Powers didn't have to submit to the authority of GDR police on the Helmstedt *autobahn*. Neither of the Western Powers surrendered any part of their status as an occupier. The agreement said all signatories were "Acting on the basis of their quadripartite rights and responsibilities, and of the corresponding wartime and postwar agreements and decisions of the Four Powers, which are not affected."[47] The Potsdam Agreement was still in force. Germany was still not officially at peace because World War II (in the Western Powers' eyes) *still* hadn't officially ended.

The agreement said all four WWII Allied powers had approved the Four-Power Agreement "Without prejudice to their legal positions." The Western Allies' legal position was that *all* Berlin was under Four-Power authority, pending the final peace settlement. The Soviets held that East Berlin was the capital of the GDR and that West Berlin sat on GDR territory. The Four-Power Agreement didn't force either side to budge on their legal interpretations of what Berlin was (or wasn't). How did the diplomats manage that? They skirted the issue.

In critical places in the text, where specific wording could be construed to have specific legal meanings—saying, for example, "West Berlin" instead of the "Western sectors of Berlin" or "Berlin" instead of "East Berlin —the text didn't use the word "Berlin" at all. Instead, it said "the relevant area." The document's preamble said the agreement took "into account the existing situation in the relevant area." Part One (General Provisions) said the "four Governments will strive to promote the elimination of tension and the prevention of complications in the relevant area."

This compromise in wording shows the Four Powers' desire to conclude a meaningful agreement on Berlin. They couldn't agree on what to call Berlin because they couldn't agree on what its international legal status was. In many diplomatic negotiations, a disagreement that serious would scuttle the talks. But the Four Powers wanted a deal. So, instead of walking away from the talks, they "agreed to disagree" and came up with a phrase (the "relevant area") that everyone could live with.

In the Four Power Agreement, all four WWII Allied powers agreed "that there "shall be no use of threat or force in the area and that disputes shall be settled by peaceful means," and "the situation which has developed in the area ... shall not be changed unilaterally." (The Berlin Blockade, for example, had been a unilateral move). The Four Powers also agreed to "mutually respect their individual and joint rights and responsibilities, which remained unchanged." The Western Powers interpreted that as a written affirmation by the USSR that the "rights and responsibilities" that the US, UK, and France exercised in West Berlin would not be challenged. In other words, the Russians wouldn't follow through on their threats to conclude a separate peace with the GDR and end Western Allied occupation rights.

The critical parts of the agreement were specific commitments made by one or more of the Four Powers. The Soviet Union declared "that transit traffic by road, rail and waterways through the territory of the GDR of civilian persons and goods between the Western Sectors of Berlin and the FRG will be unimpeded; that such traffic will be facilitated so as to take place in the most simple and expeditious manner; and that it will receive preferential treatment."[48] Here, at last, was an official, on-the-record affirmation by the Russians that ground and water access between West Berlin and West Germany would not be choked off. The "muddy" legal standing for German civilian travel to and from West Berlin was now cleaned up.

This was a major step back for the Soviet Union. This new Russian commitment to allow West German rail and road traffic to move freely *de facto* "cancels a 1955 agreement in which the Soviet Union nominally transferred control of the access routes to East Germany," wrote the *New York Times* News Service. The Four Power Agreement essentially invalidated that. The only way the Soviets could guarantee that traffic to and from West Germany would be "unimpeded," "simple," and "expeditious," as the Four Power Agreement said it would be, was for them to get tough with the GDR if necessary—i.e., infringe on the "sovereignty" that the GDR claimed it had over East German territory.

For their part, the US, UK, and French governments declared that while ties between West Berlin and West Germany would be "maintained and developed," West Berlin itself would "continue not to be a constituent part of the Federal Republic of Germany and not to be governed by it."[49] The Western Allies would use their authority as occupation powers—now newly confirmed by the Russians! —to prevent West Berlin from becoming a separate *Land* of the FRG or otherwise asserting itself as part of the West German state. The Western sectors didn't have to drop their current ties with Bonn—and there were many, with several FRG agencies (with thousands of employees) active in West Berlin. But West Berlin couldn't legally become part of the FRG as long as the occupation continued. It would have to remain a freestanding political entity.

The Four Power Agreement said that its signatories, by concluding this agreement, were "Guided by the desire to contribute to practical improvements of the situation."[50] In the agreement, the Soviets made another commitment that would tremendously improve the situation for Berlin families divided by the Cold War:

> The Government of the USSR declares that communications between the Western Sectors of Berlin and areas bordering on these Sectors and those areas of the GDR which do not border on these Sectors will be improved. Permanent residents of the Western Sectors of Berlin will be able to travel to and visit such areas for compassionate, family, religious, cultural or commercial reasons, or as tourists, under conditions comparable to those applying to other persons entering those areas.[51]

It had been hard for West Germans to visit East Berlin or East Germany, especially since the Wall appeared. But West Berliners found it especially hard. The GDR's border crossing policies made it easier for FRG residents to visit the East than West Berliners. Essentially, West Berliners could only visit the East under special circumstances, such as family emergencies. (This was one way in which the GDR emphasized that West Berliners were *not* West Germans.[52])

West Berliners felt this acutely. Many had family or friends in the Soviet Sector of Berlin. Before August 13, 1961, visiting them only required a trip across town. Since then, a visit compelled you to not only cross a *de facto* national border but also convince the often-unwilling officials of another *de facto* country to let you cross. The Four Power Agreement paved the way for West Berliners to visit friends and family in the East much more easily.

There was also very good news—life-changing news, in fact—for the people of Steinstuecken. The Four Power Agreement contained this sentence: "The problems of the small enclaves, including Steinstuecken, and of other small areas, may be solved by exchange of territory."[53]

The "other small areas" were the small meadows and patches of uninhabited land that sat in Communist territory but officially belonged to West Berlin. But there were East German "small areas," too. When the GDR divided Berlin, some small slivers of land belonging to East Berlin *Bezirkes* were chopped off by the barbed wire. These fingers of GDR territory were left behind, jutting into West Berlin. Some were real nuisances. They crossed streets or canals; West Berliners had to detour around them.[54]

The occupying powers wanted to clean up these border anomalies by having West Berlin and the GDR swap bits of land. Some of

West Berlin's exclaves would become part of *Land* Brandenburg. Not Steinstuecken, though. Not only would it remain part of West Berlin; it would receive a road of its own to the city! As part of the land exchanges, the GDR gave enough land to West Berlin so that West Berlin could build a "corridor" to Steinstuecken.[55]

A real road to West Berlin, over territory that West Berlin owned, would change life forever in Steinstuecken. The West Berlin police could come when needed. The Americans could send as many troops there as they wanted, whenever they wanted. City buses could come to the village. Repairmen and deliverymen could travel there when their customers, not the GDR, wanted them to. If the GDR tried to close the new road, they would have to encroach on part of the American Sector of West Berlin. Steinstuecken's days as an exclave would end. It would be a peninsula, to be sure. It would still be isolated, a finger of free territory jutting into the Soviet Zone. But it would no longer be severed from West Berlin.

Who would work out all the details for implementing the Four Power Agreement? Details like this: which parcels of territory would change hands, how often could West Berliners visit the GDR, how would the Vopos modify their procedures for inspecting cars and trucks on the Helmstedt *autobahn*? The wartime Allies delegated the lion's share of that work to two entities that had kept each other at arms' length for years: the FRG and the GDR. "Detailed arrangements concerning travel, communications and the exchange of territory," said the Four Power Agreement, "will be agreed by the competent German authorities."[56] The West German and East German governments would sit down, as *de facto* equals, and negotiate major agreements with sweeping impact on economic, cultural, and political matters. These agreements would "have a certain historical significance," wrote the *Los Angeles Times*. They would be "the first between the two German states which go beyond technical and economic questions into subjects of deep political consequence."[57] The Hallstein Doctrine had been swept away by *Ostpolitik*.

The Four Power Agreement didn't go into effect immediately. Signing it was only the first step. Next, the GDR and FRG would negotiate the series of agreements that would implement it. The wartime Allies would approve those FRG-GDR agreements, and then the Four Power Agreement would go into effect. Throughout the fall of 1971, FRG and GDR diplomats and government officials fleshed out the details. By the end of September, they agreed to establish more telephone lines, coordinate radio-frequency usage, and automate more of the telephone and telegraph services between them.[58]

On December 17, the two governments concluded a major agreement governing the movement of "Civilian Persons and Goods" between the FRG and West Berlin. Cargo shipments would no longer be subject to detailed searches by GDR border guards. Instead, shippers would seal cargo containers before shipping them; GDR customs personnel would then check the seals and verify they hadn't been tampered with. The border control procedures "for travelers in individual conveyances shall not involve delay," said the agreement. "The travelers, their vehicles and personal baggage will not be subject to search, detention or exclusion from use of the designated routes, except in special cases"[59] There, finally, in explicit language, was a guarantee from the GDR that civilian traffic could move relatively freely between West Berlin and West Germany. The GDR agreed to stop levying tolls on individual vehicles. The FRG would pay an annual lump sum to the GDR to cover road, rail, and waterway maintenance and repair.

The "Civilian Persons and Goods" agreement was one of two pacts the FRG and GDR concluded on December 17, 1971. The second was titled: "The Arrangement Between the Senat of [West] Berlin and the Government of the GDR on the Regulation of the Enclaves Question by Exchange of Territory." West Berlin agreed to transfer five small exclaves to the GDR. In return, West Berlin would receive:

> a strip of land, along the railway line Seddin-Berlin (West), approximately 1 kilometer long and 20 meters wide, together with the road branching west from this strip immediately before Steinstuecken, up to the western edge of the Teltower Strasse, in the width of the roadway of approximately 3 meters, including the bridge, as an access route to Steinstuecken.[60]

A Protocol Note in the agreement spelled out exactly what the land was for. "The Senat shall build a road in the strip of land along the railway line Seddin-Berlin [West] designated as access to Steinstuecken."

The Protocol Note said that "During the road construction period, the Government of the GDR shall grant access to Steinstuecken under the conditions existing at present." In other words, use of the path by

American personnel, or West Berliners without a pass, would still not be authorized until the road was finished. Also, "In order to provide for unhindered construction operations, a strip of land 5-10 meters wide shall be made available on both sides of the agreed access route to Steinstuecken for the duration of construction, on which excavation work necessary for road construction may also be carried out."[61]

The pathway to Steinstuecken wasn't the only land West Berlin received. A cemetery in the Frohnau neighborhood in the French Sector had literally been split in half by the border. The northern half lay in the Soviet Zone. When the East Germans closed their border in 1952, some West Berliners couldn't visit the graves of their relatives.[62] The "Exchange of Territory" agreement gave "the northern part of the Frohnau cemetery" to West Berlin.[63]

The British Sector got some territory, too. The British occupation force had its own pocket of land dangling in the Soviet Zone. Its name was Eiskeller. It wasn't as big as Steinstuecken—only a few farm families lived there. And it was officially an enclave, not an exclave. Eiskeller was connected by land to the Berlin *Bezirk* of Spandau. It was a tenuous connection—one strip of land just a few meters wide, over which ran an unpaved country lane. But the Soviets didn't dispute that that lane or the strip of land it sat upon belonged to West Berlin.

Eiskeller had had its own moments in the Cold War spotlight. In May 1952, when East Germany closed its borders with West Berlin, Communist forces entered Eiskeller and hindered British troops from moving freely to and from the hamlet. In August 1961, the month the Berlin Wall appeared, a boy who lived in Eiskeller reported that Vopos had harassed him as he attempted to bicycle to school one day.

In both instances, the British reacted boldly. In 1952, the Soviets still used a Radio Berlin facility, known as the *Rundfunkhaus*, in the British Sector. British Military Police surrounded it with barbed wire and guards. Many of the Soviet staff and their East German employees stayed in their building, fearing the British would seize it if they evacuated. The British move on the *Rundfunkhaus* grabbed headlines worldwide. It eventually pressured the Russians to relent in Eiskeller.

And as for the boy on the bicycle? When the British heard what happened, they decided to give him an escort to and from school. Newspapers worldwide showed pictures of the young man pedaling to class—followed by a British armored car! Years later, the boy reportedly admitted that he'd been playing hooky from school that day and made up a story about harassment by the Vopos in order to stay out of trouble.[64]

Surely the British found out, eventually. But they might not have minded being misled. Those pictures appeared in many Western newspapers. They demonstrated the UK's resolve to assert its rights as an occupying power. As part of the FRG-GDR agreement on enclaves, West Berlin received additional territory along the country lane; this made the road to Eiskeller wider and more secure.[65]

When the amount of acreage being exchanged between the GDR and West Berlin was totaled, it turned out that West Berlin was getting more land than it was giving up. The West Berliners employed a remedy that solves many problems: cash. "As the areas to be exchanged are not equal in size in value," read Article 2 of the territory exchange agreement, "the *Senat* shall pay the Government of the GDR compensation in the amount of 4 million Deutsche Marks [approximately $1.5 million U.S. dollars]"[66]

A small problem arose with the section of railway that went through Steinstuecken, splitting it into eastern and western halves. Residents (including Magrit Wiese Sanchez's father) had built a footbridge over the tracks. Because the tracks were treated as East German property, the GDR balked at recognizing the footbridge as West Berlin territory. Negotiators solved the problem by agreeing to let the bridge itself and the airspace above it become part of West Berlin, but also recognize the open area under the bridge as GDR territory.

All the FRG-GDR agreements would go into effect on June 4, 1972. That gave everyone six months to prepare. For the Steinstueckeners, they began to contemplate the actual end to their separation from West Berlin. The road that Johannes Niemeyer had implored the Western Allies to build for over twenty years was finally coming. Their neighborhood would no longer be that mysterious little spot hidden in the woods outside of Zehlendorf, the place where the people had cows—or maybe not—who knew for sure? In the months leading up to the traffic agreement going into effect, the people of Steinstuecken pondered how their lives and community would change.

Some weren't all that enthusiastic. A few were even unhappy. "Somewhat surprisingly, not all residents are happy that in the future anyone who wants to can come to Steinstuecken," reported AP writer Hubert Erb.[67] "A 59-year old woman who for years has had to bicycle her way in and out of Steinstuecken voiced her disapproval of any steps to change the status quo," wrote Joe Alex Morris in a *Los Angeles Times* article. "'Now we live in heavenly peace,' she said, 'with no salesmen pounding on our doors. Who knows, if things get better, the rents may go up as well.'"[68]

"I could go for a walk with three million marks in my handbag, and no one would take it from me," Gertrude Vogel told a Reuters reporter. "Now with strangers among us, I wouldn't be that certain."[69] "We were very cut off from the world," one resident told a German TV reporter. "For those of us with stressful jobs, Steinstuecken was like a little oasis, away from the hustle and bustle."[70] "A school bus driver said she was concerned that the city will scratch its subsidy for the bus service once access became 'normal' over a Western road," wrote Hubert Erb. Some residents were unhappy when they heard that West Berlin wanted to use some of the privately owned property in the village for turnarounds and parking areas to accommodate the higher amounts of vehicle traffic that were now sure to come.[71] Others worried that their quiet neighborhood would be "overrun by space-hungry fellow citizens from heavily-populated West Berlin areas."[72]

But others looked forward to reunion with their home city. "Two elderly women were encountered as they made their way along the Steinstuecken wall to the first East German control point," wrote Hubert Erb. "They termed as 'nonsense' criticism that open access will cut into Steinstuecken's quietly idyllic lifestyle. 'It is such a long walk through the woods,' Hildegard Manhart said. 'I hope we get a regular bus, even if it is a small one.'…'More important,' Gertrude Vogel emphasized, 'from now on, we know we really belong.'"[73] (Presumably this was the same Gertrude Vogel whom the Reuters reporter interviewed. If so, she apparently saw both good and bad in the new road). That idea of "really belonging" to West Berlin resonated among many villagers. Daily visits from a regular city bus, the ability to drive to and from work and stores in the big city without having to show a pass—all those things would make Steinstuecken feel like a real part of West Berlin.

The road would also allow Steinstuecken to be connected to West Berlin utilities. The exclave used East German sources for its water, power, and gas. That often caused problems. At peak cooking times the gas pressure often dropped sharply.[74] "On Sundays, if I want to have a roast I have to get up at seven in the morning to start," said Gertrude

Vogel. "If I begin any later the gas is likely to fail." "Power cuts were frequent," wrote UPI reporter Joseph Fleming. "In the summer, water trickled from taps."[75] And even when the utilities worked well, there was always the threat that the GDR could cut them for any reason. West Berlin authorities planned to lay water, gas, and electric lines along the new road.[76]

Most of all, the new road would provide security. Residents would no longer have to travel the *Waldweg*, where the Vopos might snatch them. "No matter how often you go across, you never get used to it," said Ursula Bohlmann, the mayor of Steinstuecken at the time. "There is always the sense of tension, of nervousness, of the feeling that it's unnatural."[77]

Frau Bohlmann's comments came in an interview with the *Washington Post* about the new road and its impact on (arguably) Berlin's most famous hamlet. The *Post* also interviewed Elsbeth Noel, who was "not among those residents experiencing a sudden nostalgia for the old privacy. 'I don't know whether access to West Berlin will be good or bad,' she said, 'but don't let all this talk fool you. We had some very frightening times here when it looked like we were lost, and no one talked about Steinstuecken being a paradise then.'"[78]

The *Washington Post* reporter who interviewed Frau Bohlmann and Frau Noel had been helicoptered into the hamlet. He was part of a group of journalists the US Army had brought to Steinstuecken to get one last look at the place while it was still a true "exclave." Stories in American papers reminded readers of the little community that UPI reporter Joseph Fleming called "a perennial trouble spot," and *LA Times-Washington Post* reporter John Goshko described as "one of the world's most hotly contested pieces of real estate."

The stories told about the little quirks of life in an exclave—no bus or taxi access, waiting days for the plumber to get GDR permission to come fix your toilet,[79] no playdates for children with their classmates from Wannsee, having to carry the village's garbage to Berlin because the Vopos wouldn't allow a garbage truck to come collect it.[80] Quirks that were about to disappear—for better or worse. "Ten years of isolation for 180 inhabitants of this tiny western enclave inside East Germany will end soon and the possible consequences are causing some concern," was Reuter's opening sentence for a Steinstuecken story on December 26. Two weeks later, John Goshko started his story this way:

> With its neat, tile-roofed houses set amid massive oaks and pines, Bernhard-Beyer Strasse might be a pleasant residential street anywhere in the Western world. Even its sounds are of a piece with the setting: the laughter of running children and the buzz of housewives chatting across fences.
>
> But walk to the end of the block-long street and this picture of cozy suburbia abruptly turns into a scene of surrealistic ugliness. There, behind a sign that proclaims 'Warning, Soviet Zone,' a high concrete wall and a tangle of barbed wire bring Bernhard Beyer Strasse to a chilling dead end.
>
> Beyond the wall lies a wide band of barren earth from which every blade of grass has been torn and replaced with barbed wire. The perimeters of the 'death strip' are studded with armament-bristling towers manned by 'Vopos' of the East German People's Police who stare constantly into the windows of the houses below.[81]

Headlines for these Steinstuecken stories weren't as sensational as those readers saw during the exclave's multiple crises in the 1950s and 1960s. (There were exceptions: "Red-Ringed Village Hoping For Freedom" appeared in *The Times-Herald*, Port Huron, Michigan, January 20, 1972). They emphasized the major changes Steinstuecken faced and the hopes and fears arising from those changes: "Steinstuecken: West Berlin's 'Offshore Island' May Come Home" (Louisville *Courier Journal & Times*, January 2, 1972); "East German Enclave Fears End to Its Privacy" (Reuters exclusive to the *LA Times*, December 26, 1971); "German Village Hopes to Rejoin West Berlin" (*Anniston Star*, Anniston, Alabama, January 19, 1972); "Wall-Encircled E. German Town May Rejoin West" (*The Bridgeport Telegram*, Bridgeport, Connecticut, January 20, 1972); "Small Village to be 'Freed'" (*Springfield News-Leader*, Springfield, Missouri, January 20, 1972).

One *Washington Post* News Service story suggested that the West's most prolific author on Steinstuecken had helped the village finally get its road. This appeared in the *Tucson Citizen* on January 4, 1972:

> *Thesis Aid in Freeing Berliners? Student's Study Possible Key.*
>
> A doctoral candidate at American University here believes that he may have played an important role in changing the lives of 180 citizens in West Berlin whose homes are in a hamlet sur-

rounded by Communist territory. The student is Honore' Marc Catudal Jr., 26, a native Washingtonian.

Catudal told the Post reporter "that he reminded American officials" who were exploring solutions to the Berlin problem "that the Steinstueckeners themselves once had unsuccessfully put forward" a proposal to give the GDR uninhabited exclave plots of land in return for a corridor to Steinstuecken.[82] This refers to the suggestions exclave residents made after the GDR's October 1951 attempt to absorb the village. "A State Department official said that he was unaware of any role that Catudal might have played in the development of the proposal, but didn't dispute the possibility that some of Catudal's research may have helped."[83]

Finally, the big day arrived. On June 4, 1972, a Sunday, the Four Power Agreement went into effect. The previous day, the four occupying powers, satisfied that the FRG-GDR agreements met their requirements, had applied their final signatures. "West Berliners Crowd Offices for Wall Passes," read the headline in a *Los Angeles Times* article on the pact's first day of operation. "Hundreds of West Berliners lined up on Sunday to apply for passes to visit the Communist East." Eager applicants "began to line up at the two East German pass offices in West Berlin at 4 a.m. When they opened at 9 a.m., there were 150 persons waiting at one pass office and about 100 at the other. Many were disappointed, because they had hoped to get passes in time to visit relatives in East Berlin or East Germany Sunday. But Communist officials told them it would take five days to get the passes, except in case of emergency." West Berlin officials promised to try to speed up the process.

A West German diplomat demonstrated that GDR control procedures on the Berlin-Helmstedt *autobahn* really had been relaxed. He "drove the 110-mile autobahn through East Germany to the city without leaving his car. He was required to show his identity card at East German highway checkpoints, but his automobile and baggage were not searched as they used to be. 'At last, what we waited for for years has become reality,' he said."[84]

As for Steinstuecken, the all-important "approximately 1 kilometer long and 20 meters wide" strip of land became the property of West Berlin on midnight, June 4. For the first time ever, Steinstuecken was legally connected to its parent *Bezirk*. That morning, Western dignitaries marked the historic occasion with a short but symbolic walk. This comes from the *Berlin Observer*'s account of the event:

> *A Sunday Stroll: Steinstuecken Opens For Visit*
>
> It was a blazing hot Sunday afternoon and in West Berlin proper hundreds of people were out sunning themselves and bathing in the cool water of the Berlin lakes.
>
> However, in nearby Steinstuecken, the enclave of 31.5 acres and home for nearly 200 people, the scene was quite different. For on this Sunday they were to be visited by a group of distinguished guests....
>
> Major General William W. Cobb, U.S. Commander in Berlin, joined with West Berlin Mayor Klaus Schuetz and other officials to walk the once treacherous and heavily-guarded kilometer-long and 20 meters-wide strip. As a result of their Sunday stroll they were bringing the citizens of Steinstuecken new hope that, because of the important signing between the four powers, they will finally have a road of their own which will remain unguarded and allow them to travel unimpeded.
>
> 'It is always nice to take a walk on a nice Sunday morning,' Cobb observed.... As the mayor and the American commandant reached the edge of the village, a crowd of residents greeted them. 'We bid you welcome, very welcome,' a spokesman said.[85]

The AP wrote that the mayor and general "walked over the newly-acquired access route—a death strip before, where anyone setting foot was shot at. People's Army officers scurried about. On a knoll, two East German soldiers, no older than 18, sat with a machine gun pointing it along the edge of Eastern territory, ready to cut down any Easterner who might try and escape to the West."[86] UPI's Joseph Fleming said that the mayor and general "walked out to the hamlet ... to show it is no longer an island."[87]

Steinstuecken finally had its corridor to its home city. But, no paved road—yet. West Berlin had to build it. Over the summer, West Berlin construction firms graded the land and laid pavement and sidewalks. During the construction, Steinstuecken residents still used the *Waldweg* to reach Berlin; the Vopo checkpoints continued to operate.[88] The East Germans were busy building, too. They erected a new stretch of the Berlin Wall along each side of the new road. During construction, the opening in the Wall was closed with a temporary iron gate.[89]

Three months later, both construction efforts were finished. A paved road, complete with sidewalks and bike paths, connected Steinstuecken to Wannsee, a Zehlendorf suburb. On either side, new sections of the Berlin Wall sealed the road off from East Germany.

The new road officially opened on August 30. Time to celebrate again. Bands played, as the mayor of Berlin and the wife of the USCOB cut a red ribbon. The first vehicle to use the road—a beer truck, carrying free kegs. A city bus followed it.[90] Mayor Schutz and General Cobb took another stroll to Steinstuecken, this time on the brand-new paved street. Crowds joined them.

When the visitors reached Steinstuecken, the exclave's longest-standing business establishment wasn't open to receive them. Walter Steinweg had closed his restaurant in protest. For years, GDR border barriers had blocked direct access to his shop. People had to enter it through the back door. Herr Steinweg asked that when the Four Power Agreements went into effect, part of the Berlin Wall be moved back to reopen his front door. That didn't happen, so Herr Steinweg wasn't open for business on Steinstuecken's first day as a *de facto* West Berlin suburb in over twenty years. "That did not place a damper on the celebration," wrote a UPI wire reporter,[91] because Steinweg "had competition again for the first time since the war. Heinz Pieper, a 50 year-old mason, converted a barn into a café called the 'Dovecote,' the entrance to which is not blocked by the wall. He is hoping that West Berliners will flood out to what was once forbidden territory. 'If they do, I will stop working and devote all my time to the café,' he said."

Heinz Pieper got his wish. Over the next few weeks, months, and years, West Berliners came in droves to Steinstuecken. "For years, the village was remote and inaccessible, a fascinating and forbidden fruit for all but the privileged few who lived there," wrote *Los Angeles Times* reporter Joe Alex Morris in a 1973 article. "Now, on a sunny Sunday, the curiosity-seekers arrive in droves, on regular buses, in special sight-seeing buses, on foot and by car."[92] Ralph Sanchez recalls that so many tourists came on the weekends that the few parking spaces in Steinstuecken itself quickly filled. People ended up parking on both sides of the new road.

Many residents bristled at their new notoriety. "The inhabitants—especially on weekends—felt like exotic animals at some strange zoo being stared at," recalled Elke Hammer. "They peer over fences and into living rooms," Joe Alex Morris wrote of the tourists. "They fill the only tavern and occasionally get drunk."[93] "'Now we have to park the car in the garden or they'll steal everything off of it,' a housewife told Morris. 'There's so much traffic you have to watch the kids all the time. We never did that before.'" Another resident echoed the housewife's irritation. "Fritz Bohlmann, a Berlin city official, moved to Steinstuecken 10 years ago because 'it was the best place in Berlin.' Now he is less sure. 'On Sundays, I often wonder whether we are monkeys in a cage,'" he said.[94]

Morris noticed that a distinct group of West Berliners had taken a liking to the village. "The West Berlin motorcycle gangs have added Steinstuecken to their ports of call. The villagers have learned to their sorrow what it is like to be awakened at 3AM by the deep-throated roar of powerful bikes." The new road, a long, straight stretch of modern pavement surrounded by sound-echoing walls, was irresistible to bikers.

But other Steinstueckeners Morris spoke with focused on the big picture. "'It's wonderful now,' said postal worker Werner Neumann, who's been a Steinstueckener since 1944. 'Free entry is 100 times more important than peace and quiet.'"[95]

Free entry. No more need to show a pass to guards to go to and from home. No more fears that the GDR could snatch you on the *Waldweg.* No more waiting to see if the Vopos would eventually get around to allowing the Wannsee plumber to come to your house. After more than twenty years, a Steinstueckener could go to and from home, school, or the store as easily as any other West Berliner.

The West Berlin police could now come to Steinstuecken. That meant that one of Berlin Brigade's most unique missions could end. A month after the road opened, it did. This headline appeared in the European edition of *Stars and Stripes* on October 25, 1972: "Quiet Fadeaway: US Army Withdraws Tiny Garrison From Steinstuecken Berlin Exclave." The mission of the 287th MP Company ended much more quietly than it had begun:

> The US Army has withdrawn its garrison from the West Berlin exclave of Steinstuecken, a spokesman confirmed Tuesday.

The closing down of a permanent watch over the village and its 200 inhabitants ended 11 years of GI presence aimed at preventing encroachment from surrounding East Germany.

The American presence has been supplanted since Oct. 4 by West Berlin city police patrols who do not stay in the village overnight.

The building that housed the American GIs stood empty in the rain but with the back door to their living quarters open.

A neighbor said he could not recall when the Americans pulled out. 'They just moved out,' he said. 'There was no farewell celebration from us.'[96]

The Four Power Agreement made it possible for the men of the 287th to return to more routine police missions. It also made it possible for one of Berlin's most famous American benefactors to pay a visit—Gail Halvorsen, the US Air Force colonel who commanded Templehof Air Force Base. Millions of Berliners knew Halvorsen by the colorful nickname he earned during the Berlin Airlift: the "Candy Bomber."

In his autobiography, *The Berlin Candy Bomber,* Halvorsen tells how he got the nickname. After landing at Templehof on an airlift mission one day, he took a break and pulled out his movie camera. Aircraft landing at Templehof had to execute a risky approach. As they neared the airstrip, their wingtips were actually level with buildings at the end of the airfield. Halvorsen wanted a movie of those aircraft flying literally under the rooftops, "seemingly popping out of the chimneys."

"The first thing that caught my eye," as he prepared his camera, he writes, "was about thirty kids standing near the airfield fence watching the planes swoop over the rooftops." They noticed the American pilot with the movie camera. Soon "half of the kids were right up against the fence, across from me." Halvorsen gave them a polite greeting in elementary German ("*Guten Tag. Wie geht's*?") Their response, and the conversations that followed moved him.

"I was immediately greeted with a torrent of responses that were geared to someone with a greater command of the language." They peppered Halvorsen with questions about the airlift—surprisingly technical questions. "'One of the first questions was, 'How many sacks of flour does each of the aircraft carry?' There has been some discussion about how many equivalent loaves of bread came across the fence with each aircraft. Were we really flying in fresh milk for the younger children? What about the other cargo? How many tons? One question came right after the other." Halvorsen learned that some of the children were "timing aircraft arrivals, and could tell of the weekly increases in the number of landings." Several spoke English well, and they translated for the others.

What really moved Halvorsen, though, was the children's priorities and beliefs.

> They were interested in freedom more than flour. They fully recognized that, between the two there was a real relationship, but they had already decided which was preeminent. I was astonished with the maturity and clarity that they exhibited in advising me of what their values were and what was of greatest importance to them in these circumstances.
>
> In the years between the time the aircraft over Berlin changed their cargo from bombs to flour, the children had witnessed an accelerated change in international relations. These young kids began giving me the most meaningful lesson in freedom I had ever had. Here I was, an American, almost bald-headed at the age of 27, yet I was learning about something I obviously took too much for granted.[97]

Halvorsen decided to thank the children with some candy. But he only had two sticks of gum with him. He tore them in half and handed them to the children at the fence. "In all my experience, including Christmases past, I had never witnessed such an expression of surprise, joy and sheer pleasure that I beheld in the eyes and faces of those four young people" who got one of the pieces of gum. "Nor do I remember seeing such disappointment, as was evident in the eyes of those who came so close." But, there "was no fighting or attempts to grab away" the gum from the four lucky ones.[98]

Halvorsen came up with a unique idea to bring more candy to the children around the airfield. He told the group that the next time he flew into Templehof, he would drop candy attached to a parachute. (He made them promise to share the candy). He was true to his word. Halvorsen convinced his co-pilot and crew chief to combine their chocolate ration with his, and they fastened the candy to parachutes made of handkerchiefs. As Halvorsen's plane approached the Templehof runway, the crew chief tossed the parachutes out.

As they taxied to fly back to West Germany, Halvorsen and his crew saw they'd hit their target. "Protruding through the fence were three little parachutes extended by several animated arms attached to three vibrant bodies. The little parachutes were being waved without discrimination at every crew as each aircraft taxied by. Behind the three with the parachutes were the rest of the cheering section, with both arms waving above their heads and every jaw working on a prize."[99]

Halvorsen didn't stop. He and his crew kept dropping candy parachutes on subsequent flights. Other Berlin Airlift pilots joined in. The media took notice, and soon Halvorsen was famous. The project captured the imagination of the American people. Sympathy for children, even the children of a nation that was your sworn enemy just a few years earlier, is a natural thing. The sight of American airplanes dropping sweets to Berlin youngsters did much to make Americans more sympathetic to the German people.

Halvorsen's book is filled with heartwarming stories of how the Berlin children (and their parents) reacted to the candy drops. Children would race each other to catch parachutes as they fluttered down. One boy jumped into a lake and swam out to get a package that had landed offshore. One night a father sat sadly in his apartment. His son's birthday was coming up, and he couldn't get the boy a decent present in a still-devastated West Berlin. He looked out his window and saw what seemed like a miracle: A fluttering candy parachute, with its precious cargo still attached, snagged on a nearby rooftop. The Russians complained that candy parachutes landing in the Soviet Sector were "'a capitalist trick to influence the minds of the young people against them.'"[100]

One of the candy parachutes ended up in Steinstuecken. A boy named Gert Knecht caught it.[101] Years later, after he'd grown up and started a family, he bought a house in Steinstuecken while it was still officially an exclave. Once the road was built, Knecht started writing to then-Colonel Halvorsen at Templehof, urging him to visit. Eventually Halvorsen did. He and his wife drove to Steinstuecken, met with Gert Knecht and other Steinstueckeners, and shared memories of the airlift and the candy drops. Knecht showed Halvorsen the parachute he'd caught decades ago. He'd saved it as a keepsake.

To this day, Halvorsen fondly remembers his trip to Steinstuecken. When interviewed for this book, he said that he'd been impressed by the spirit and determination of the village's residents. "They had a certain esprit de corps about them."[103]

That *esprit de corps* had sustained Steinstuecken through more than twenty years of isolation and intimidation. As 1972 drew to a close, those years were finally, thankfully, behind them. W.R. Smyser said this about Steinstuecken and its isolation from the rest of Berlin.

> For the Steinstueckeners, the important thing was not to be forgotten. The important thing was for people to remember that they were part of Berlin, and to have people act on that assumption. That was what mattered. That was what mattered also to Clay. The Berliners and Clay were on the same page on this matter. They would have been very unhappy if Clay had said 'No, I cannot go to Steinstuecken, it is outside the area of Berlin.' Because it wasn't outside of Berlin, it was part of Berlin. It was part of the administrative area of Berlin. And so, the key to them was, they did not want to be abandoned. And what Clay did was to make clear to them that they were still part of Berlin, they were still part of the system, that one day they would return, one day everything would revert, and they would be back. I think that was what mattered to them.[103]

Smyser was right. Frau Vogel ("from now on, we know we really belong") undoubtedly spoke for many of her neighbors in the village that was now no longer an island, but once again a neighborhood of Greater Berlin. Everything had, as Smyser put it, finally reverted. Steinstuecken was part of the system, and part of the great city of Berlin, again.

CHAPTER ELEVEN

I wish to express my admiration for your courage to remain free in a democratic society while surrounded by a Communist land. We Americans stand ready to guarantee your freedom today as we have in the past.
—Major General Raymond Haddock,
USCOB, to the citizens of Steinstuecken, May 6, 1989

Until December 1976, this site was a helicopter-landing-zone of the U.S. Forces. Since the construction of the wall in August 1961, it served to protect the freedom of the former exclave of Steinstuecken.
—Inscription on the rotor blade memorial

On July 28, 1945, less than one month after the US Army occupied Berlin, the first American military newspaper appeared. The first edition was one page long. As time passed and the American presence in West Berlin grew, the newspaper grew with it. On November 15, 1946, the paper adopted the name it would keep until the Cold War ended and the American military went home—the *Berlin Observer*. For forty years the *Berlin Observer* "[gave] an account of American Military activities in the Divided City."[1] It became the local paper for the American military community. Many of its issues are preserved online at *http://www.theberlinobserver.com*. It is a wonderful source for learning more about life in Cold War West Berlin.

On September 18, 1977, the *Observer* ran an article with this headline: "Zehlendorf Memorial Unveiled." Two main rotor blades from a UH-1 "Huey" helicopter had been mounted on a pedestal as a memorial to the decade-long airlift of MPs into Steinstuecken. It stood on the field that was once the former exclave's helipad. For its dedication ceremony, as American, West German, and Berlin flags flew nearby, an Army helicopter landed on the field. It carried the Zehlendorf *Bezirk* mayor and the commander of the American military community. The *Observer* described the flight as "one last official helicopter flight into Steinstuecken."[2]

By September 1977, the airlift into Steinstuecken had been over for five years. For five years, residents of the *enclave* (no longer an *exclave*) had had uninterrupted access to West Berlin. And West Berlin's economy and government had extended its reach into Steinstuecken. "The value" of property in Steinstuecken "has skyrocketed since unhindered access was established," wrote the *Los Angeles Times*' Joe Morris. "One Zehlendorf official said it has increased by seven to eight times."

But "unhindered access" also had its drawbacks. "The city, which already owns a lot of Steinstuecken property, is planning to buy more," wrote Morris. "The purpose, as one official revealed, is to build low-income housing in the former enclave." Berlin had a housing shortage, the official said. "This will unquestionably change the village's present rural atmosphere and further exacerbate such problems as rowdiness and juvenile delinquency, which came as part of the price of freedom," wrote Morris. "'Time marches on,' the city official said curtly." The headline of Morris' article? "West German Enclave Pays for Freedom." (It also had this sub-headline: "Tiny Enclave Loses Peace, Wins Freedom."[3])

Time did march on. The MPs were long gone from Steinstuecken. However, there were still reminders of the former exclave here and there in the Berlin Brigade. The kilometer-long corridor to Steinstuecken, bounded closely by walls and watchtowers on both sides, made for an interesting route for a road march. On July 15, 1977, the *Observer* covered a squad of infantry marching to the village—with East German watchtowers in the background.

The artillerymen of the Berlin Brigade also remembered the village. Berlin Brigade had one battery of cannons. In the 1960s and 70s, that battery was named C ("Charlie") Battery, 94th Artillery Regiment, or "C/94" for short. Brigade units often painted the names of Berlin neighborhoods on Army vehicles. An *Observer* article on November 22, 1963, said that one of the battery's 105mm self-propelled howitzers was named "Steinstuecken."

More than ten years later, Charlie Battery still remembered Steinstuecken. The Armed Forces Network (AFN) reported on a C/94 field training exercise in the late 1970s. The video showed two soldiers attaching antennas to the top of an armored command post (CP) vehicle. The

CP housed fire direction specialists who computed the firing commands for the cannon crews.[4] The CP's name? "Steinstuecken."

Throughout the 1970s and 1980s, Steinstuecken still got regular visits from the Berlin Brigade—by air. Chief Warrant Officer (retired) Darrell Pope was an Army aviator, assigned to the Berlin Brigade's Aviation Detachment from 1987 to 1991. "We flew the Wall in the helicopters on a daily basis," he recalls. They followed the trace of the Wall, as a routine security and "show-the-flag" patrol. The helicopter flights allowed the Americans to continue asserting their privilege as occupiers to fly into Steinstuecken. "After the access road was opened, there was no operational requirement to fly" to the village, said Doug Powell, a detachment commander. "But we still did. Why? Solely to exercise the right or privilege to do so."

"Out of 365 days of flying the Berlin Wall each year," said Pope, "about 360 of those days we'd all circle Steinstuecken." The new road into the "enclave" was easy to see from the air; the pilots followed it into and out of the village. "Steinstuecken was a place where we could actually go over the East-West border wall," because of the Americans' rights as occupation forces.

The meadow that was the helicopter landing zone, or "LZ," in the days of the MP airlift was still a meadow in the late 1970s and 1980s. It wasn't maintained as an LZ anymore, but American helicopters could still use it. Frequently, the Americans made what they called an "approach" into the LZ. Normally they patrolled the Wall at an altitude of 500 feet, said Pope. Over Steinstuecken, though, often they'd approach the hamlet's LZ as if they were going to land, dropping to approximately 100 feet.

This allowed the Aviation Detachment to engage in some *schadenfreude* at the expense of the Vopos watching Steinstuecken. The helicopter approach "used to drive the East German border guards in the tower nuts," recalled Pope. "You could tell that they were disturbed that we did that. It was our way of poking them in the eye." The Vopos "would get their binoculars out—we were close enough that we didn't need binoculars—they would get on the phone, you could see them dialing whoever it was they dialed up and they were writing things down and they were scrambling around. I'm sure they were documenting the aircraft tail number, the number of people aboard—we'd have the back of the Huey open, so [the aircrew] could do surveillance. I know it was a real irritant to them. But I don't know, it may have been the highlight of their day—you just never know."

The Steinstuecken residents often came out to greet them. "The citizens would come out and they would wave to us," said Pope. "The citizens of Steinstuecken loved" it when the Berlin Brigade Hueys approached the hamlet.[5] Occasionally one would land. Locals—especially the children—would swarm the helicopter.

By June 1988, the MPs had been gone from Steinstuecken for almost sixteen years. Life had moved on, both for the Berlin Brigade and Berliners. The village that had once been a little pocket of freedom, isolated in Communist territory, was now accepted as a suburb of Berlin. An odd suburb, to be sure. Not many neighborhoods have soldiers from another country watching them from watchtowers. But Steinstuecken had been integrated into the regular flow of life in West Berlin. The city bus came and went daily; motorcyclists and other tourists came to visit and eat a snack in one of the village's restaurants. That ongoing sense of unease, even fear, which Steinstueckeners felt during the early decades of the Cold War, had faded.

The close ties between the village and the American occupation forces faded, too. The MP Christmas dinners stopped, as did Santa's visits by chopper. As time passed, the rotor blade memorial fell into disrepair. Brush and vines grew up to obscure it, and vandals painted graffiti on the helicopter blades. The *Berlin Observer* ran a story on May 23, 1986, headlined "Girl Scouts Put New Face on Memorial." A Girl Scout troop from the Berlin military community had gone out to the rotor blade monument to clean it. They carted away "several truckloads of weeds and brush" and removed the tarnish from the bronze commemorative plaque on the memorial's base.[6]

The Girl Scouts' effort was apparently the exception, not the rule. Neither the American military community nor the Zehlendorf government appears to have expended much effort to keep the monument clean. The brush and graffiti soon returned. (It should be pointed out that graffiti and overgrown brush was common in West Berlin. The Divided City's residents included many strong environmentalists; that made Berliners hesitant to trim almost any vegetation. Especially if that vegetation covered a monument whose upkeep was viewed to be an American responsibility.) It was almost as if the MP airlift had faded from official memory.

The author can attest to this. In the spring of 1988, I was an Army lieutenant assigned to an artillery unit south of Frankfurt. I toured the Steinstuecken enclave with some of my fellow officers and their wives and girlfriends. We rode down the street to the village with our mouths agape, stunned as the sight of concrete walls and watchtowers hemming in one little local road. In the village, the tour guide described the history of Steinstuecken, the MP presence, and the helicopter airlift.

We young lieutenants and our companions stared at the railroad track that was East German property, then looked up at a nearby Vopo watchtower. We engaged in a little *schadenfreude* of our own. Two Vopos watched us from the tower. Whenever one of us pointed a camera at the tower, the Vopos would obscure their faces—one held up binoculars, the other hid behind a telephone handset.

We made a game of it. Anytime one of us lifted a camera lens, the Vopos would "hide." When the lens dropped, the Vopos would relax—and we would whip out the cameras again. We treated the Vopos like marionettes—lift the binoculars/phone, drop them, lift them again—until the novelty wore off. Childish, perhaps, but an irresistible bit of fun, all courtesy of the Cold War. The tour guide didn't take us to see the rotor blade memorial, though. He must have known it was there. Most likely, he knew it was overgrown and graffiti-covered and, thus, not a good choice for a stop on the tour.

The monument's fortunes soon improved. In the summer of 1988, the Berlin Brigade's Aviation Detachment got a new commander, Major Douglas ("Doug") Powell. Shortly after arriving, Powell took an orientation tour of the city and the American Sector. He'd read a few books on Berlin, so he already knew a little about Steinstuecken. In fact, Powell recalls, "I found that I knew more about it than the tour guide." The detachment had an aviation technician named Billy Johnson. He spoke German and "had made a connection with the people out in Steinstuecken. And he took me out there and introduced me to everybody."

"We went out there and we looked at the rotor blade memorial. It had become overgrown with vines." That didn't totally surprise Powell. "The city was filled with environmentalists who would rather see grass two feet tall than allow it to be cut and trimmed."[7] Nevertheless, Powell and his soldiers "were embarrassed at the monument. The condition of it didn't speak well of the American presence here."[8] As the Aviation Detachment commander, Powell also headed the local chapter of the

Army Aviation Association of America (AAAA)—the "Checkpoint Charlie" chapter. Accordingly, Powell organized a chapter event—a weekend trip to Steinstuecken to clean up the memorial.

"I told my men, let's just deal with the rotor blades. They were covered with graffiti, and we'd better not touch any of the vegetation. So we went out there, and we tried to make it a fun occasion. We built a scaffold next to the rotor blades, I got my maintenance guys out there, and we were doing some sandblasting, and refinishing of the blades, and tightening up anything that needed to be tightened up. We had the grill going, too."

No one in the detachment told anyone in Steinstuecken they were coming. "Pretty soon the residents started coming out, trying to determine what we were doing. One of the guys who came out was a resident by the name of Gert Knecht." Knecht was the same man who'd caught Gail Halvorsen's "Candy Bomber" parachute as a child and hosted Colonel Halvorsen. "He came up to me and we had a conversation through Billy Johnson, who interpreted for us."

"Gert said 'I know what you're thinking, You're thinking that, if we could take down some of the vegetation and vines, that would present the monument in a better manner.' I replied, 'That's exactly what I'm thinking.'" Powell told Knecht that he'd been advised that environmentalists in Berlin might get upset if the Americans cleared away any vegetation.[9] "He said to me 'Well, as long as I'm here you can cut down anything you want.' And he disappeared, and came back ten minutes later with a chainsaw."

Other Steinstueckeners joined in. They helped the aviators free the monument of vines and branches. "These rotor blades were literally covered. You couldn't see them from a distance." It took the whole weekend to make the memorial look good again.[10] That weekend cleanup turned out to be the spark that rekindled the close relationship between the people of Steinstuecken and the American soldiers in Berlin. This time, though, the village would bond with the Berlin Brigade's aviators instead of its MPs.

The people of Steinstuecken responded to the Americans' cleanup efforts by inviting Powell and his fellow "Quad-A" association members to join the villagers in their annual summer festival. Germany is cloudy much of the year. When summer's sunshine comes, Germans celebrate. Communities across the country put on mini-festivals, or "fests." There is food and music and lots of beer and wine. Steinstueckeners traditionally held their *Sommerfest* every August. For the 1988

Sommerfest, the aircrews of the Berlin Brigade Aviation Detachment were their guests of honor.

This was exactly the kind of activity that the *Berlin Observer* liked to cover. On August 5, the paper ran an article on preparations for the fest: The headline: "Aviators Assist Exclave. Detachment prepares area for local event."

> Members of the Army Aviation Association of America have been sprucing up a memorial in Steinstuecken to prepare for the exclave's annual festival.
>
> This is the first time the Americans have been invited to participate in the fest-that takes place August 20–21.
>
> "We've been asked to participate in their festival and integrate our soldiers with the citizens of Steinstuecken," said Major Douglas Powell.

The *Observer* also interviewed the fest's organizer—Gert Knecht.

> 'We've been connected with the Americans since 1948. During the years since the war, the relationship between Steinstuecken and the U.S. has developed into a friendship,' said fest organizer Gert Knecht. Americans were invited to the fest to strengthen that connection, Knecht said.
>
> The aviation detachment will have a static display at the fest, working in booths and will be participating with some Steinsteucken residents in a bike ride around the Wall in the American sector. The purpose of the 80-mile bike ride is to 'foster the spirit of unity with the citizens of Steinstuecken and the Aviation Detachment,' Powell said. The bike riders are planning to conclude their trip between 2 p.m. and 3 p.m. in Steinstuecken as the fest is going on.
>
> 'We would like to see many of our American friends at the festival,' Knecht said. Steinstuecken can be reached by bus #18.

Between twenty and thirty Americans, mostly AAAA members and their families, made the trip down the Wall-and-watchtower-lined road to the fest. "We opened the fest by riding the Berlin Wall from Checkpoint Charlie along the American sector, all the way out to Steinstuecken," recalled Powell. "We came in, cut the ribbon and sort of started the fest."

Waiting for the bike riders was a UH-1 Huey, which had flown into the enclave to be part of a static display. Enclave residents, especially the children, did what anyone would do—they climbed in, around and all over the helicopter. Cameras clicked repeatedly.

Once the pictures were taken, the Americans directed people to a table where Quad-A members had a mini-production line set up. They attached the photos to a certificate and typed in the person's name, creating a customized memento of the person's time on an American Huey. Translated, the caption reads: "____________________________ is designated an Honorary Pilot of Steinstuecken, in remembrance of the resolute resistance of Steinstuecken as an exclave of liberty, and the airlift by US Army aviators from 1961 to 1972, which preserved the freedom of the proud residents of Steinstuecken."

Doug Powell convinced the Army to allow the Huey on static display to have the name "Steinstuecken" painted on it. Normally, said Powell, authorization to put a personalized label on a piece of Army equipment had to come from high up the command chain—in this case, the US Army command in Europe. However, the senior operations officer ("G3") in Berlin Brigade recognized the idea's merit and gave the go-ahead himself. Gert Knecht used a stencil to paint the village's name on the cargo bay doors of the Huey.

The *Berlin Observer* covered the fest. "Residents of Steinstuecken got together for the first time in recent history with members of the Army Aviation Association Saturday and Sunday to renew old ties and celebrate their annual summer festival." The article admitted that "the friendships developed" between the (now) enclave's residents and the Americans during the Cold War had "drifted off" in recent years. It then described how Billy Johnson and Doug Powell worked "to bring the two groups together again." "'We want to continue to tell the story of Steinstuecken,' said Major Powell during the small and informal ceremony," where the UH-1 on display was officially named for the hamlet. "'We would like to see this become an annual event, due to the good reception on both sides,' said Captain Thomas Gainey, helicopter pilot and co-organizer of the festival."[11]

Tom Gainey got his wish. "We sort of connected to the Germans who had hosted us," said Powell. "As a result of that, in October, they had a thank-you dinner and a bonfire for us. They brought us all out. That was where the relationship was cemented."

In July 1989, Powell sent helicopters over the village to take pictures of it. He turned them into 8x10 prints and took the prints to the enclave. "We went around to each house in Steinsteucken and knocked on the doors. I introduced myself as the commander of the aviation detachment, handed them a photograph of their village, and pointed out their house. Billy Johnson came with me, and was my interpreter. I think we got a lot of momentum out of that from the villagers."

Some Steinstueckeners didn't know what to make of this US Army major's sudden interest in their neighborhood. One of the residents—Elke Hammer, whose anecdotes about Steinstuecken's Cold War experiences appear in earlier chapters—decided to find out. "Out of nowhere she wrote me a letter," recalled Powell, "and wanted to know what my motives were. I just told her that, truly, my motive was just getting to know the Germans better." Also, Powell said in an interview for this book, he was "trying to revive a connection between that rotor blade memorial and the Aviation Detachment."[12]

Several Steinstueckeners became members of the AAAA. "We had about half-a-dozen residents join the organization," said Powell. "I suspect that was a return of respect for us." Some enclave residents also came to the detachment's base at Templehof Airfield to lend a helping hand of their own.

Periodically the detachment participated in German-American outreach events. The USAF staged regular German-American "Open Houses" at Templehof. Berliners came in droves to view military equipment and enjoy American food and beverages. The Army Aviation Detachment operated the American Beer concession—which was built to resemble a UH-1 helicopter. Outreach events gave the aviators a rare opportunity to connect with Berliners. (The Berlin Brigade's ground soldiers had plenty of chances to meet locals as they conducted maneuvers in the city or went to and from training areas. Pilots and aircrews, though, were isolated on Templehof.) Steinstueckeners helped the aviators run some of these events. "We would share beer and wine, lots of discussion, good camaraderie, we would give them tours of the aircraft we had in the hangar," said Darrell Pope. "They came out and helped us, like we had helped them," said Powell. "And we became really close."

The Aviation Detachment upped its game for the 1989 fest. They brought back the "Steinstuecken" helicopter, along with the photo-

and-certificate booth. This time, though, they also brought a VIP—the USCOB himself. In May, Doug Powell coordinated with Major General Raymond Haddock, the American commander in Berlin, to visit Steinstuecken. The enclave residents took General Haddock to the Berlin Wall—which ran through their *backyards*—and hosted him in the village clubhouse. He signed their visitor book, and they presented him with a framed picture of Steinstuecken, taken from the air. They also gave him a letter, signed by more than thirty enclave residents:

> From the Citizens of Steinstuecken, May 6th 1989.
> Dear Major General Haddock,
> The citizens of Steinstuecken are pleased to welcome you here.
> We would like to express our appreciation to our American friends for having stood by us since the opening up of Steinstuecken to West Berlin in 1972, and for the close ties which have been established.
> May we ask that you inform the West Berlin Senate and the District Council of Zehlendorf that the citizens of Steinstuecken would like the American Forces to continue using the Heliport as frequently as in the past. Our need for security makes this indispensable.

That year, the Berlin government floated the idea of building new houses on the helipad area.[13] But even in the late 1980s, almost twenty years since Steinstuecken had received a road to Zehlendorf, the little neighborhood still felt a need to keep the helipad. It also, as their letter to MG Haddock showed, felt some need to ask the Americans for reassurances of their safety.

Major General Haddock obliged. In his own note to the hamlet, on the same day, he said this:

> To the Citizens of Steinstuecken.
> I wish to express my admiration for your courage to remain free in a democratic society while surrounded by a Communist land. We Americans stand ready to guarantee your freedom today as we have in the past.
>
> Raymond Haddock
> Major General, U.S. Army
> StadtKommandant Berlin

For the 1989 *Sommerfest*, Doug Powell arranged for General Haddock to open the event. He cut the ribbon and led a toast. Haddock arrived by helicopter, along with four Steinstueckeners. Powell secured Army approval for Gert Knecht, Kurt Behrendt, and two other enclave residents to fly in with the general. It was the first time any of the Germans had flown in a helicopter.

Almost 4,000 people attended the fest. Kurt Behrendt displayed a collage of his photos from Steinstuecken's days as a Cold War hotspot. Fest organizer Brigitta Rossnagel told the *Berlin Observer* that "the friendship with the Americans had really grown over the last year."[14] The article's headline: "Steinstuecken Summerfest Commemorates U.S. Ties."

"Around Christmas of 1988," recalls Powell, "I was approached by some citizens in Steinstücken, who asked what they could give the Aviation Detachment for Christmas. I suggested a streamer for our detachment guidon." The residents didn't know what a guidon was. "I recall trying to explain it to them." Eventually, the message got through, and a needle-point crochet streamer ended up on the detachment's guidon, which it used in physical training runs and brigade ceremonies.

Wilbur Wolf was Doug Powell's operations officer. Now a retired brigadier general, he remembers how the people of Steinstuecken made the aviators feel like part of their community.

"We met them, and it wasn't like we were complete strangers. It was like we had jumped back in time 30 years to those soldiers and airmen who were providing their mini-airlift. It was like that for the rest of our time there." Villagers invited aviators and their families to their houses for birthdays, anniversaries, or just dinner. "My feeling was, this would have been like my coming home to visit with my family in Pennsylvania, when we'd go to visit with the residents of Steinstuecken. They were that welcoming, that thankful. We weren't the ones who had protected them 30 years prior, but it was like we were those same people, who had maintained their freedom when the Soviets had cut off the access."[15]

Doug Powell shared another Steinstuecken memory with the author. "If you orbited Steinstücken at night, the villagers, in response to hearing our rotor blades, would rush to their light switches and flash lights on and off. It was fun to watch from above." Powell also noted that Steinstuecken was one of the few places the Americans overflew in Berlin that never complained about the noise.[16]

In August 1990, the Aviation Detachment came back to the Steinstuecken *Sommerfest*. The 1990 fest featured the same attractions as the previous two years—pictures in the helicopters, certificates, and lots of food and drink. But in the summer of 1990, the aviators and their Steinstuecken friends had something else to celebrate. The Berlin Wall was coming down.

CHAPTER TWELVE

Barriers once thought to be insurmountable have crumbled and been carried off.
—MG Raymond Haddock, USCOB,
on the day that US Berlin Command inactivated, October 3, 1990

"There are at the present time two great nations in the world, which started from different points, but seem to tend towards the same end. I allude to the Russians and the Americans."

Those aren't the words of FDR, Dwight Eisenhower, George C. Marshall, or any of America's leaders during World War II. They're not from any of our Cold War presidents. Lucius Clay didn't say them, and neither did Ernst Reuter. John J. McCloy didn't say them either, but he did mention them in *The Challenges to American Foreign Policy*, a book he wrote that outlined America's post-WWII challenges in the early 1950s.

Alexis de Tocqueville said them. He wrote them in *Democracy in America*, his landmark study of the United States. De Tocqueville wrote them more than one hundred years before the Cold War. His enthusiasm for the American people, and how they lived and governed themselves, is obvious when he compares them to the Russians.

De Tocqueville said that both America and Russia were young nations, just starting to come of age in the mid-nineteenth century. "All other nations seem to have nearly reached their natural limits, and they have only to maintain their power; but [America and Russia] are still in the act of growth. All the others have stopped, or continue to advance with extreme difficulty; these alone are proceeding with ease and celerity along a path to which no limit can be perceived."

De Tocqueville felt the two nations had drastically different philosophies for government. "The Anglo-American relies upon personal interest to accomplish his ends, and gives free scope to the unguided strength and common sense of the people; the Russian centers all the authority of society in a single arm. The principal instrument of the former is freedom; of the latter, servitude. Their starting-point is different, and their courses are not the same; yet each of them seems marked out by the will of Heaven to sway the destinies of half the globe." By the late 1980s, no one could deny that the destinies of half the globe—the Eastern Hemisphere—had been swayed by the conflict between America and the Soviet Union.

The tone of American-Soviet relations in the 1980s was much harsher than the optimistic days of *détente*. Ronald Reagan was determined to press back against a Soviet Union that he felt had turned aggressive. He fielded new theater ballistic missiles in Europe and called the Soviet Union an "evil empire." Reagan's boldness rattled nerves in many Western capitals. They feared the Soviet Union might retaliate; that would disrupt (or end) peace on the European continent.

Prisoners in the Soviet gulags, on the other hand, were thrilled to hear an American president speak about the Soviet Union in harsh but honest terms. Dissident Natan Sharansky said that, when news of Reagan's "Evil Empire" speech reached his cellblock, the prisoners celebrated.[1] Ronald Reagan made himself part of Berlin's Cold War legacy with one of his most famous speeches: the "Tear Down This Wall" speech on June 12, 1987.

The man Reagan challenged to tear down the Wall was Soviet leader Mikhail Gorbachev. Gorbachev felt that the Soviet Union and its East European satellite states needed reforms in order to make communism more efficient and effective. Gorbachev launched a reform program, which came to be known by two catchphrases: *perestroika* and *glasnost*. *Perestroika* literally means "restructuring." The Library of Congress (LOC) described it as Gorbachev's attempt to "revitalize the economy, party and society by adjusting economic, political and social mechanisms."[2] Soviet industry was managed through a complex, highly centralized control system. *Perestroika*, writes the LOC, "called for wholesale revision of the industrial management system and decentralization of policy making in all ministries."[3] As for *glasnost*, which means "openness," the LOC describes it this way:[4]

> In the late 1980s, the Soviet regime, first that of Andropov and then that of Gorbachev, relaxed their monopoly on the press and

> modern communications technology and eased the strictures of socialist realism, thus permitting open discussion of many themes previously prohibited. The implementation of the policy of glasnost made much more information about government activities, past and present, available to ordinary citizens, who then criticized not only the government but also the CPSU and even Lenin, founder of the Soviet Union.... Editors, journalists and other writers transformed newspapers, journals and television broadcasts into media for investigative reports and lively discussion of a wide variety of subjects that had been heavily censored before glasnost.

Perestroika and *glasnost* opened Pandora's Box for the Communist Bloc. Russian citizens began demanding widespread changes in society. "These policies led to a renewed ferment among the nationalities throughout the Soviet Union," wrote the LOC. "By 1987 the Baltic nationalities, Armenians, Ukrainians, Soviet Muslims, Belorussians, Georgians and others, including ethnic Russians themselves, were expressing their national and religious grievances and calling on the regime to redress them."[5] The Soviet government "began to lose control of the policy of *glasnost*, and the censors began to lose control of the mass media."[6]

The ferment spread to the satellites—where there had already been trouble in the 1980s. In Poland, the Solidarity labor union led a campaign of protest and pushback against government repression. The Polish Communist regime declared martial law and jailed many of the protesters, but they couldn't quash the movement. Eventually they were compelled to negotiate with Solidarity. *Perestroika* and *glasnost* made it much easier to discuss (and protest against) communism's shortcomings. And Soviet communism had many, many shortcomings, which Eastern Europeans had suffered under for decades.

The GDR government resisted *perestroika* and *glasnost.* It preferred the existing policies of tight government control over virtually everything—industry, academia, the press. J.D. Bindenagel, deputy chief of the US Mission in Berlin in 1989, described GDR head Erich Honecker as a "stalwart to Stalinism."[7]

But Gorbachev had unleashed a wave of change, and East Germany wasn't immune. "Although the GDR leadership tried to deny the reality of these developments, for most East Germans the reforms of Soviet leader Gorbachev were symbols of a new era that would inevitably also reach the GDR," writes the LOC in its country study of East Germany. "The GDR leadership's frantic attempts to block the news coming out of the Soviet Union by preventing the distribution of Russian newsmagazines only strengthened growing protest within the population."[8]

In May 1989, East Germany held local elections. The political party the GDR favored, the SED, won resoundingly, scoring almost 99% of the vote—as it always did in GDR elections. This time, though, GDR citizens didn't accept the results quietly. In its country study of East Germany, the LOC writes that the public was "enraged." "In the next months, persistent public complaints against the prevailing living conditions and lack of basic freedoms, voiced by church groups and by opposition groups, inspired the population to take to the streets in large numbers."[9]

"The demonstrations were too massive to be quelled by intimidation or even mass arrests," writes the LOC. The GDR had no problem with cracking down on protesters, violently if need be. But Gorbachev was not Stalin. "Shooting at the demonstrators was out of the question because of the sheer size of the crowds and the absence of Soviet support for draconian measures."[10] The mass demonstrations not only continued; by the fall of 1989, they occurred almost every Monday in the GDR's largest cities.

The demonstrations weren't the only spectacles rattling the GDR. That summer, Hungary allowed several hundred GDR citizens, who were supposedly "vacationing" in Hungary, to cross the border into Austria, a neutral nation aligned with the West. Word spread, and thousands of East Germans flocked to Hungary. The Hungarian Communist government didn't turn them back or arrest them. Instead, on September 11, the Hungarians opened their border to Austria. 15,000 East Germans crossed into Austria—and freedom—in just a few days.[11]

The foundations of the GDR government started to wobble. On October 7, Gorbachev came to East Germany for the celebration of the fortieth anniversary of the founding of the German Democratic Republic. GDR leader Erich Honecker defiantly proclaimed that "Socialism will be halted in its course neither by ox, nor ass."

In his remarks, though, Gorbachev didn't offer the Pankow regime unflinching support. "He who comes too late," the Soviet leader said, "will suffer the consequences of history." Many took Gorbachev's remarks as a criticism of the GDR for resisting reforms. Two days later, over 70,000 East Germans protested the regime. One week later, there were over 100,000.[12] The next day, on October 17, Erich Honecker was removed from office.

The new GDR leadership searched for ways to quell the rising unrest. They wanted to "establish legitimacy and get the people with them," said Bindenagel. "They were nervous about the demonstrations, dissident activity and so many youth escaping their paradise. We [in the US State Department] focused on how the SED would address the concerns of the people out on the street who wanted the freedom to travel. The idea created by the Politburo was to revise the travel law, allowing more travel with the hope that changes would take care of the question of the refugees and so forth. On the 6th of November, the GDR announced a revised travel law in their newspaper."[13]

What followed was extraordinary. Richard Barkley, the US Ambassador to the GDR at the time, recalled what happened. On November 9, a GDR official held a press conference. State Department officials didn't expect anything important to come out of it. They couldn't have been more wrong.

> It was a rather unremarkably uneventful press conference for a long time, to the point where I gave up watching it on television, got in my car and drove home. I didn't see anything new coming out of the whole thing. By the time I got home I immediately put on the news. During that interim, [the GDR official] was handed a piece of paper where he announces that forthwith, or in a very short period of time, there will be no travel restrictions on East German citizens between East and West Germany and East and West Berlin.
>
> The question was asked at that time, what does this mean. He said, 'Well just what I said. Everybody will have a right to a visa. You can get that visa. There will be no exceptions and they can move back and forth.' One of the journalists said, 'Does that mean immediately?' He looked at the paper and said, 'Yes, that means immediately.'[14]

The GDR had planned to institute a measured, controlled visa program, starting the next day. But no one told the official who was briefing the press. Apparently he assumed the program started immediately.[15] And that's what he told the press—who then told the world.

East Berliners could watch West German TV and hear West German radio. When the West German press announced the border openings, thousands of East Berliners flocked to Checkpoint Charlie and other crossing points. The GDR border guards were surprised and overwhelmed. They were also under orders not to harm the crowds. "They were told for God's Sakes don't shoot anybody and don't do anything, and if they push you, get out of the way,"[16] recalled Ambassador Barkley. When the crowds pushed forward, asking to go through the checkpoints, the Vopos let them.

"November 9, 1989 will be remembered as one of the great moments of German history," writes the Library of Congress. "On that day, the dreadful Berlin Wall, which for twenty-eight years had been the symbol of German division, cutting through the heart of the old capital city, was unexpectedly opened by GDR border police. In joyful disbelief, Germans from both sides climbed up on the Wall, which had been called 'the ugliest edifice in the world.' They embraced each other and sang and danced in the streets."[17] Lester Feutz was a fixed-wing aircraft pilot in the Berlin Aviation Detachment. The trains and roads were so crammed, he said, you couldn't move anywhere.[18]

November 9 was a Thursday. The GDR still planned to implement their plan to require a visa before visiting the West. But the crush of East Berliners overwhelmed them. On Friday morning, November 10, they moved the start time for the visa requirement from 8 a.m. to noon. At noon they delayed it until the following Monday. This allowed East Germans to go through the border, essentially unimpeded, for a whole weekend.[19] That Monday, Doug Powell read this headline in a German newspaper: "Good Morning Berlin. Wasn't That A Wonderful Weekend?"[20]

Powell wrote a memorandum describing how he and his detachment reacted to the news that the Wall was open. Here are some excerpts:

> The initial news was passed to the detachment commander's wife as she returned from an evening at the theater. Her neighbor came running up to her saying 'The Wall is down! I just heard the news on AFN.' In turn, she entered the house and relayed

the news to her husband. Feeling a bit skeptical, the Major, determined to get to the truth of the matter, called the Emergency Operation Center. As soon as he got through, the Operations Sergeant indicated the Chief of Staff, Colonel Counts, was trying to reach him on another line. At that point he decided something unusual was going on and in a matter of minutes was coordinating an airplane and flight crew to fly the West Berlin Mayor, Herr Momper to Bonn and back at 0600 the next morning. But finding a crew and airplane was a story in itself.

For the first time in 18 months, the detachment's warrant officers had decided to go down to the Kurfurstendamm (Berlin's liveliest nightspot) for a much deserved night on the town. [Note to the reader: in an Army aviation unit, most of the pilots are warrant officers. This meant that most of Major Powell's pilots were out on the town the night the Wall opened.] The commander knew and approved of their absence but did not know their exact location. This was the first weekend in well over a month that the Aviation Detachment was not on call.

The C-12, the unit's VIP transport plane, was down for programmed maintenance: both engines had been scheduled for replacement and a new navigation package was being installed. The irony of this was that it was fully coordinated six months prior, with all agencies and it was determined to be the best time with the least impact on the command. The Air Force managed to scare up a C-141 and crew that just happened to be in town from Charleston S.C. [and it flew the Berlin mayor to West Germany the next morning.]

At daybreak, Berlin Brigade sent helicopters to scout the entire 102-mile circumference of the Berlin Wall. Fixed-wing aircraft flew reconnaissance missions. By 1964 the Soviets and Western Allies had agreed to not overfly East Berlin with helicopters. (Because Steinstuecken was surrounded by the territory of *Land* Brandenburg, not East Berlin, this restriction didn't apply there). Fixed-wing aircraft, however, could fly anywhere within the twenty-five-mile radius of the Berlin Control Zone. Hence, the Aviation Detachment used fixed-wing aircraft for reconnaissance missions over and around Berlin.

With exception of the downtown area, everything was pretty much 'ops normal.' The city center's five crossing points were another story. At each location on the East side, vehicles were backed up for about a mile while lines of pedestrians, five abreast, stretched for a quarter mile. It was a flood of humanity. On the west side, Berliners had formed massive rows of cheering people, welcoming each car and border-crosser to the city. Downtown city streets were choked with thousands of pedestrians.

While the men and women of the detachment performed their jobs, their spouses were informed that the whole affair (in and around the Wall) was pretty much non-threatening, so they, individually, participated in experiencing the historic events downtown. The Commander released the detachment's Local National employees at 1100 hours to allow them to witness this historic moment.

That night, members of the detachment went downtown to see it all from the ground. Some tried to take the bus but it only went a few blocks toward the Ku'damm when it was forced to turn around. The streets were packed with people; no more than two wheels could get through. They then began to walk to their destination. The Ku'damm was lined on both sides with DDR cars. They were so small that two could fit into one parking space.

After walking a bit, they decided it best to go underground to the catch the U-bahn to Checkpoint Charlie. Since they were traveling opposite the flow of traffic, they had no problem finding a place on a U-bahn car.

The first thing they encountered at Checkpoint Charlie was a line of West Germans greeting DDR cars coming across the border. The West Germans were banging their hands on car roof tops, offering flowers, chocolate, money and hugs. The faces of the car occupants revealed a mixture of joy and uncertainty. You could see lines of people pouring out across the border, just as we had seen from the air earlier in the day. The exodus was continuous.

The group (from the Aviation Detachment) continued to walk along the Wall towards the Brandenburg Gate.

> Upon reaching the Brandenburg Gate, they observed, literally, thousands of people who had climbed up on top of the Wall—including some members of the detachment. [Unbeknownst to the commander, at least two crew chiefs, one avionics technician and one dependent son were among the crowd upon the wall]. There were old and young alike; East and West together. It was like a New Year's Eve party and Christmas all rolled up into one.
>
> The news media … had erected banks of flood lights which illuminated the place to a level much brighter than a sunlit day. People in the crowd were wearing sun glasses! Occasionally, a chorus would emerge from the crowd, '*Die Mauer Muss Weg*!' (The Wall must go!)[21]

Heike Behrendt was a grown woman when the Wall opened. She still lived in Steinstuecken and worked in Berlin. Like many Berliners, she skipped work on Friday, November 10. Before she had Heike, Heike's mother had worked for a tailor in Berlin. Two of her mother's former colleagues lived in Kleinmanchow, a suburb in the Soviet Sector. When the Berlin Wall went up, these two women were sealed behind it.

On that Friday, Heike's mother called to tell her that one of the ladies had called. The lady said to Heike's mother, "Guess where we are?" Heike's mother replied, "You must be in West Berlin." They were—in the living room of a friend.

The woman had brought her daughter with her, a student. "Her daughter was just a little bit younger than I was," said Heike. "Because they were not sure that the situation would not change, they asked if the daughter could stay in Steinstuecken with us. They were afraid that [the GDR] might close the border a second time. So the daughter came home and stayed with me. The following Monday, when I went back to work, I heard from many of my colleagues that many of their relatives from the East had stayed with them too. If the situation changed, they wanted to be in the West when the border closed again."

Heike took the young East German woman on a walk through Steinstuecken. She saw the death strip, the watchtowers—and Heike learned that this was the first time the woman had ever seen the border fortifications. The GDR prevented its citizens from getting close to the frontier. This woman was seeing sights that, for Heike Behrendt and the other children in Steinstuecken, were commonplace.[22]

Soon people were chopping chunks out of the Berlin Wall. In some places they removed whole panels. The GDR border guards replaced some of the panels but not all of them. Steinstuecken residents got in on the act, as Doug Powell remembers. "The people of Steinstucken created a hole in the wall and, using beer as a lure, managed to convince an East German soldier he should spend his Sunday afternoon drinking instead of guarding the wall. I happened by and the soldier was in such an inebriated state, he offered me his uniform. I settled for his epaulets, which now hang on my kitchen wall."[23]

Powell collected some other souvenirs from the Vopo border guards around Steinstuecken. Hanging in the branches of a tree, he found two bottles. Inside each was a note, written by (presumably) a Vopo. Powell later learned that it was a tradition for Vopos who were nearing the end of their service in the GDR border forces to toss bottles with notes into the enclave. A larger object (a spoon, stick, shoe, etc...) tied to the bottle would catch in the tree branches, letting the bottle dangle. Doug opened the bottles and found these two handwritten messages:

> 'Resig' cigar was lit at 11:50 AM and finished by Buby at 12:20 and by Wolfchen at 12:25 on 25 October 1989. 'Keep it up, the end is near.' Signed: Buby and Wolfchen
>
> Best wishes for a healthy New Year 1986, our discharge year. He, who finds this message, perhaps has never experienced what we have. Endure Boys. Before us there were 1,000 and after us will come 100,000. Signed: [By both guard's numerical codes.]

The bottles "were found within days of the Berlin Wall falling," said Powell, in an email to the author. (Although, according to the dates on both notes, they'd been hanging in the trees for some time). "Had they been found prior, they could have lent a bit of intelligence value. From the notes, it is clear that two guards threw them from their guard tower perch, over the wall to be caught by tree branches." One was wrapped around a cigar. The counterweights used to catch them in the tree branches were, respectively, a canteen and a flattened spoon. The flattened spoon was apparently a token symbol for a "short-timer" in the GDR armed forces.

On Saturday, November 11, Berlin Aviation Detachment pilots flew the US Ambassador along the East-West Berlin border, so he could see the crowded crossing points. The helicopter carrying the ambassador then flew on to Wannsee, so he could see the Gleinicke ("Freedom") Bridge—the bridge that U-2 pilot Francis Gary Powers had crossed when released from Soviet captivity. Doug Powell followed in another helicopter. As the ambassador's Huey went to Wannsee, Doug's landed at Steinstuecken.

"As usual, residents came out of the woodwork to greet the helicopter and its occupants," recalls Powell. "But this day there were three guests present—residents of East Germany. One, a bearded man of about 50 years, came forward and threw his arms around both crew members. The man's wife immediately joined her husband and the two of them hugged the American officers. Things started to calm down and the third guest came forward with his greetings."

"The three East Germans lived only a stone's throw away. They had spent 28 years living in homes with adjacent back yards separated by the Wall." (The western edge of the exclave butted up against the eastern edge of the Babelsberg suburbs.) These East Germans probably lived there. "They had seen the people, the helicopters, the Americans and now for the first time they could share, touch and experience what they could only before imagine. These people were brothers, neighbors, and the like. Their emotions toward each other, after 28 years of separation, spoke for itself. They couldn't believe it when we allowed them to sit in our aircraft."[24]

A month later, on December 2, Brigadier General Jim Hesson, president of the Army Aviation Association of America, visited Steinstuecken. "Using sledgehammers provide by Steinstuecken citizens," recalls Doug Powell, they punched their own hole through the Berlin Wall. This concerned Powell because US Forces had recently been ordered not to desecrate the Wall. But by early December, Wall desecration was the thing to do in West Berlin. "An entire section of the Wall collapsed," recalls Powell. "Later that same day, East German engineers replaced the panel."[25]

"The Wall had not only become irrelevant," said J. D. Bindenagel, "the East German government had become irrelevant. They lost the authority of government to do basic things like issue visas. They had no control over that crucial aspect of their authority. The Soviets didn't intervene. We thought they would do something. They were clearly taken by surprise, as the East German government was taken by surprise over what had occurred."[26]

There's an old saying about rotten systems. When they collapse, it happens slowly at first but finishes suddenly. With the border crossings open, the German Democratic Republic began to collapse quickly. Not everyone in East Germany wanted to be rid of socialism. Some reformers wanted to modernize and improve it, as Gorbachev wanted. But a critical mass of East Germans did want to do away with the German Democratic Republic.

Enter West German chancellor Helmut Kohl. At the end of November, he gave the *Bundestag* a detailed plan for German reunification. In December, East Germany's political parties began discussions on the GDR's future. In March 1990, East Germany held elections for its parliament, the *Volkskammer*. The SED—the party of the Communists, the party that had ruled East Germany since the end of World War II, the party that got well over 90% of the "official" vote in elections—was replaced by a coalition led by the CDU, the sister party of West Germany's CDU.[27]

One month later, the East and West German governments began negotiations with the four WWII occupying powers on a treaty that would finally end the Second World War and allow Germany to reunite. These came to be known as the "Two Plus Four" talks—the "Two" being the FRG and GDR and the "Four" being the wartime Allied Powers. The British and French raised concerns about a reunited Germany and its impact on the European continent. (When you think about it—could you blame them?) But the US and West German governments pushed for a quick conclusion to the treaty. Gorbachev removed major stumbling blocks to ratification when he agreed to not oppose German reunification, full restoration of its sovereignty, or the membership of a reunified Germany in NATO.[28]

The treaty was signed in September. The FRG agreed to reduce the size of its armed forces, and both the FRG and GDR pledged not to develop nuclear, chemical, or biological weapons. The reunited Germany pledged to honor its existing border with Poland and renounce any claims to prewar German territories. The Allied Powers agreed to relinquish all occupation rights once Germany reunified. The reunified Germany would have full sovereignty once again. Soviet troops were to depart from Germany territory by the end of 1994; Western Allied forces could stay in West Berlin until the Soviets left.[29]

As the East and West Germans negotiated with the Allies, they also pressed forward with reuniting their country. In July the two countries adopted the Deutsche Mark as their common currency. The FRG began sending financial aid to East Germany.[30] It also proposed a plan for bringing the two halves of Germany back together. The FRG's Basic Law had a provision in it, which allowed individual *Laender* (states) to join the country. The Germans would use this provision to allow Brandenburg and the other GDR states to join the FRG. The GDR would simply go out of existence. October 3, 1990 was set as the date for reunification.

Four days before reunification, on September 29, the Berlin Brigade Aviation Detachment conducted one last flight over territory that was still officially the GDR. "Four helicopters filled with dignitaries and news media" flew to Steinstuecken, remembers Powell. The dignitaries included General Haddock, the USCOB, and Berlin City Councillor Ingrid Stahmer. The Hueys also carried several Steinstueckeners, including Gert Knecht, Kurt Behrendt, and Guenter Rossnagel. The Commander in Chief, USAREUR, authorized the enclave residents to fly.

In Steinstuecken, General Haddock and Frau Stahmer attached a new plaque to the rotor blade memorial. The inscription read:

> On 3 October 1990, the freedom of Steinstuecken was assured by German reunification. In commemoration, a final U.S helicopter flight over East German airspace landed here on 29 September 1990. This memorial remains as a testimony to the will to preserve freedom.

Gunter Rossnagel and Major Powell received awards, and a Steinstuecken citizen presented each American aircrew member a silver commemorative Airlift coin.[31]

When the ceremony was over, the dignitaries and media boarded the helicopters, and everyone flew back toward West Berlin. As they departed, Doug Powell realized that the last aircraft to leave Steinstuecken airspace were the ones carrying the media. This was the last official flight of Americans as protectors of West Berlin from the hamlet they had safeguarded for decades. As it stood, the last people to officially fly out of the American Sector enclave of Steinstuecken and over East German airspace would be reporters. This, said Doug Powell, was a "totally inappropriate situation."

The helicopters delivered General Haddock, Frau Stahmer, and the media representatives to Army headquarters. But the helicopters did not shut down, and their crews did not deplane. They lifted off again. This time, they only carried Army aviators and one Air Force photographer. The helicopters joined into a formation of four over West Berlin's Grunewald Forest and flew back to Steinstuecken. They orbited the village three or four times, then flew home. The Army aviators wanted to make absolutely sure there would be, as Doug Powell put it, "no historical misunderstandings as to who actually made the *last* flight to the "West Berlin" enclave of Steinstuecken.[32]

On October 3, 1990, Germany became one nation again. World War II had finally ended. The GDR, whose leader Erich Honecker had boasted just one year earlier that "Socialism will not be halted in its course, either by ox or ass,"[33] was swept away.

"Unification celebrations were held all over Germany," writes the LOC, "especially in Berlin, where leading figures from West and East joined the joyful crowds who filled the streets between the *Reichstag* building and Alexanderplatz to watch a fireworks display. Germans celebrated unity without a hint of nationalistic pathos, but with dignity and in an atmosphere reminiscent of a country fair. Yet the world realized that an historic epoch had come to an end."[34]

With the GDR in history's trashcan, the Wall and the areas on both sides on it became a tourist attraction. Former "West" Berliners, Allied soldiers, and their families explored old Vopo bunkers and fighting positions. One of Doug Powell's pilots, Ken Breeden, found a notebook in an East German command bunker near Steinstuecken. It listed the tail numbers of all the Aviation Detachment Hueys that had flown to the hamlet.[35] The Wall vanished steadily, bit by bit, ending up as decorative centerpieces in memorials and parks across the West or smashed into chunks and sold as souvenirs. Graffiti flourished on what was left.

In July 1991, Doug Powell's tour of duty in Berlin ended. Before he departed, the Aviation Detachment installed new rotor blades on the memorial. The new blades came from Frank Radespinner, the director of Bell Textron's European Division. (Bell Helicopter built the Hueys the Aviation Detachment flew). Radespinner himself is noteworthy. He was the first person to fly a helicopter to the South Pole. Detachment members and Steinstueckeners installed the new blades at a farewell celebration for Doug and his family. The mayor of Zehlendorf came to thank Powell and the detachment for all its efforts.

In July 1991, even though the Wall was vanishing and the GDR had vanished, the American military was still in Berlin. It would stay for three more years. Those were times of constant change. The archives of the *Berlin Observer* are a wonderful source for learning how the American military community in Berlin closed down operations and eventually went home.

Stories started to appear about contacts between American personnel and the Soviets, East Berliners, and East Germans. In its February 7, 1992 issue, the Berlin military community travel office advertised bus tours to Prague, Budapest, and Dresden—all in former Soviet satellites. There was also a notice for signups for the Berlin Half-Marathon, which that year would start at … Karl-Marx Allee.

That same issue covered a visit by forty sixth-grade students to the town of Neustrelitz. Neustrelitz was in the former GDR. The following month, a photo in the *Observer* showed an elementary school exchange student eating a cupcake at a US military elementary school. The girl wasn't German. "A student from Russian School #3 in Potsdam enjoys a cupcake during Thomas A. Roberts School's Valentine's Day celebration. Approximately 100 students from the Russian school visited TAR. The children were treated to pizza parties, Burger King and other typically American cuisine during their visit. On March 20 Mary Lou Neumann's third-grade class will travel to the Russian school to spend the day with the students and experience Russian culture."[36]

In 1993, American connections to the Soviet Zone took a huge step forward. Or, to be more precise, eastward. The Americans staged a German-American Culture Fest ("*Kulturfest*") in the former GDR. "The first German-American festival to be held in former East German territory will be held April 30–May 2 in Neubrandenburg [part of the Land of Mecklenburg-Vorpommern]," reported the *Observer* on April 23. "Neubrandenburg officials will conduct English-speaking tours of the town each afternoon. Local officials and American representatives are also scheduled to plant a linden tree of friendship." Coca-Cola helped sponsor the festival. Lenin, who claimed the capitalists would sell the Communists the rope they'd use to hang the capitalists with, must have been spinning in his grave. (Stalin, too).

Lester and Jan Feutz ventured into East Berlin and East Germany. "Initially, if you wanted to go over to the East, you had to pay a visa fee—about 60 West German marks for an adult," recalled Les. "And we had to declare, when we crossed over into East Germany, to Potsdam, everything. If we had a radio in the car, we had to declare how much money we had in the car, if we had anything of value. Then as time went on, and this happened fairly fast, things got kind of relaxed. I think it was the next year, where we were allowed to drive through East Germany, down to the Elbe River, so we could see the American and Russian bands celebrating at Torgau."

Torgau was the spot where American and Soviet forces had met in World War II. When the Feutzs tried to drive to Torgau, they had American military license plates. Initially, the Vopos were unsure if they could let them enter East Germany with those plates. "They were debating on what to do with us, and they finally said 'Just let them go with the [plates] they had on the car.' We [might have been] the first ones to drive through East Germany with the old American license plates."[37]

As the months passed, the former GDR officials relaxed more and more restrictions. "One day, it reached the point where you could drive anywhere, you didn't need any additional paperwork, you could drive into East Berlin, you could drive anywhere you wanted to go," said Les Feutz. The Feutzs even made friends with a couple from the former East, who they'd met while walking in Potsdam. When it came time for them to leave Berlin and move back to the United States, the Feutzs hired the husband to paint their apartment.[38]

The Berlin Brigade's mission changed. "We're no longer the Berlin city guard," said Colonel Jimmy Banks, the brigade commander in August 1992.[39] Brigade units began to train for out-of-Germany, and even overseas, deployments. One of its infantry companies went to Macedonia for UN peacekeeping duties. The artillery battery, E/320 Field Artillery (re-designated from C/94 FA) traded its heavy tracked cannons for lighter wheeled howitzers that helicopters could carry in slings. During the Cold War, Berlin Brigade soldiers had became experts at city fighting. They had learned to block alleyways with barbed wire and call in artillery strikes with street intersections instead of map coordinates. With the Cold War won, the brigade morphed into a more typical Army unit, capable of deploying anywhere in the world.

By 1994, the *Observer's* reporting had one overriding theme: going home. 1994 was the year that all Allied forces were to be out of Berlin. The *Observer* started a regular feature column: "Drawdown Update." Throughout 1992 and 1993, the Berlin commands had to deal with an endless stream of rumors about units departing Berlin on short notice or community support facilities closing. The Army and Air Force commanders in the city spent lots of their time reassuring nervous Americans (and the Berliners who worked for them). "The rumor for the week is that the base exchange will be closing in June," wrote the Templehof AFB commander in the March 20, 1992 issue of the *Observer*. "Not so. The month may be correct, but the year will be 1993, not 1992."

By 1994, though, the closings started in earnest. The *Observer* was filled with stories about "the last ____________________ in Berlin for the US military community. [The last Association of the US Army ball, the last Winterfest, etc.]," Berlin military community agencies sold off excess property. By spring, articles about unit farewell ceremonies started to appear. Many of the Berlin Brigade's units had partnerships with specific Berlin neighborhoods—similar to the Aviation Detachment partnership with Steinstuecken. As the brigade's departure drew near, these communities held parades and festivals to bid their American friends farewell. Even Russians attended.

Steinstuecken held a farewell for the Aviation Detachment and all the Americans who helped the community and protected it over the previous four decades. Doug Powell, now retired from the Army, came back for the ceremony. The same Huey helicopter that Gert Knecht had named "Steinstuecken" five years earlier returned to the small cluster of houses and fields that had been a suburb of Babelsberg, then the Cold War's most famous exclave, then a West Berlin enclave, and was now a suburb of Greater Berlin once again. One of the guests was one of the first Army pilots to ever enter Steinstuecken—Tom Clark, the copilot for General Clay's historic flight into the exclave on September 22, 1961.

Doug Powell met Tom Clark while he still commanded the Berlin Aviation Detachment. "I was taking a day of leave at my quarters, when the phone rang. It was Nic Davidson, our flight operations officer. He said there was a man standing in front of him who said he flew General Lucius D. Clay into Steinstucken in 1961. Thank God for good people. Many would have said, 'Too bad, you missed the boss. He's not here.'"

"Within the next hour I was standing together with Tom Clark in the basement of the detachment going over our unit's archives. I had many questions; he had many answers. He had tail numbers. He had names of pilots who flew the first flight mission the day the Wall went up. He had the flight route. He had aerial photos of the tanks facing off at Charlie. I wrote as he talked. Tom was re-living his past assignment to Berlin."

"Eight hours later, well into the evening, I asked Tom if he wanted to return to Steinstucken." Clark seemed a bit surprised by Powell's offer. "Tom's brain was thinking a bit different from mine. He left Berlin in 1962 or 63, prior to the 1972 Four Power Accords, and thus was not aware of the 1,200 meter access road. So here is Tom; thinking we're about to make a night flight and he's not even on active duty. I can't imagine what he was thinking. When we got into my car, he realized things had changed in the 26 years since he was assigned to Berlin."

Powell and Clark drove to Steinstuecken. "Tom was totally amazed. Soon we were standing in Kurt Behrendt's living room viewing photos of Tom and his aircraft from the day he flew General Clay in 1961. It was an emotional time for Tom. Later that evening, we used the headlights of our car to illuminate original barbed wire and wood posts from the evening of August 13, 1961."[40]

Richard Boehm had been an economics officer for the State Department in Berlin from 1959 to 1962. He witnessed Clay's efforts to guarantee Steinstuecken's security during the Berlin Wall crisis. He returned to Berlin in 1990—unaware that the 1972 Four Power Agreement had led to a new road from the village to Zehlendorf. "I was itching to go to Steinstuecken," said Boehm, to a State Department interviewer. "I drove to it. I thought that I had to cross to it through East Germany. I came back. The Ambassador in Bonn… had invited me to stay at his Berlin residence. He was in Bonn or somewhere. I had the whole residence to myself. I told the butler that I had made it to Steinstuecken, fulfilling a longstanding ambition to drive there through East Germany. He said, 'That isn't East Germany at all. We bought that road.'"[41]

Three days after the Aviation Detachment's farewell, the Berlin Brigade held its deactivation ceremony on July 12. President Clinton and *German* Chancellor Helmut Kohl presided as the brigade cased its colors and paraded for the last time. President Clinton reviewed the brigade in a WWII-vintage Jeep. Later that day, he, First Lady Hillary Clinton, Chancellor Kohl, and his wife took a ceremonial walk through the Brandenburg Gate, now free of any trace of the hideous Berlin Wall.

President Clinton didn't mention Steinstuecken in his formal remarks. But he almost did. A preliminary draft copy of those remarks had the president commending "General Lucius D. Clay, who rallied

Western support for the city during the Airlift and after the building of the Wall. When the 200 residents of the tiny exclave farming village of Steinstuecken were walled off from west Berlin in 1961, General Clay flew into Steinstuecken by helicopter over hostile east German territory and stationed a detachment of military police there. For more than ten years U.S. forces were rotated in and out by helicopter and saved Steinstuecken from being sucked into communist east Germany."[42]

"The Americans came and freed us from a totalitarian system," said Berlin Mayor Eberhard Deepen at the farewell ceremony. "They fed us. They protected us. They built a new future together with us, and for that we should thank them." The mayor of Zehlendorf, Ulrich Mendel, published a farewell letter to the American troops, many of whom had lived in his *Bezirk*. "With the drawdown of the U.S. Army in Europe, an era in the history of Berlin comes to an end," he wrote. "Berliners are well aware that their freedom and prosperity depended on the presence and the firm stand of the Americans during many years of East-West confrontations.... So it is with sadness that we now see our American friends and neighbors leave. We will not forget them, and the friendships will outlast the separation."

When the American military left Berlin, the Steinstueckeners took over the leadership of the Checkpoint Charlie chapter of the AAAA. With few Americans left in the city, they searched for a way to generate interest (and membership) in the club. They came up with a unique idea: Send Gert Knecht's "Candy Bomber" parachute into space. They wanted one of the joint US-Russia space shuttle missions to take the parachute with them.

On November 12, 1995, the space shuttle *Atlantis* lifted off from Kennedy Space Center. The mission was designated STS-74, and its destination was the Russian *Mir* space station. The mission lasted for eight days, completed 129 Earth orbits, and flew 3.4 million miles.[43] On board was Gert Knecht's parachute. From his home in Utah, Colonel Halvorsen signed it and gave it a special inscription: "Out of the C-54 to Berlin's Children in 1948—Out of space in 1995, in memory of those who died for freedom." Unfortunately, the parachute's trip into space didn't lead to additional members for the Checkpoint Charlie chapter of the AAAA. It did, however, add one more interesting element to the story of Steinstuecken. The parachute is now in Steinstuecken, with Gert Knecht's son Lorenz.

Gail Halvorsen kept in touch with Gert Knecht and the people of Steinstuecken. Many veterans of the Brigade Aviation Detachment and the 287th MP Company have also made their way back there. Several of the Cold War-era Steinstueckeners have paid visits of their own. Guenter and Gitte Rossnagel and Kurt Behrendt all traveled to see Les and Jan Feutz in their retirement home—Sierra Vista, Arizona, a small town southeast of Tucson near the Mexican border. Jan Feutz recalled how the Berliners marveled at the warm, dry climate and the striking desert vegetation. Kurt Behrendt, ever the photographer, found several especially photogenic cactus plants and photographed them repeatedly from multiple angles and differing levels of shading and sunlight.[44] (Les Feutz passed away in 2015).

Steinstuecken has changed dramatically. With the Cold War over, its fields and wooded areas—and the cleared areas around it—became prime targets for real estate developers.

Wilbur Wolf, Doug Powell's former executive officer, saw the changes in Steinstuecken when he and his family visited the village in December 2017. The helipad is now covered with houses. The helicopter playset is still there, though, entertaining a new generation of Steinstuecken children. The community club still operates. Technically, it's a *Tierverein*, translated as "a club for small animals." The Steinstuecken residents raise rabbits, poultry and small birds. They gather at the clubhouse for archery, art lessons, card games and to share memories.

Only a few families from the Cold War days live in Steinstuecken now. The neighborhood now has residents from America, Russia, and India. And some of the *Tierverein's* regulars are former East Germans. This has led to some surprising reactions when the Cold War comes up in conversation. One weekend's discussion centered on a new documentary of former GDR border guards. One guard talked about how he was shocked at the prospect that some of his colleagues might actually try to kill someone fleeing across the border. Lifelong Steinstueckeners, whose sympathies align with the West, were surprised to hear former East German club members grumble that the soldier shouldn't have been troubled by doing his duty. Nowadays, the *Verein* shies away from politics in its weekend discussions. But the reminders of the Americans are still there. A section of a Huey tail rotor hangs above one of the clubhouse's windows, and a huge American flag covers the ceiling of the anteroom.

The US Army hasn't forgotten Steinstücken. On December 14, 2016, representatives of the 16th Combat Aviation Brigade travelled to the *Verein* to present the village of Steinstuecken and Guenter Rossnagel with the Order of Saint Michael Award on behalf of the Army Aviation Association of America. Normally awarded to individuals, this was the first time the Order of Saint Michael was bestowed upon an entire village.

The rotor blade memorial is still there and in good shape—but it's easy to miss. The blades are tall, but the suburbs of Berlin have grown up around them. Life has marched on from the days of the Berlin Wall and the Cold War. Steinstuecken has blended into the rest of metropolitan Berlin. Thousands of people drive by the neighborhood each day, most likely unaware of its noteworthy and tumultuous past.

That's too bad because Steinstuecken deserves to be remembered. Its history is colorful, and many of the events arising from its days as a little pocket of freedom are worthy of being told. In closing this book, please allow the author to share three themes that reoccur throughout the nearly half-century of American and Berliner partnership in Steinstuecken. They are determination, persistence, and courage.

A March 1967 CIA report on the exclaves of West Berlin said that they were "significant mainly because they provide the USSR with a ready means of testing Western resolve." Steinstuecken remained free because several Americans were determined (or resolved) that it remain free. In the years immediately following World War II, American occupation officials like Karl Mautner and Ulrich Biehl resisted suggestions to give the neighborhood to the Russians. When the Communists tried to swallow the exclave in October 1951, General Lemuel Mathewson put his foot down and the Communists backed away. And in 1961, when many thought that Steinstuecken might be washed away in the waves of confusion and angst caused by the Berlin Wall crisis, Lucius Clay stepped forward. He made it clear that the Americans were determined to protect it.

The "persistence" came from the Army MPs and aviators and the OMGUS, HICOG, and State Department officials who looked out for the little village. Over nearly fifty years of Communist harassment, Americans went to bat for Steinstuecken. For nearly a half-century, US Army soldiers guarded Western Europe and West Berlin. Teddy Roosevelt said, "Speak softly, but carry a big stick." The "big stick" in NATO and in West Berlin was the American military. The Communists saw that stick and were wary of it. The MP outpost in Steinstuecken and the Army helicopter airbridge that made it possible were symbols of that stick. For more than ten years, the US Army maintained its tiny-but-meaningful "boots on the ground" presence in Steinstuecken until it was no longer needed.

Lastly, the "courage" came from the Steinstueckeners themselves. For ten years, from 1951 to 1961, they lived surrounded by and virtually unprotected from a hostile power. Until the MPs showed up in 1961, nothing prevented the Soviets or Vopos from crossing the street from Babelsberg and snatching any Steinstueckener they pleased. Nothing could stop the Vopos from grabbing a village resident as they walked along the *Waldweg.* Yet the Steinstueckeners didn't back down. They were defiant, even at times where there was no guarantee the Americans could (or would) come to their aid.

When the Vopos surrounded the village in October 1951, almost all Steinstueckeners refused the "offer" to come meet the mayor of Potsdam or shop at the GDR food trucks. In 1952 they wouldn't accept GDR identity cards. When the West Berlin mayor tried to visit in 1956 and the Vopos blocked him, most of the villagers marched up the *Waldweg* to meet him at the Kohlhasenbrueck checkpoint. If the Vopos, Stasi, or KGB wanted to single out the "malcontents" in Steinstuecken for future reprisals, the people of the village gave the Communists plenty of targets to choose from. Yet throughout it all, Steinstueckeners worked together and banded together to keep their community strong and healthy. When the Soviet Union and the GDR finally melted away, they were the ones left standing.

The story of Steinstuecken is a wonderful episode in the history of the partnership between Americans, Germans, and Berliners during the Cold War. In his farewell message, Zehlendorf mayor Ulrich Menzel said that he hoped that the "friendships" that Berliners had developed with Americans "would outlast the separation" as their former American neighbors went home. It's been more than a quarter-century since the Berlin Wall fell and over twenty years since the last American soldier left Berlin. Here's hoping that the memories of the struggles that Americans and Berliners endured together and the values they shared and protected will sustain those friendships and keep them strong.

ENDNOTES

Chapter 1

1 Interview with Jacques Reinstein, *Germany Country Reader* (Arlington, VA: Association of Diplomatic Studies and Training [ADST]), 338.

2 Nowhere in Reinhart's interview does he specifically name Steinstuecken as being "that little place." However, as this book will show, Steinstuecken was, far and away, the detached section of West Berlin that most preoccupied American, Allied, and German officials during the Cold War. Reinstein's unedited quote was "What was that little place that was disconnected with an exclave of Berlin?"

3 US Department of State, William Z Slany (Historian), *Documents on Germany 1944-1985*. Department of State Publication 9446. (Washington D.C.: US Government Printing Office, 1985), 2.

4 US State Department, *Documents on Germany*, 33.

5 Tilman Reine, "The Battle for Berlin in World War II" (http://www.bbc.co.uk/history/worldwars/wwtwo/berlin_01.shtml) and Lucy Ash, "The Rape of Berlin," (http://www.bbc.com/news/magazine-32529679), both accessed on February 1 2018.

6 Richard Davis, *Bombing the European Axis Powers: A Historical Digest of the Combined Bomber Offensive 1939–1945*. 2006. (Maxwell Air Force Base Alabama: Air University Press, 2006.), 497 (Disrupt reinforcements and break will of the German people), 498, 522, 524, and 558 (bombing tonnage).

7 Lucius D. Clay, *Decision in Germany* (New York: Doubleday, 1950), 21.

8 Clay, *Decision*, 31.

9 Clay, *Decision*, 32.

10 Clay, *Decision*, 32.

11 Clay, *Decision*, 15.

12 Clay, *Decision*, 16.

13 Office of the U.S High Commissioner for Germany [HICOG] memorandum dated October 24, 1951, subject "Steinstuecken." Copy retrieved from National Archives.

14 Honore' Marc Catudal Jr., *Steinstuecken: A Study in Cold War Politics* (New York: Vantage Press, 1971), 33.

15 CIA Directorate of Intelligence, *Intelligence Report: The Exclaves of West Berlin*. (Washington D.C.: CIA, March 1967), 1-2.

16 Interview with Frederick Sackstedter, *Germany Country Reader*, 445.

17 HICOG memorandum, dated October 24, 1951, subject "Steinstuecken." Copy retrieved from National Archives.

18 CIA Directorate of Intelligence, *The Exclaves of West Berlin*, 2.

19 "The cosmopolitan city of the Weimar Republic." Official web portal of the city of Berlin (Berlin.de), https://www.berlin.de/berlin-im-ueberblick/en/history/the-cosmopolitan-city-of-the-weimar-republic/. Accessed February 3, 2018.

20 CIA Directorate of Intelligence, *The Exclaves of West Berlin*, 2.

21 Catudal, *Steinstuecken*, 18 and 48.

22 It may seem irrelevant to note that Honore' Mark Catudal, the Steinstuecken author, is a "Jr." But in this case, it's important. His father, Honore' Mark Catudal Sr., was an influential State Department diplomat. In this book, presume that any mention of "Catudal" refers to the son, not the father.

23 Catudal, *Steinstuecken*, 38.

24 U.S. Department of State, Frederick Aandahl (Editor), *Foreign Relations of the United States* [FRUS] 1951, Volume III part 2—European Security and the German Question. (Washington D.C: Government Printing Office, 1951). Hereafter referred to as "FRUS," 1894 and 1955.
25 Memorandum from COL William Babcock dated April 27, 1949. Copy retrieved from National Archives.
26 Interview with Karl Mautner, *Germany Country Reader*, 973.
27 HICOG memorandum of October 19, 1951, subject "Steinstuecken."

Chapter 2

1 Special Blotter for Steinstuecken Crisis, HICOG Berlin Element, dated October 18, 1951. Copy retrieved from National Archives.
2 Catudal, *Steinstuecken,* Appendix D.
3 Catudal, *Steinstuecken*, 47–49.
4 Memorandum from Chief HICOG Berlin Element Public Safety Division, subject "Soviet Zonal Authorities Annex U.S. Sector Enclave Steinstuecken," dated October 18, 1951. Copy retrieved from National Archives.
5 FRUS 1951 Volume III, part 2, 1895.
6 "Reds Occupy Area in Berlin," *Stars & Stripes*, February 3, 1951.
7 "Reds Occupy Area in Berlin," *Stars & Stripes*, February 3, 1951.
8 FRUS 1951 Vol III part 2, 1895.
9 FRUS 1951 Vol III part 2, 1894.
10 Catudal, *Steinstuecken,* 46.
11 *Der Tagesspiegel,* October 19, 1951. Undated HICOG summary of West German press reporting.
12 *Der Kurier,* October 20, 1951. Undated HICOG summary of West German press reporting.
13 *Der Tagesspiegel,* October 21, 1951. Undated HICOG summary of West German press reporting.
14 *Der Tagesspiegel,* October 19, 1951. Undated HICOG summary of West German press reporting.
15 Undated HICOG summary of West German press reporting.
16 *Der Telegraf,* October 19, 1951. As quoted in Catudal, *Steinstuecken,* 51.
17 Undated HICOG summaries of West German press reporting.
18 Catudal, *Steinstuecken,* 52.
19 *Berliner Zeitung,* October 20, 1951. Accessed via ZEFYS Newspaper Information System (http://zefys.staatsbibliothek-berlin.de/).
20 *Neues Deutschland,* October 20, 1951. Accessed via ZEFYS.
21 HICOG memorandum dated October 24, 1951, subject "Steinstuecken."
22 Ibid.
23 HICOG memorandum dated October 19, 1951, for Mr. Lyon, subject "Steinstuecken."
24 HICOG memorandum dated October 19, 1951, for Mr. Lyon, subject "Steinstuecken."
25 HICOG memorandum dated October 19, 1951, from C. J. Scarvada, subject "Steinstuecken, US Sector Enclave of Soviet Zone."
26 HICOG memorandum dated 19 October 1951, for Mr. Lyon, subject "Steinstuecken."
27 Personal recollection of Wilfried Hammer, Steinstuecken resident, in interview with the author.
28 "Steinstuecken: Lifestyles of West Berlin." *Der Spiegel,* October 31, 1951, 12–13. Accessed via ZEFYS.
29 Memoirs of Herbert Steinweg.
30 Ibid.
31 Ibid.
32 HICOG memorandum for Mr. Lyon, October 19, 1951.
33 "Control Council Law Number 46 (25 February 1947) Abolition of Prussia," *Wikisource.* (https://en.wikisource.org/wiki/Control_Council_Law_No_46_(25_February_1947)_Abolition_of_Prussia), accessed March 18, 2018.
34 Mathewson message to Hays and Handy, undated.
35 Mathewson message to HICOG Frankfurt, undated.
36 Mathewson message to Hays and Handy, undated.
37 Mathewson message to HICOG Frankfurt, undated.
38 Ibid.
39 Ibid.

40 Howley, General Frank. *Berlin Command,* (New York; Putnam, 1950) 148.
41 Karl Mautner, *Germany Country Reader*, 100.
42 Martha Mautner, *Germany Country Reader*, 501.
43 Howley, 224.
44 "City Councellor Ernst Reuter Appeals to the 'People of the World'", *German History in Documents and Images.* http://www.germanhistorydocs.ghi-dc.org/sub_image.cfm?image_id=1009. Accessed February 20, 2018.
45 Martha Mautner, *Germany Country Reader*, 501.
46 OMGUS Information Bulletin #159 (April 1949), 7–8.
47 HICOG Information Bulletin May 1951, 3–4.
48 Mathewson message to Hays and Handy, undated.
49 British Control Commission telegram, undated
50 Central Intelligence Agency (CIA) Office of Current Intelligence Daily Digest, October 25 1951, 13
51 Cecil Lyon, *Germany Country Reader*, 539.
52 Text of General Mathewson's protest letter to Soviet Control Commission, dated October 19, 1951.
53 "The 'Vopo' Intermezzo," *Die Zeit,* November 1, 1951.
54 Catudal, *Steinstuecken,* 55.
55 Ibid, 52-55.
56 "The Vopo Intermezzo," *Die Zeit,* November 1, 1951.
57 HICOG Special Blotter on Steinstuecken, time entry 2200.
58 Catudal, *Steinstuecken*, 60.
59 HICOG Special Blotter on Steinstuecken, time entry 2200.
60 Memoirs of Walter Steinweg.
61 FRUS 1951-1952, Vol VII, Part 2, 1242.

Chapter 3

1 FRUS 1950, Vol IV, 634.
2 NATO Archives, "NATO the first five years 1949–1955. Chapter 4—Lord Ismay." (1954; Paris). Accessed August 18, 2018.
3 FRUS 1951, Vol III Part 1, 656.
4 FRUS 1951, Vol III Part 1, 673.
5 FRUS 1951, Vol III Part 1, 665.
6 FRUS 1951, Vol III Part 1, 668–669.
7 FRUS 1951, Vol III Part 1, 680.
8 FRUS 1951, Vol III Part 2, pg. 1333.
9 Manuel Abrams, *Germany Country Reader*, 481.
10 FRUS 1951, Vol III, Part 2, 1328.
11 Office of the US High Commissioner for Germany (HICOG). *Report on Germany.* (Washington D.C.; US Government Printing Office). 6th quarterly report, 29. Hereafter referred to as "HICOG #Quarterly Report.
12 HICOG 1st Quarterly Report, 3.
13 OMGUS Information Bulletin #161, 30.
14 HICOG 1st Quarterly Report, 10.
15 HICOG 2nd Quarterly Report, 9.
16 HICOG 8th Quarterly Report, v.
17 FRUS 1948, Vol II, 261–2.
18 Harry Odell, *German Country Reader*, pg. 410.
19 Taylor Seeyle, *German Country Reader*, pg. 418.
20 Charles Stuart Kennedy, *Germany Country Reader*, pg. 183.
21 Wikipedia page on "Council of Europe."
22 FRUS 1950, Volume III, 817.
23 FRUS 1950, Volume IV, 597–8.
24 HICOG 5th Quarterly Report, iii.
25 HICOG 6th Quarterly Report, 23.
26 Ibid, 83.
27 Ibid.

28 HICOG 2nd Quarterly Report, 9.
29 HICOG 8th Quarterly Report, 15-17.
30 FRUS 1951, Vol III Part 2, 1328.
31 FRUS 1950, Vol III, 1236.
32 Wikipedia page on "Rationing in the UK."
33 OMGUS Information Bulletin #91, 2.
34 FRUS 1950, Vol IV, 600-601.
35 Smith, Jean Edward. *Lucius Clay: An American Life.* (New York; Henry Holt & Company, 1990), 573.
36 Mathewson message to Hays and Handy, undated.
37 Letter from Dengin to Mathewson, April 17, 1951.
38 Letter from Mathewson to Dengin, April 23, 1951.
39 Letter from Dengin to Mathewson, June 12, 1951.
40 Letter from Mathewson to Dengin, June 18, 1951.
41 Letter from Dengin to Mathewson, June 26, 1951.
42 Recollections of Betsy Bailey.
43 Letter from Dengin to Mathewson, August 17, 1951.
44 "West to Act on Berlin Grab." *Stars and Stripes,* European edition, October 22, 1951, 1.
45 "Reds Take Over Area in Berlin." AP wire story in *Ft Lauderdale News,* October 19, 1951.
46 "Berlin Reds Take Part of US Zone," AP report in *Des Moines Register,* October 19, 1951.
47 "US Protests Red Grab in Berlin." UPI wire story in *Pittsburgh Press,* October 19, 1951.
48 "Protest Filed with Soviet Over Seizure of Hamlet in West Berlin." New York Times cable report in *Cincinnati Enquirer,* October 20, 1951.
49 *Neues Deutschland,* October 21, 1951, accessed via ZEFYS.
50 Catudal, *Steinstuecken,* 56.
51 FRUS 1951, Vol III, Part 2, 1954–1956.
52 Recollections of Cecil Lyon, ADST, *Germany Country Reader,* 539.
53 FRUS 1951, Vol III, Part 2, 1957.
54 CIA Office of Current Intelligence Daily Digest, October 25 1951, 13
55 "Red Cops Yield Control of Seized Berlin Area." *Stars and Stripes,* October 24, 1951, 1,
56 "Disputed Berlin Area Returned to Yanks." UPI wire report in *Green Bay Press-Gazette,* October 23, 1951.
57 "East's Police Quit Village: Russia Orders Germans Out after US Protest. AP wire report in *Baltimore Sun,* October 24, 1951.
58 Catudal, *Steinstuecken,* 58.
59 US Army Berlin, *Steinstucken—A West Berlin Exclave in the U.S. Zone* (Berlin: Public Information Office, 1960, 2). As referenced in Catudal, *Steinstuecken,* 58.
60 *Der Tag,* October 24, 1951. As referenced in Catudal, *Steinstuecken,* 58.
61 "East Police Quit Village."
62 HICOG Memorandum for Cecil Lyon dated October 23, 1951, 2.
63 "East's Police Quit Village."
64 HICOG memo of report from Zehlendorf police, October 23, 1951.
65 Catudal, *Steinstuecken,* 59.
66 "Red Cops Yield Control of Seized Berlin Area."
67 *Der Tagesspiegel* and *Berliner Anzeiger,* both on October 24, 1951. As related in Catudal, *Steinstuecken,* 60.
68 "Red Cops Yield Control of Seized Berlin Area."
69 Memoirs of Walter Steinweg.
70 Ibid.

Chapter 4

1 HICOG memorandum from C.J. Scavarda, dated October 19, 1951.
2 HICOG Press Summary, section titled "The Steinstuecken Incident," undated.
3 "Protest Filed with Soviet Over Seizure of Hamlet in West Berlin." NY Times cable in *Cincinnati Enquirer,* October 20, 1951.
4 HICOG Public Safety Division memorandum dated October 24, 1951.

5 Ibid.
6 HICOG Special Blotter for Steinstuecken Police Crisis, October 24, 1951.
7 Ibid.
8 Ibid.
9 Ibid.
10 Ibid.
11 "Unexplained Move Leaves American Officials Baffled." UPI, in *Honolulu Star-Bulletin*, October 25, 1951.
12 Ibid.
13 Ibid.
14 *Der Tag*, October 26, 1951. As noted in Catudal, *Steinstuecken*, 62.
15 "Berlin Territory Dispute Put Up to Zonal Chiefs." AP wire report, in *St. Louis Post Dispatch*, October 25, 1951.
16 Catudal, *Steinstuecken*, 62.
17 Ibid, 63.
18 "Red Zone Cops Free Reporter Held 3 Days." UPI wire report in *Brooklyn Daily Eagle*, October 28, 1951.
19 Ibid.
20 Text of ADN news report, October 23, 1951, from HICOG files.
21 *Neue Zeit*, November 6, 1951. Accessed via ZEFYS.
22 "Reds Ignored During Grab of Berlin Suburb, Girl Says." *European Stars and Stripes*, October 28, 1951, 6.
23 Soviets Hand Back Seized Berlin Area: Russia Backs Down After Threats." UPI, in the *Times of Shreveport LA*, October 24, 1951.
24 "East Police Quit Village." AP wire report in *Baltimore Sun*, October 24, 1951.
25 "Soviets Hand Back Seized Berlin Area: Russia Backs Down after Allied Threats."
26 HICOG transcription of UPI report. Report dated October 24, transcription dated October 25, 1951.
27 HICOG transcription of UPI report. Report dated October 25, 1951.
28 "Lifestyles of West Berlin," *Der Spiegel*, October 31, 1951. Accessed via ZEFYS.
29 FRUS 1951, Vol III Part 2, 1878.
30 Ibid.
31 "Future Status of Steinstuecken." *Guardian*, November 6, 1951.
32 "Disputed Berlin Area Gets Chief." AP report in *Los Angeles Times*, October 28, 1951.
33 "In and Out of Steinstuecken," *Guardian*, October 28, 1951.
34 Catudal, *Steinstuecken*, 65.
35 *New York Times*, October 20, 1951. As related in Catudal, *Steinstuecken*, 53.

Chapter Five

1 FRUS 1952–1954, Vol VII Part 2, 1262.
2 HICOG Information Bulletin June 1952, 27.
3 FRUS 1952-1954 Vol VII Part 2, 1239.
4 "The Soviet Harassment Campaign in Germany." US Department of State (DOS) *Bulletin*. Volume 27, number 688 (Washington D.C.: US Government Printing Office, September 1, 1952), 311–312.
5 Memoirs of Walter Steinweg.
6 Message from Mathewson to Dengin, June 28, 1952, from National Archives.
7 FRUS 1952–1954, Vol VII Part 2, 1270.
8 Catudal, *Steinstuecken*, pg. 71.
9 FRUS 1952–1954, Vol VII Part 2, 1255.
10 Catudal, *Steinstuecken*, 66.
11 HICOG Information Paper, titled "The Problem of the Enclaves and of Certain Contested Areas On The Border," undated.
12 Ibid.
13 Catudal, *Steinstuecken*, 69.
14 Ibid, 74.
15 Recollections of Johannes Niemeyer, dated July 1952.

16 HICOG Information Paper, "The Problem of the Enclaves."
17 "US Protests Red Squeeze in Berlin." UPI report in *Great Falls Tribune*, June 6, 1952.
18 HICOG Information Paper, "The Problem of the Enclaves."
19 Catudal, *Steinstuecken*, 76.
20 "Reds Beat Deadline by 24 Hours." UPI wire report in *Akron Beacon Journal*, June 6, 1952.
21 FRUS 1952-1954, Vol VII Part 2, 1271.
22 Niemeyer recollections, no date.
23 Catudal, *Steinstuecken*, 83.
24 Niemeyer, document dated July 1952.
25 Recollections of Magrit Wiese.
26 Recollections of Niemeyer, document dated July 1952.
27 Ibid.
28 Recollections of Wilfried Hammer, as translated by Elke Hammer.
29 Recollections of Elke Hammer.
30 Ibid.
31 Recollections of Elke Hammer.
32 Letter from Niemeyer to US HICOG Walter Donnelly, dated September 1952.
33 Letter from Niemeyer to USCOB Timmerman, February 1954.
34 Catudal, *Steinstuecken*, 84.
35 Niemeyer document, dated July 1952.
36 Memo from HICOG Protocol Element, subject "Conversation with Soviets Concerning Steinstucken," dated March 30, 1953.
37 Ibid.
38 Memo from HICOG Protocol Element to State Department in Washington, subject "Additional Developments Concerning Steinstuecken," dated April 9, 1953.
39 English translation of Zehlendorf Police report, subject "Women ordered to get the mail for Steinstucken was checked by Vopo," dated April 9, 1953.
40 "This Postman Doesn't Even Ring." Reuters wire report in *Minneapolis Star Tribune*, June 28, 1952.
41 HICOG memorandum, subject "Additional Developments Concerning Steinstuecken," dated April 9, 1953.
42 HICOG Information Bulletin, December 1952, 25.
43 Letter from Dengin to Mathewson, dated November 4, 1952, subject lights for Waldweg.
44 Letter from Mathewson to Dengin, dated November 12, 1952.
45 *Die Neue Zeitung*, November 5, 1952. As reported in Catudal, 86.
46 "U.S. Continues Presentation of Western Peace Plan In Second Week of Foreign Ministers' Conference." DOS *Bulletin* Vol 40 Number 1041, June 8, 1959, 819–820.
47 FRUS 1952–1954, Vol VII Part 2, 1321.
48 FRUS 1955–1957, Vol XXVI, 349.
49 FRUS 1958–1960, Vol VIII, 37.
50 PublicDomainFootage.com. Accessed from YouTube, https://www.youtube.com/watch?v=P3ZLRzxO4hQ.
51 FRUS 1958-1960, Vol VIII, 37.
52 Ibid.
53 "France, UK and US Protest Travel Restrictions in Berlin." DOS *Bulletin*, Vol 43 Number 1116, November 14, 1960, 748-749.
54 FRUS 1955–1957, Vol XXVI, 446.
55 FRUS 1958–1960, Vol VIII, 36.
56 "Chronology of Statements and Documents Concerning the Berlin Crisis for the Period 1 November 1959 to 31 January 1960." US State Department Bureau of Intelligence and Research (BIR) Intelligence Information Brief (IIB) 114–8, April 20, 1960, 179.
57 Catudal, *Steinstuecken*, 87. He lists *Der Tagesspiegel*, 16 September 1955, as his source.
58 Catudal, *Steinstuecken*, 88. He lists *Der Tagesspiegel*, 16 September 1955, as his source.
59 US Army Berlin, "*Steinstucken—A West Berlin Exclave in the Soviet Zone*." Berlin; Public Information Office, 1960, pg.3. As referenced in Catudal, *Steinstuecken*, 88.
60 *Nachtdepesche*, April 19, 1956. As referenced in Catudal, *Steinstuecken*, 89.
61 Catudal, *Steinstuecken*, 91.

62 *Der Telegraf*, April 27 and May 8, 1956. As referenced in Catudal, *Steinstuecken*, 89–92.
63 "West Berlin Mayor Blocked by Reds." New York Times news service report in *Des Moines Register*, April 27, 1956.
64 *Der Telegraf*, April 27. As referenced in Catudal, *Steinstuecken*, 89–92.
65 *Der Tagesspiegel*, 3 November 1956. As referenced in Catudal, *Steinstuecken*, 93.
66 Niemeyer document, dated July 1952.
67 Ibid.
68 Niemeyer document, undated.
69 Recollections of Elke Hammer.
70 Catudal, *Steinstuecken*, 19.
71 Niemeyer document, undated.
72 Recollections of Magrit Wiese.
73 Niemeyer letter dated July 1952.
74 "Tiny Village Braved Forces of Communism." Reuters wire report in *Daily Press of Newport News, Virginia*, December 21, 1952.
75 Ibid.
76 Recollections of Magrit Wiese.
77 *Der Tagesspiegel*, August 14, 1958. As referenced in Catudal, *Steinstuecken*, 94.
78 *Der Tagesspiegel*, August 8, 1958. As referenced in Catudal, *Steinstuecken*, 94.
79 *Der Abend*, August 13, 1948. As referenced in Catudal, *Steinstuecken*, 95.
80 Catudal, *Steinstuecken*, 95.
81 FRUS 1958–1960, Vol VIII, 40.
82 "West Germans Urge Buildup of US Troops." UPI wire report in the *Times Recorder of Zanesville Ohio*, August 11, 1958.
83 "US Berlin Moves Weak, Germans Say." Bynum Shaw, *Baltimore Sun*, August 12, 1958.
84 FRUS 1958–1960, Vol VIII., 33.
85 Ibid., 40.
86 Lloyd Stearman, *Germany Country Reader*, 756.
87 State Department BIR IIB 1959–1960, 4.
88 Wikipedia entry, "Nikita Khrushchev." Accessed October 26, 2016.
89 Whitman, Alden. "Khrushchev's Human Dimensions Brought Him to Power and His Downfall." *New York Times*, September 12, 1971.
90 "Berlin-Germany Group: S/P—George C. McGhee". State Department reference document, undated, 25.

Chapter Six

1 "Decree of the German Democratic Republic Imposing Restrictions on Travel Between East and West Berlin," August 13, 1961. *Documents in Germany, 1944–1985*, 775.
2 CIA Intelligence Weekly Summary (CIWS), October 12, 1961.
3 Steury, Dr. Donald P. "Bitter Measures: Intelligence and Action in the Berlin Crisis, 1961," 12.
4 "Note from the Soviet Commandant in Berlin to the Western Commandants, Defending Erection of the 'Berlin Wall,'" August 18, 1961. *Documents on Germany 1944-1985*, 779.
5 Steury, "Bitter Measures," 12.
6 "Berlin-Germany Group: S/P—George C. McGhee", 78.
7 Steury, "Bitter Measures," 12.
8 Ibid.
9 "Summary of Orders Issued by the East German Ministry of the Interior Governing Entry of West Berliners into East Berlin, August 22, 1961." *Documents on Germany, 1944–1985*, 782.
10 "Border Controls," CIWS August 24, 1961.
11 "Summary of Orders Issued by the East German Ministry of the Interior Governing Entry of West Berliners into East Berlin, August 22, 1961." *Documents on Germany, 1944–1985*, 782.
12 *Washington Post*, August 26, 1961. As related in Smith, Jean Edward, *The Defense of* Berlin (Baltimore; Johns Hopkins Press, 1960), 301.
13 "Note from the Soviet Union to the United States Protesting the Transport of West German officials to West Berlin Through The Allied Air Corridors, August 23 1961." *Documents on Germany, 1944–1985*, 783–784.

14 CIWS August 31, 1961, 2.
15 Ibid, 5.
16 FRUS 1961–1963, Vol XIV, Item 130.
17 FRUS 1961–1963, Vol XIV, Item 128.
18 Karl Mautner, *Germany Country Reader*, 106.
19 FRUS 1961–1963, Vol XIV, Item 114.
20 FRUS 1961–1963, Vol XIV, Item 117.
21 Howley, *Berlin Command*, 195.
22 OMGUS Four Year Report, 10.
23 Howley, *Berlin Command*, 201.
24 OMGUS Four Year Report, 10.
25 Ibid.
26 Universal Newsreels, *Berlin Airlift, General Clay speaks, 1948/10/21*. https://www.youtube.com/watch?v=zjIMi3ofn1I. Accessed February 15, 2018.
27 Universal International Newsreel, *1949-Cold War Germany 221752-44*. https://www.youtube.com/watch?v=7QqTcG5HvqI. Accessed February 15, 2018.
28 Howley, *Berlin Command*, 206.
29 OMGUS Information Bulletin #148, 10.
30 Portion of a period newsreel on the Berlin Airlift, in YouTube video "The Berlin Blockade (10m)", exact source unknown. https://www.youtube.com/watch?v=CZidBq8QS-g&list=PLqp0G9VLdu0St0U57Iodx0Ge95ZDXhNh5. Accessed October 5, 2018.
31 Howley, *Berlin Command*, 118.
32 OMGUS Information Bulletin #62, 8.
33 Ibid., 9.
34 Howley, 118.
35 Howley, 126.
36 Howley, 119.
37 Howley, 134.
38 OMGUS Weekly Bulletin #35, 21.
39 FRUS 1946, Vol V, 704.
40 Ibid.
41 Howley, *Berlin Command*, 165.
42 Ibid.
43 Karl Mautner, *Germany Country Reader*, 103.
44 OMGUS Information Bulletin #65, 14.
45 Howley, 131.
46 OMGUS Information Bulletin #67, 20.
47 OMGUS Information Bulletin #151, 14.
48 Ibid., 13.
49 Ibid, 13–14.
50 Ibid.,15.
51 OMGUS Information Bulletin #152, 27.
52 FRUS 1961-1963, Vol XIV, Item 133.
53 Smith, Jean Edward. *Lucius D. Clay: An American Life*. (New York; Henry Holt & Company, 1990), 650.
54 Jack Sulser, *Germany Country Reader*, 640.
55 FRUS 1950, Vol IV, 595.
56 Joseph Greene Jr., *Germany Country Reader*, 653.
57 Ibid.
58 O'Ballance, Major Edgar, British Army. "The Bundeswehr." *Military Review*. Volume 40, Number 2. (Fort Leavenworth; US Army Command and General Staff College, May 1960), 15.
59 Ibid., 7–18.
60 Frederick Flott, *Germany Country Reader*, 770.
61 FRUS 1961-1963, Vol XIV, Item 139.
62 Catudal, *Steinstuecken*, 103.
63 Recollections of Magrit Wiese.

64 Ibid.
65 *Documents on Germany,* 786-787.
66 Ibid.
67 FRUS 1958–1960, Vol VIII, Item 21, 42.
68 Commander in Chief US Forces Europe (CINCEUR) Message dated September 5, 1961. The message contained US Forces Europe's defense plan for Steinstuecken.
69 FRUS 1961–1963, Volume XIV, Item 148.
70 General Lemnitzer's meeting notes.
71 FRUS 1961–1963, Vol XIV, Item 148.
72 FRUS 1961–1963, Vol XIV, Item 129.
73 Memorandum of Conversation, subject: Tripartite Foreign Minister's Meeting, September 14, 1961. Retrieved from National Archives.

Chapter Seven

1 FRUS 1961–1963, Volume XIV, Item 276.
2 Ibid.
3 FRUS 1961–1963, Volume XIV, Item 181.
4 Wikipedia page on "Berlin Wall," accessed February 19, 2017.
5 "Flowers Engulf Clay in Berlin." UPI wire report in *The Democrat and Chronicle,* Rochester, NY, September 19, 1961.
6 "General Clay Says West Berlin Shall Always Be Free." AP wire report in *Greely Tribune,* Greely Colorado, September 20 1961.
7 FRUS 1961-1963 Volume XIV, Item 181.
8 Ibid.
9 FRUS 1961-1963 Volume XIV Item 159.
10 Smith, Jean Edward. *Lucius D. Clay: An American Life,* 650.
11 Catudal, *Steinstuecken,* 105. Catudal cites his source for this as *Die Welt,* September 21, 1961.
12 FRUS 1961–1963, Item 161.
13 Catudal, *Steinstuecken,* 105. Catudal sites his source for this as being Hermann Zolling, *Kalter Winter im August,* pg. 172.
14 Catudal, *Steinstuecken,* 105.
15 Ibid, 106.
16 Richard Boehm, *Germany Country Reader,* 888.
17 Ibid.
18 Ibid.
19 Catudal, *Steinstuecken,* 105–106. Catudal's cited source is Hermann Zolling, *Kalter Winter im August,* pg. 172.
20 FRUS 1961–1963, Vol XIV, Item 181.
21 Ibid, item 161.
22 Smith, *Clay: An American Life,* 656
23 Catudal, 106, footnote.
24 Ibid, 16. Catudal's cited source appears to be the *New York Times,* September 22, 1961.
25 Photo album of Kurt Behrendt.
26 Clark, Christine. *Letters from Berlin: A Memoir.* Published by Christine Clark, 2014, 28.
27 Army G2 Berlin Intelligence Summary (ISUM) 12-005, covering the period September 15–26, 1961. Copy retrieved from National Archives.
28 Catudal, *Steinstuecken,* 16–17. Catudal's cited source is the *New York Times,* September 22, 1961.
29 *Berliner Morgenpost,* September 22, 1961.
30 Pacific *Stars and Stripes,* September 22, 1961, pg. 5.
31 "Berlin Reds Continue Evictions." AP wire report, in *Arizona Daily Star,* September 21, 1961.
32 Clark, Christine, *Letters,* 28.
33 *Berliner Morgenpost,* September 22, 1961.
34 Smith, Jean Edward, *The Defense of Berlin,* 310.
35 Smith, Jean Edward, *Clay: An American Life,* 659.
36 Clark, *Letters,* 28.
37 *Berliner Morgenpost,* September 22, 1961.

38 Bailey, George. "The Gentle Erosion in Berlin." *The Reporter,* April 26, 1962, 15. As quoted in Smith, *The Defense of Berlin,* 310.
39 FRUS 1961–1963, Volume XIV, Item 161.
40 Ibid.
41 FRUS 1961–1963, Volume XIV, Item 161.
42 Ibid., Item 181.
43 Ellis, William and Cunningham, Thomas. *Clarke of St. Vith: The Sergeants' General.* (Cleveland; Dilland/Leiderbach Inc. 1974.) 268.
44 Ibid.
45 Ibid., 269.
46 Ibid.
47 Ibid.
48 Smith, *Clay: An American Life,* 657.
49 Catudal, Honore Marc. *Kennedy and the Berlin Wall Crisis* (1980; Berlin Verlag), 134.
50 Interview with W.R. Smyser.
51 Ibid.
52 Ibid.
53 Ibid.
54 Catudal, *Kennedy and the Berlin Wall Crisis,* footnote #32, 134.
55 "Martin J. Hillenbrand, 89, A State Dept. Europe Expert." Obituary in *New York Times,* February 18, 2005.
56 Hillenbrand, Martin J. *Fragments Of Our Time.* (1998: University of Georgia Press, Athens GA.), 192.
57 Ibid., pg. ???
58 Ibid.
59 Ibid.
60 Ibid.
61 Catudal, *Steinstuecken,* 20.

Chapter Eight

1 "Unique Jobs for Berlin MPs." AP article by Hubert Erb in *Stars and Stripes,* August 15, 1967.
2 Ibid.
3 Interview with Vern Pike.
4 "US Soldiers Land in Area of Red Ring." AP, in *Kansas City Times,* Sept 23, 1961.
5 "3 GIs 'Occupy' Red-Encircled Town." NY Herald Tribune wire service in *Minneapolis Star-Tribune,* September 23, 1961.
6 Interview with Vern Pike.
7 Interview with Ed Hamborski.
8 AP wire service report in *Bridgeport Telegram,* Bridgeport, Connecticut, September 23, 1961.
9 Interview with Ed Hamborski.
10 Interview with Herbert Judd.
11 Interview with Ed Hamborski.
12 FRUS 1961–1963, Volume XIV, Item 181.
13 Ibid, Item 161.
14 Interview with Vern Pike.
15 Berlin Command G2 Intelligence Summary covering September 26 to October 31, 1961, 10.
16 Berlin Command G2 Intelligence Summary covering the period ending November 16, 1961, 7.
17 Interview with Ed Hamborski.
18 Interview with John Montour.
19 Ibid.
20 Interview with Ed Hamborski.
21 Note in the photo albums of Kurt Behrendt.
22 "Assign 3000 to Toil on Death Strip." UPI story in *Stars and Stripes,* October 1, 1961.
23 "5 Germans Escape in US Copter." UPI story in *Stars and Stripes,* October 5, 1961.
24 "3 Airlifted from Berlin Enclave." UPI story in *Stars and Stripes,* February 8, 1962.
25 "Reds Tighten Squeeze on Berlin Outpost." Scripps-Howard wire report in *El Paso Herald-Post,* October 2, 1962.

26 Diary of Dieter Mueller. Courtesy of Leland McCaslin.
27 "Weekly chronology of reports concerning the Berlin situation received during the week of 21–27 November. Dated November 27, 1961. Downloaded from CREST.
28 Interview with Vern Pike.
29 "Unique Jobs for Berlin MPs."
30 FRUS 1961–1963, Volume XIV, Item 161.
31 "Reds Revive Threat to Air Corridors." UPI report in *Democrat and Chronicle*, October 2, 1961.
32 "New Peril Point Developing at Steinstuecken." UPI report in *St. Louis Post-Dispatch*, October 2, 1961.
33 Interview with Keith Koziba.
34 Recollections of Heike Behrendt.
35 Recollections of Heike Behrendt.
36 Interview with Herbert Judd.
37 Interview with Charlie Smith.
38 Ibid.
39 Ibid.
40 Interview with Ralph Sanchez.
41 Interview with Ed Hamborski.
42 Interview with Herbert Judd.
43 Interview with Ed Hamborski.
44 Interview with Charlie Smith.
45 Interview with Keith Koziba.
46 Interview with Ralph Sanchez.
47 Interview with Herbert Judd.
48 "I suggested then replacing the helicopter service by a truck moving on the ground. This action was turned down even though there had been no Soviet reaction to our helicopter service." Telegram from Clay to Rusk, Sept. 28, 1961. FRUS 1961–1963, Volume XIV, Item 161.
49 Recollections of Heike Behrendt.
50 Interview with Herbert Judd.
51 Interview with Jerome Weilmuenster.
52 Interview with Herbert Judd.
53 Interview with Ralph Sanchez.
54 Recollections of Heike Behrendt.
55 Interview with Herbert Judd.
56 Interview with Ralph Sanchez.
57 Interview with Jerome Weilmuenster.
58 "West German Town Menaced By Reds." UPI, in *The Town Talk*, Alexandria, LA, May 25, 1963.
59 "Vopos Reopen Road to Exclave of West Berlin." AP wire report in *St. Louis Post-Dispatch*, May 27, 1963.
60 "Reds Back Down on German Road." UPI wire report in *Pittsburgh Press*, May 27, 1963.
61 Interview with Bill Bacon.
62 Ibid.
63 "West 'City' in East Berlin Looks to Future," AP story by Hubert Erb, *Stars and Stripes*, December 25, 1971.
64 http://www.chronik-der-mauer.de/en/victims/180543/marzahn-willi
65 By OTFW, Berlin—Own work, CC BY-SA 3.0, https://commons.wikimedia.org/w/index.php?curid=11459830.
66 Interview with Ralph Sanchez.
67 *Stars and Stripes*, September 26, 1963.
68 Interview with Keith Koziba.
69 Ibid.
70 *Stars and Stripes*, September 26, 1963.
71 "GI Faces Court-Martial for East Germany Shooting." UPI wire report in *The Morning News*, Wilmington, Delaware, July 10, 1963.
72 *Stars and Stripes*, September 26, 1963.
73 Letter from Keith Koziba.

74 E-mail comment from Elke Hammer, dated April 8, 2017.
75 *Stars and Stripes*, September 5, 1963.
76 "Berlin Exclave Reinforced." AP wire story in *Stars and Stripes*, October 4, 1963.
77 "Steinstuecken GIs Reinforced After Stone-Throwing Incident." AP wire report, in *Daily Press of Newport News VA*, October 4, 1963.
78 "Steinstuecken: Berlin's Own Little Island." Peter Kurt, *Stars and Stripes*, May 4, 1967.
79 Ibid.
80 Interview with Ed Hamborski.

Chapter Nine

1 Recollections of Heike Behrendt.
2 Interview with W. R. Smyser.
3 Recollections of Annemarie Knecht, as told to Leland McCaslin.
4 Ibid.
5 Recollections of Gudrun Neumann, as told to Leland McCaslin.
6 Recollections of Heike Behrendt.
7 Recollections of Heike Behrendt, from e-mail.
8 Recollections of Johannes Niemeyer.
9 Clark, Christine, *Letters,* 30.
10 Recollections of Dieter Gertz, via e-mail from Elke Hammer.
11 Recollections of Magrit Wiese.
12 Recollections of Heike Behrendt, from e-mail.
13 Report from Zehlendorf Administrative Representative, January 5, 1962.
14 Report from Zehlendorf Administrative Representative, January 5, 1962.
15 Report from Zehlendorf Administrative Representative, November 1, 1968.
16 Report from Zehlendorf Administrative Representative, April 7, 1962.
17 Report from Zehlendorf Administrative Representative, January 5, 1962.
18 Report from Zehlendorf Administrative Representative, January 5, 1962.
19 Report from Zehlendorf Administrative Representative, October 17, 1962.
20 Report from Zehlendorf Administrative Representative, May 18, 1966.
21 Report from Zehlendorf Administrative Representative, August 9, 1962.
22 Report from Zehlendorf Administrative Representative, September 1, 1962.
23 Report from Zehlendorf Administrative Representative October 17, 1962.
24 Recollections of Wilfried Hammer, as told to Leland McCaslin.
25 Recollections of Heike Behrendt.
26 Recollections of Wilfried Hammer
27 "Berlin's Own Little Island." *Stars and Stripes*, May 4, 1967.
28 Recollections of Wilfried Hammer, as told to Leland McCaslin.
29 Ibid.
30 Recollections of Herbert Judd.
31 Recollections of Jerome Weilmunster.
32 Recollections of Heike Behrendt.
33 Diary entry of Dieter Gertz, courtesy of Leland McCaslin.
34 Recollections of Ralph Sanchez.
35 Recollections of John Mentor.
36 Diary entry of Dieter Gertz, courtesy of Leland McCaslin.
37 Recollections of Heike Behrendt.
38 "Christmas in Berlin-Steinstuecken, December 1969." Video by RBB media. Accessed via YouTube, June 24, 2017. URL: https://www.youtube.com/watch?v=XMd0EPl1NlY.
39 Recollections of Heike Behrendt, as relayed by Elke Hammer in an e-mail dated September 19, 2014.
40 Recollections of Ralph Sanchez.
41 "Courting in Steinstuecken." *Stars and Stripes*, January 28, 1986.
42 Ibid.
43 Recollections of Heike Behrendt.

Chapter Ten

1 "West Germany and the Berlin Wall," *Deutsche Welle*, November 4, 2014. Accessed online July 8, 2017. http://www.dw.com/en/west-germany-and-the-berlin-wall/a-18035420
2 Lucian Heichler, *Germany Country Reader*, 904–905.
3 Letter from Ulbricht to Khrushchev, 15 September 1961. SED Archives, IfGA, ZPA,Central Committee files, Walter Ulbricht's office, Internal Party Archive, J IV 2/202/130." Woodrow Wilson International Center for Scholars. https://digitalarchive.wilsoncenter.org/document/116212. Accessed January 17, 2021.
4 Arthur Day, *Germany Country Reader,* 1014.
5 Brandon Grove, *Germany Country Reader*, 1145.
6 *Documents on Germany 1944–1985*, 1060.
7 Ibid., 1059.
8 German History in Documents and Images (GHDI). Chapter 8, Document 5, "Two States, One Nation (October 28, 1969. Accessed online July 9, 2017.) http://germanhistorydocs.ghi-dc.org/sub_document.cfm?document_id=168.
9 Interview with Gail Halvorsen.
10 FRUS 1958–1960, Vol VIII, Item 19, 37.
11 FRUS 1958–1960, Volume IX, Item 91, 227.
12 *Documents on Germany*, 221.
13 FRUS 1958–1960, Volume IX, Item 91, 227.
14 Ibid.
15 Ibid, 229.
16 Lucian Heichler, *Germany Country Reader*, 904.
17 William Bodde Jr., *Germany Country Reader*, 1425-1426.
18 Arthur Day, *Germany Country Reader*, 1014.
19 Lucian Hechler, *Germany Country Reader,* 904.
20 GDHI, "Two States, One Nation."
21 Lucian Hechler, *Germany Country Reader,* 905.
22 GHDI, Chapter 1, Document 1, "Change Through Rapprochement." Accessed online July 9, 2017. http://germanhistorydocs.ghi-dc.org/sub_document.cfm?document_id=81
23 Bing.com definition of the word "rapprochement," July 9, 2017.
24 GHDI, "Change Through Rapprochement" speech.
25 Arthur Day, *Germany Country Reader,* 1014.
26 Brandon Grove, *Germany Country Reader,* 1142.
27 GHDI, "Two States, One Nation."
28 Ibid.
29 *Documents on Germany*, 1061.
30 Lucian Heichler, *Germany Country Reader*, 904.
31 GHDI, "Two States, One Nation."
32 *Documents on Germany*, 1059.
33 Ibid., 1061.
34 GHDI, "Two States, One Nation."
35 Definition taken from the Free Dictionary, accessed via the Bing search engine, July 15, 2017.
36 *Documents on Germany*, 1031.
37 Ibid., 1034.
38 Ibid., 1053.
39 Ibid., 1037.
40 Ibid., 1054.
41 "Germany: The Jigsaw Puzzle of Exclaves," by Joe Alex Morris Jr., *Los Angeles Times,* September 18, 1971.
42 *Documents on Germany,* 1081.
43 Ibid., 1160.
44 Ibid.
45 Ibid.
46 Ibid.
47 Ibid., 1136.

48 Ibid.
49 Ibid.
50 Ibid.
51 Ibid., 1136-1137.
52 "East Germans Initial Berlin Access Pacts," by Joe Alex Morris Jr., *LA Times* staff writer. *Los Angeles Times*, December 12, 1971, 27.
53 *Documents on Germany*, 1137.
54 "Germany: The Jigsaw Puzzle of Exclaves," by Joe Alex Morris Jr. *Los Angeles Times*, September 18, 1971.
55 "East Berlin Surrounds West's 'Islands.'" Brigitte Falbe, *Baltimore Sun*, September 5, 1971.
56 Documents on Germany, pg. 1137.
57 "East Germans Initial Berlin Access Pacts." *LA Times*, Joe Alex Morris Jr., Dec 12, 1971.
58 *Documents on Germany*, 1167.
59 Ibid., 1173.
60 Ibid., 1182.
61 Ibid., 1184.
62 Catudal, Honore' Marc. "Berlin's New Boundaries." *Cahiers de géographie du Québec.* Volume 18, number 43, 1974, 218.
63 *Documents on Germany*, 1182.
64 "The tank boy and the scooter man." "Journey to Berlin" website. http://journeytoberlin.com/content/the-tank-boy-and-the-scooter-man-encounters-in-eiskeller. Accessed August 5, 2017.
65 Catudal, "Boundaries," 217.
66 *Documents on Germany*, 1183.
67 "West's 'City" in East Berlin Looks To Future," by Hubert Erb, AP. *Stars and Stripes*, Dec 25, 1971.
68 "Germany: The Jigsaw Puzzle of Exclaves."
69 "East German Enclave Fears End to Its Privacy." Reuters exclusive to the *Los Angeles Times*, December 26, 1971.
70 RBB media clip on Steinstuecken from 1972. (https://www.youtube.com/watch?v=TuK0nwW5sxM)
71 "West's 'City" in East Berlin Looks To Future."
72 "Red-Ringed Village Hoping For Freedom." AP wire story in *The Times-Herald,* Port Huron, Michigan, January 20, 1972.
73 Ibid.
74 "East German Enclave Fears End to Its Privacy."
75 "Hamlet Realizes Dream of 27 Years." UPI story in the *Independent,* Long Beach, California, June 15, 1972.
76 Interviews with Steinstuecken residents.
77 "Steinstuecken: West Berlin's 'Offshore Island' May Come Home." LA Times-Washington Post News Service article in the *Louisville Courier-Journal and Times,* January 2, 1972.
78 Ibid.
79 "Hamlet Realizes Dream of 27 Years."
80 "West German Enclave Pays For Freedom," by Joe Alex Morris Jr., *Los Angeles Times,* April 26, 1973.
81 "Steinstuecken: West Berlin's 'Offshore Island' May Come Home."
82 "Thesis Aid in Freeing Berliners? Student's Study Possible Key." Washington Post News Service, January 4, 1972.
83 Ibid.
84 "West Berliners Crowd Offices for Wall Passes." UPI story in *Los Angeles Times*, June 5, 1972.
85 *Berlin Observer*, June 5, 1972.
86 "Eased Access to East Germany Marked by First-Day Snarls," AP wire report in *The Morning Call,* Allentown, PA, June 5, 1972.
87 UPI wire report, June 15, 1972.
88 Recollections of Elke Hammer.
89 Recollections of Heike Behrendt.
90 "Road Opens To West Berlin's Island Town in East." UPI wire report in *Arizona Republic,* Phoenix, September 24, 1972.
91 Ibid.

92 “West German Enclave Pays For Freedom.”
93 Ibid.
94 Ibid.
95 Ibid.
96 “Quiet Fadeaway: US Army withdraws tiny garrison from Steinstuecken Berlin exclave.” By Hubert Erb, AP. *Stars and Stripes*, October 25, 1972.
97 Halvorsen, Gail. *The Berlin Candy Bomber* (Bountiful, Utah; Horizon Publishers, 2002), 98–99
98 Ibid.
99 Ibid., 111–113.
100 Ibid., 117–134.
101 Ibid., 216.
102 Interview with Gail Halvorsen.
103 Interview with W.R. Smyser.

Chapter Eleven

1 *Berlin Observer* archive website. http://www.theberlinobserver.com. Accessed November 19, 2017.
2 “Zehlendorf Memorial Unveiled.” *Berlin Observer,* September 15, 1977.
3 “West German Enclave Pays for Freedom.” Joe Alex Morris, *Los Angeles Times*, April 26, 1973.
4 “C Btry 94th FA Berlin Brigade.” YouTube video of Armed Forces Network (AFN) video. https://www.youtube.com/watch?v=QS7vE3aiWZg&feature=youtu.be
5 Interview with Darrell Pope.
6 “Girl Scouts Put New Face on Memorial.” *Berlin Observer,* May 23, 1986.
7 Interview with Doug Powell.
8 “Aviators Assist Exclave.” *Berlin Observer*, August 5, 1988.
9 Notes of Doug Powell, originally compiled for Leland McCaslin’s book.
10 Interview with Doug Powell.
11 “Exclave Spotlights Aviators.” *Berlin Observer,* August 26, 1988.
12 Ibid.
13 Notes of Doug Powell, originally compiled for Leland McCaslin’s book.
14 “Steinstucken Summer Fest Commemorates U.S. Ties.” *Berlin Observer*, August 28, 1989.
15 Interview with Wilbur Wolf.
16 E-mail from Doug Powell to author, November 27, 2017.

Chapter Twelve

1 “The View From The Gulag.” Interview with Natan Scharansky in the *Weekly Standard.* June 21, 2004.
2 Library of Congress. *Soviet Union: a country study.* 1991, 998.
3 Ibid., 492.
4 Ibid., lxxii.
5 Ibid., 201.
6 Ibid., lxxiii.
7 J.D. Bindenagel, *Germany Country Reader*, 2200.
8 Library of Congress. *Germany: a country study.* 1996, 124.
9 Ibid., 122.
10 Ibid., 123.
11 Ibid., 124.
12 Ibid., 124.
13 J.D. Bindenagel, *Germany Country Reader*, 2205.
14 Richard Barkley, *Germany Country Reader*, 2132.
15 Wikipedia entry on “Berlin Wall,” accessed December 12, 2017.
16 Richard Barkley, *Germany Country Reader,* 2132.
17 LOC country study of Germany, 125.
18 Interview with Les Feutz.
19 J.D. Bindenagel, *Germany Country Reader*, 2207.
20 Recollections of Doug Powell.
21 Personal notes of Doug Powell.

22 Recollections of Heike Behrendt.
23 Recollections of Doug Powell.
24 Recollections of Doug Powell.
25 Ibid.
26 J.D. Bindenagel, *Germany Country Reader*, 2207.
27 LOC Germany country study, 126.
28 Ibid.
29 GHDI, "Two-Plus-Four Treaty on Germany (September 12, 1990)." Accessed online December 15, 2017. http://germanhistorydocs.ghi-dc.org/sub_document.cfm?document_id=176.
30 LOC Germany country study, 127.
31 Notes of Doug Powell, for Leland McCaslin's book.
32 Ibid.
33 LOC Germany country study, 124.
34 Ibid., 128.
35 Recollections of Doug Powell.
36 *Berlin Observer,* March 13, 1992.
37 Interview with Lester Feutz.
38 Ibid.
39 *Berlin Observer,* August 28, 1992.
40 Recollections of Doug Powell, as told to author Leland McCaslin.
41 Paul McCusker, *Germany Country Reader*, 889.
42 Copy of President Clinton's draft remarks, retrieved online from the National Archives.
43 Personal notes and photo collection of Doug Powell.
44 Recollections of Jan Feutz.

BIBLIOGRAPHY

Books

- Carter, Donald and Stivers, William. *The City Becomes A Symbol.* Washington D.C.; Center of Military History, U.S. Army, 2017
- Catudal, Honore Marc. *Kennedy and the Berlin Wall Crisis.* Berlin; Berlin Verlag, 1980
- Catudal, Honore Marc. *Steinstuecken: A Study in Cold War Politics.* New York; Vantage Press, 1971
- Clark, Christine. *Letters from Berlin: A Memoir*. Published by Christine Clark, 2014
- Clay, Lucius D. *Decision in Germany*. New York: Doubleday, 1950
- Davis, Richard. *Bombing the European Axis Powers: A Historical Digest of the Combined Bomber Offensive 1939-1945.* Maxwell Air Force Base Alabama: Air University Press, 2006
- Ellis, William and Cunningham, Thomas. *Clarke of St. Vith: The Sergeant's General.* Cleveland; Dilland/Leiderbah Inc., 1974
- Halvorsen, Gail. *The Berlin Candy Bomber.* Bountiful, Utah; Horizon Publishers, 2002
- Hillenbrand, Martin J. *Fragments Of Our Time.* Athens GA: University of Georgia Press, 1988
- Smith, Jean Edward. *The Defense of Berlin.* Baltimore: Johns Hopkins Press, 1960
- Smith, Jean Edward. *Lucius D. Clay: An American Life.* New York; Henry Holt & Company, 1990

U.S. Government Publications and Records

- U.S. Government Publications and Records
- U.S. Department of State *Bulletin.* Washington D.C.: U.S. Government Printing Office. https://catalog.hathitrust.org/Record/000598610
  - Volume 27, Number 688 (September 1, 1952)
  - Volume 40, Number 1041 (June 8, 1959)
- U.S. Department of State, Frederick Aandahl (Editor). *Foreign Relations of the United States.* (FRUS). Washington D.C: Government Printing Office, 1951.
  - 1946, Volume V (The British Commonwealth, Western and Central Europe)
  - 1948, Volume II (Germany and Austria)
  - 1950, Volume III (Western Europe)
  - 1950, Volume IV (Central and Eastern Europe; The Soviet Union)
  - 1951, Volume III, Part 1 (European Security and the German Question)
  - 1951, Volume III, Part 2 (European Security and the German Question)
  - 1952-1954, Volume VII, Part 2 (Germany and Austria)
  - 1952-1954, Volume VIII (Eastern Europe: Soviet Union: Eastern Mediterranean)
  - 1955-1957, Volume XXVI (Central and Southeastern Europe)
  - 1958-1960, Volume VIII (Berlin Crisis 1959-1960)
  - 1958-1960, Volume IX (Germany and Austria)
  - 1961-1963, Volume XIV (Berlin Crisis)
- OMGUS Information Bulletin
  - #62 (October 1946)
  - #65 (October 1946)
  - #91 (May 1947)
  - #148 (November 1948)
  - #151 (December 1948)
  - #152 (January 1949)
  - #159 (April 1949)
  - #161 (May 1949)

- HICOG Information Bulletin
  - May 1951
  - June 1952
  - December 1952
- CIA Intelligence Weekly Summaries (CIWS)
  - August 24, 1961
  - August 31, 1961
  - October 12, 1961
- *Intelligence Report: The Exclaves of West Berlin.* CIA Directorate of Intelligence, March 1967. Report # CIA-RDP84-00825R000100670001-2
- Documents from the U.S. High Commission for Germany (HICOG), retrieved from National Archives, College Park MD.
  - Letter from Sergei Dengin to General Lemuel Mathewson, April 17, 1951
  - Letter from Dengin to Mathewson, April 23, 1951
  - Letter from Dengin to Mathewson, June 12, 1951
  - Letter from Dengin to Mathewson, June 18, 1951
  - Letter from Dengin to Mathewson, June 26, 1951
  - Letter from Dengin to Mathewson, August 17, 1951
  - Special Blotter for Steinstuecken Crisis, HICOG Berlin Element, dated October 18, 1951
  - Memorandum from Chief HICOG Berlin Element Public Safety Division, subject "Soviet Zonal Authorities Annex U.S. Sector Enclave Steinstuecken," dated October 18, 1951.
  - Memorandum dated October 19, 1951, subject "Steinstuecken."
  - Memorandum dated October 19, 1951, for Mr. Lyon, subject "Steinstuecken."
  - Memorandum dated October 19, 1951, from C.J. Scarvada, subject "Steinstuecken, US Sector Enclave of Soviet Zone."
  - Public Safety memorandum, dated October 19, 1951
  - Undated summary of West German press reporting
  - Message from General Lemuel Mathewson to Generals George Hays and Thomas Handy, undated
  - Message from General Lemuel Mathewson to HICOG Frankfurt, undated
  - British Control Commission telegram, undated
  - Text of General Mathewson's protest letter to Soviet Control Commission, dated October 19, 1951
  - Memorandum for Cecil Lyon dated October 23, 1951
  - Memorandum of report from Zehlendorf police, October 23, 1951
  - Text of ADN news report, October 23, 1951
  - Memorandum dated October 24, 1951, subject "Steinstuecken"
  - Press Summary, section titled "The Steinstuecken Incident," undated
  - HICOG Special Blotter for Steinstuecken Police Crisis, October 24, 1951
  - Transcription of UPI report. Report dated October 24, transcription dated October 25, 1951
  - Information Paper, titled "The Problem of the Enclaves and Certain Contested Areas on the Border," undated
  - Memorandum from HICOG Protocol Element, subject "Conversation with Soviets Concerning Steinstucken," dated March 30, 1953
  - English translation of Zehlendorf Police report, subject "Women ordered to get the mail for Steinstucken was checked by Vopo," dated April 9, 1953
  - Memorandum from HICOG Protocol Element, subject "Additional Developments Concerning Steinstucken," dated April 15, 1953
  - Letter from Dengin to Mathewson, dated November 4, 1952
  - Letter from Mathewson to Dengin, dated November 12, 1952
- "Chronology of Statements and Documents Concerning the Berlin Crisis for the Period 1 November 1959 to 31 January 1960." U.S. State Department Bureau of Intelligence and Research (BIR) Intelligence Information Brief (IIB) 114-8, April 20, 1960
- "Berlin-Germany Group: S/P---George C. McGhee". State Department reference document, undated
- Steury, Dr. Donald P. "Bitter Measures: Intelligence and Action in the Berlin Crisis, 1961." Paper written for the National Archives' conference, "The Berlin Crisis of 1961." https://www.archives.gov/research/foreign-policy/cold-war/1961-berlin-crisis/2011-conference.html

- U.S. Army Command and General Staff College (CGSC), et al.. *Military Review.* Fort Leavenworth, Kan.: Command and General Staff School. https://catalog.hathitrust.org/Record/006194109
- Commander in Chief US Forces Europe (CINCEUR) Message dated September 5, 1961. (Subject of message: Defense plan for Steinstuecken)
- Memorandum of Conversation, subject: Tripartite Foreign Minister's Meeting, September 14, 1961. Retrieved from National Archives.
- Army G2 Berlin Intelligence Summary (ISUM) 12-005, covering the period September 15 to 26, 1961. Copy retrieved from National Archives
- Berlin Command G2 Intelligence Summary covering September 26 to October 31, 1961
- Berlin Command G2 Intelligence Summary covering the period ending November 16, 1961
- *Weekly chronology of reports concerning the Berlin situation received during the week of 21-27 November.* CIA CREST database, November 27, 1961. Report # CIA-RDP79S00427A000200060001-1.
- Association for Diplomatic Studies and Training (ADST). *Germany Country Reader.* Arlington, VA; ADST.
  - Manuel Abrams
  - Richard Barkeley
  - J.D. Bindenagel
  - William Bodde Jr.
  - Arthur Day
  - Frederick Flott
  - Brandon Grove
  - Lucian Hechler
  - Charles Stuart Kennedy
  - Cecil Lyon
  - Karl Mautner
  - Martha Mautner
  - Harry Odell
  - Jacques Reinstein
  - Frederick Sackstedter
  - Taylor Seelye
  - Lloyd Stearman
  - Jack Sulser
  - Thomas Weston

Magazine and Newspaper Articles

- Reds Occupy Area in Berlin," *Stars & Stripes*, February 3, 1951
- "Reds Take Over Area in Berlin." AP wire story in *Ft Lauderdale News*, October 19, 1951
- "Berlin Reds Take Part of US Zone," AP report in *Des Moines Register*, October 19, 1951
- "US Protests Red Grab in Berlin." UPI wire story in *Pittsburgh Press*, October 19, 1951
- "Protest Filed with Soviet Over Seizure of Hamlet in West Berlin." New York Times cable report in *Cincinnati Enquirer*, October 20, 1951
- "West to Act on Berlin Grab." *Stars and Stripes,* European edition, October 22, 1951
- "Disputed Berlin Area Returned to Yanks." UPI wire report in *Green Bay Press-Gazette*, October 23, 1951
- "Red Cops Yield Control of Seized Berlin Area." *Stars and Stripes*, October 24, 1951
- "East's Police Quit Village: Russia Orders Germans Out after US Protest. AP wire report in *Baltimore Sun*, October 24, 1951
- Soviets Hand Back Seized Berlin Area: Russia Backs Down After Threats." UPI, in the *Times of Shreveport LA*, October 24, 1951
- "Unexplained Move Leaves American Officials Baffled." UPI, in *Honolulu Star-Bulletin*, October 25, 1951
- "Berlin Territory Dispute Put Up to Zonal Chiefs." AP wire report, in *St. Louis Post Dispatch*, October 25, 1951
- "Red Zone Cops Free Reporter Held 3 Days." UPI wire report in *Brooklyn Daily Eagle*, October 28, 1951
- "Reds Ignored During Grab of Berlin Suburb, Girl Says," European Stars and Stripes, October 28, 1951, page 6
- "Disputed Berlin Area Gets Chief." AP report in Los Angeles Times, October 28, 1951
- "In and Out of Steinstuecken," *Guardian*, October 28, 1951
- Title of article unavailable, *Berliner Zeitung,* September 22, 1961
- "US Soldiers Land in Area of Red Ring." AP, in *Kansas City Star*, September 23, 1961
- "3 GIs 'Occupy' Red-Encircled Town." NY Herald Tribune wire service in *Minneapolis Star-Tribune*, September 23, 1961
- "U.S. Protests Detention of GI By Reds," AP wire service report in *Bridgeport Telegram*, Bridgeport Connecticut, September 23, 1961

- "Reds Cut Off Tiny Enclave," UPI story in *Stars and Stripes*, October 1, 1961
- "3000 Widen Death Strip in East Berlin." UPI story in *Stars and Stripes*, October 1, 1961
- "Reds Revive Threat to Air Corridors." UPI report in *Democrat and Chronicle*, October 2, 1961
- "New Peril Point Developing at Steinstuecken." UPI report in *St. Louis Post-Dispatch*, October 2, 1961
- "5 Germans Escape in US Copter." UPI story in *Stars and Stripes*, October 5, 1961
- "3 Airlifted From Berlin Enclave." UPI story in *Stars and Stripes*, February 8, 1962
- "West German Town Menaced By Reds." UPI, in *The Town Talk*, Alexandria LA, May 25, 1963
- "Vopos Reopen Road to Exclave of West Berlin." AP wire report in *St. Louis Post-Dispatch*, May 27, 1963.
- "Vopos Reopen Road to Exclave of West Berlin." AP wire report in *St. Louis Post-Dispatch*, May 27, 1963.
- "GI Faces Court Martial for East Germany Shooting," UPI wire report in *The Morning News*, Wilmington Delaware, July 10, 1963
- "Red Guards Stone GI Patrol in West Berlin Enclave," *Stars and Stripes*, September 5, 1963
- "Gun Firing Costs MP Sergeant," *Stars and Stripes*, September 26, 1963
- "Berlin Exclave Reinforced." AP wire story in *Stars and Stripes*, October 4, 1963
- "Steinstuecken GIs Reinforced After Stone-Throwing Incident." AP wire report, in *Daily Press of Newport News VA*, October 4, 1963
- "Steinstuecken: Berlin's Own Little Island." Peter Kurt, *Stars and Stripes*, May 4 1967
- "Unique Jobs for Berlin MPs," AP article by Hubert Erb, in *Stars and Stripes*, August 15, 1967
- "East Berlin Surrounds West's 'Islands.'" Brigitte Falbe, *Baltimore Sun*, September 5, 1971
- "Khruschev's Human Dimensions Brought Him to Power and His Downfall." *New York Times*, September 12, 1971
- "Berlin Confusion: The Jigsaw Puzzle of Exclaves," by Joe Alex Morris Jr. *Los Angeles Times*, September 18, 1971
- "East Germans Initial Berlin Access Pacts," by Joe Alex Morris Jr., LA Times staff writer, *Los Angeles Times*, December 12, 1971
- "West 'City' in East Berlin Looks to Future," AP story by Hubert Erb, *Stars and Stripes*, December 25, 1971
- "East German Enclave Fears End to Its Privacy." Reuters exclusive to the *Los Angeles Times*, December 26, 1971
- "Steinstuecken, West Berlin's 'Offshore" Island, May Come Home," John M. Goshko, LA Times-Washington Post News Service. From the *Louisville Courier-Journal and Times*, January 2, 1972
- "Thesis Aid in Freeing Berliners? Student's Study Possible Key." Washington Post News Service, January 4, 1972
- "Red-Ringed Village Hoping for Freedom," AP wire story in the *Times-Herald*, Port Huron Michigan, January 20, 1972
- "West Berliners Crowd Offices for Wall Passes." UPI story in *Los Angeles Times*, June 5, 1972
- "Eased Access to East Germany Marked by First-Day Snarls," AP wire report in *The Morning Call, Allentown PA*, June 5, 1972
- "A Sunday Stroll: Steinstuecken Opens Up For Visit," *Berlin Observer*, June 5, 1972
- "Hamlet Realizes Dream of 27 Years," UPI wire report in *The Independent*, Long Beach California, June 15, 1972
- "Road Opens to W. Berlin Island Town in East," UPI wire report in the *Arizona Republic*, September 24, 1972
- "Quiet Fadeaway: US Army withdraws tiny garrison from Steinstuecken Berlin exclave." By Hubert Erb, AP. *Stars and Stripes*, October 25, 1972
- "Zehlendorf Memorial Unveiled." *Berlin Observer*, September 15, 1977
- "Courting in Steinstuecken." *Stars and Stripes*, January 28, 1986
- "Girl Scouts Put New Face on Memorial." *Berlin Observer*, May 23, 1986
- "Aviators Assist Exclave." *Berlin Observer*, August 5, 1988
- "Exclave Spotlights Aviators." *Berlin Observer*, August 26, 1988
- "Steinstucken Summer Fest Commemorates U.S. Ties." *Berlin Observer*, August 28, 1989
- Photo caption, *Berlin Observer*, March 13, 1992
- "New Brigade Commander Praises Quality of Berlin Soldiers." *Berlin Observer*, August 28, 1992

- ZEFYS Online Newspaper Information Service. http://zefys.staatsbibliothek-berlin.de/
  - *Berliner Zeitung,* October 20, 1951
  - *Neues Deutschland,* October 20, 1951
  - *Neues Deutschland,* October 21, 1951
  - "Steinstuecken: Lifestyles of West Berlin." *Der Spiegel,* October 31, 1951
  - *Neue Zeit,* November 6, 1951

Professional Publications

- Catudal, Honore' Marc. "Berlin's New Boundaries." *Cahiers de géographie du Québec.* Volume 18, number 43, 1974

Interviews with the author

- William Bacon
- Betsy Mathewson Bailey
- Heike Behrendt
- Christine Clark
- Jan Feutz
- Lester Feutz
- Edward Hamborski
- Elke Hammer
- Wilfried Hammer
- Herbert Judd
- Keith Koziba
- John Mentor
- Verner Pike
- Darrell Pope
- Doug Powell
- Ralph Sanchez
- Charlie Smith
- W.R. Smyser
- Jerome Weilmunster
- Wilbur Wolf
- Magrit Wiese

Online Sources

- Archives of the *Berlin Observer* and *Berlin Grooper*, the U.S. military community newspaper in Berlin. http://theberlinobserver.com/
- "German History in Documents and Images" (GHDI). http://germanhistorydocs.ghi-dc.org/index.cfm
- Chapter 1, Document 1, "Change Through Rapprochement."
- Chapter 8, Document 5, "Two States, One Nation."
- "Letter from Ulbricht to Khrushchev, 15 September 1961." SED Archives, IfGA, ZPA, Central Committee files, Walter Ulbricht's office, Internal Party Archive, J IV 2/202/130. Woodrow Wilson International Center for Scholars Digital Archive, https://digitalarchive.wilsoncenter.org/document/116212.
- Remme, Tilman. "The Battle for Berlin in World War II" (http://www.bbc.co.uk/history/worldwars/wwtwo/berlin_01.shtml)
- Ash, Lucy. "The Rape of Berlin," (http://www.bbc.com/news/magazine-32529679)
- "The tank boy and the scooter man." *Journey to Berlin* website. http://journeytoberlin.com/content/the-tank-boy-and-the-scooter-man-encounters-in-eiskeller.
- "Berlin-Steinstücken exclave, 1972. " *RBB Media.*
- https://www.youtube.com/watch?v=TuK0nwW5sxM
- "Berlin Airlift, General Clay Speaks. 1948/10.21" *Universal Newsreels.* https://www.youtube.com/watch?v=zjIMi3ofn1I.
- "1949 Cold War Germany 221752-44." *Universal Interational.* https://www.youtube.com/watch?v=7QqTcG5HvqI.
- "The Berlin Blockade." Portion of a period newsreel on the Berlin Airlift, in YouTube video (10m)", exact source unknown. https://www.youtube.com/watch?v=CZidBq8QS-g&list=PLqp0G9VLdu0St0U57Iodx0Ge95ZDXhNh5.
- "Victims At The Wall." *Chronik Der Mauer* website. http://www.chronik-der-mauer.de/en/victims/180543/marzahn-willi
- "File:GedenktafelKönigsweg326(Wann)WilliMarzahn.jpg." *WikimediaCommons.*https://commons.wikimedia.org/w/index.php?curid=11459830
- "1958 Cold War Reds hike Tariff on Berlin Supplies Newsreel." *PublicDomainFootage.com.* Accessed from YouTube, https://www.youtube.com/watch?v=P3ZLRzxO4hQ

ACKNOWLEDGMENTS

I am a lucky man. I'd always wanted to write a history book, and in the spring of 2014, I decided to go ahead and do it. I found a part of America's and Berlin's Cold War history that hadn't been fully explored—the story of the Steinstuecken "exclave." Seven years later, I'm proud to have had the opportunity to tell the story of this village and the people who lived there and protected it.

Elke Hammer was my primary contact with the Steinstuecken residents. She gathered records and searched local archives. Heike Behrendt allowed me to use the invaluable photographs her father Kurt took of life in the exclave.

On the American side, Doug Powell, the Berlin Brigade's Aviation Detachment commander, put me in touch with other aviators who told me their stories and let me use their photographs. Doug also was my proofreader; he read and "sanity-checked" every chapter of this book. Jan Feutz trusted me for years with her copy of the detachment's history book, as well as a treasure trove of irreplaceable family photos.

Jesse Archbold and Alan Benson translated some of the memoirs of key Steinstuecken residents. Without those translations, I couldn't have included the insights from those memoirs in the book. Alan also helped Elke Hammer with her search of the Zehlendorf *Bezirk* archives. Wood Powell, of the Goethe Institut (and Doug's son) also arranged (at Doug's expense!) for other translation efforts.

Berlin veterans have a friend in Michael Notbohm. A Berliner, he's worked for years to help preserve the memories of the Allied presence in the city. Michael led the "Berlin Patrol," a group of Berliners who paid tribute to the Western Allies. He used his own equipment to copy many of Kurt Behrendt's pictures, and he's been a good advisor to me as I've worked through this project. All Americans who are proud of our country's accomplishments in Berlin should thank Michael and his colleagues for their efforts.

Tim Fitpatrick, a Berlin veteran, has been instrumental in helping me market the book. Thanks also to Janneck Herre of the Checkpoint Charlie Foundation, an organization dedicated to the fostering of good ties between America and Berlin.

I was honored to have the opportunity to personally interview two of the major figures in this book—the late W.R. Smyser, adviser to General Lucius Clay during the Berlin Wall crisis, and COL (Retired) Gail Halvorsen, the "Berlin Candy Bomber." Thanks to both of them for their time and patience with me. I'm also honored to have had the help of General Clay's grandson, Lucius Clay III and others in the Clay family. COL Halvorsen, Victor Davis Hanson, former Ambassador to Germany John Emerson and Dr. Marcel Rotter took a chance on a first-time book author and furnished me with promotional quotes for the book cover. The family of "Oskar," the famous Berlin political cartoonist Hans Bierbrauer, allowed me to reprint his cartoon on the 1951 Steinstuecken crisis.

Honore' Marc Catudal Jr.'s book *Steinstuecken: A Study in Cold War Politics* is the source for much of my information about the early years of Cold War Steinstuecken. He's written several books on the Cold War, all of which are worth your time to read.

The University of Wisconsin's "Germany Under Reconstruction" collection in its digital archives was invaluable. Several people asked me if I had to go to Germany to research this book. I didn't, because of the extensive collection of documents from the U.S. occupation commands that UW has placed online, for *all* of us to see and use. Also, the "Germany Country Reader," from the Association of Diplomatic Studies and Training, was incredibly useful. It contains the recollections of U.S. diplomats who served in Germany at all stages of the Cold War.

Thanks to *Stars and Stripes* and *Foreign Policy* magazine for letting me reprint some of their photos and graphics. Thanks also to ESRI, the Geographic Information Systems (GIS) software company, for letting me use the satellite images of Steinstuecken before and after the Cold War.

Lastly, my wife Tracy and son Ryan were patient with, and supportive of, me as I pursued this project.

I cannot thank all of y'all enough.

— Donald Smith, Author

ABOUT THE AUTHOR

Don Smith is a retired Army Reserve officer who served in Germany from 1986-89. He visited Berlin (West and East) three times. On one of those trips, he saw Steinstuecken and never forgot it. Don has a B.A. in History from the University of Virginia and a Masters in Strategic Intelligence from the Joint Military Intelligence College (now the National Intelligence University). He has been published in *Military History* magazine, *World War II* magazine, *Civil War Times* magazine, and the U.S Army Intelligence Center's (USAIC) *Military Intelligence Professional Bulletin.* He is a Geographic Information Systems (GIS) Instructor for USAIC at Fort Huachuca, Arizona. Don lives in Tucson.

INDEX

Endnotes and Bibliography are not included in the index.

C

H

I

J

K

T

U

V

W

Z